Cognitive Coaching:
A Foundation for
Renaissance Schools

Second Edition

Arthur L. Costa

and

Robert J. Garmston

with Preface by Robert H. Anderson
and Foreword by Carl D. Glickman

CREDITS

Christopher-Gordon Publishers, Inc.
1502 Providence Highway, Suite #12
Norwood, Massachusetts 02062
800-934-8322
781-762-5577

Printed in the United States of America
10 9 8 7 6 5 4   07 06 05 04 03

ISBN: 1-929024-41-X
Library of Congress Catalogue Number: 2001095882

Contents

Preface

In the introduction to the previous edition of this truly impressive book, I likened the reader's encounters with its many messages to the experience of taking an intensive and invigorating tour, often through familiar territory but even more often through eye-opening and mind-boggling ideas and observations that can only enrich the reader's understanding of enabling practices (such as supervision and coaching), and also inspire and guide a higher level of such practices. Browsing through this new edition has not only reinforced my own excitement about a rapidly maturing dimension of professional service, which dates back only about 17 years, but it has helped me to appreciate how far our profession has come in such a brief period of time in identifying (and often implementing) top-flight ideas and procedures. Although it is never automatic or guaranteed, the acquisition and application of Cognitive Coaching skills by those leaders seeking to improve schooling offers great promise for the making of dramatic educational progress.

Especially those readers who are not thoroughly familiar with the exciting history of cognitive coaching, and in fact veteran users of the practice as well, might well begin exploring this volume by carefully reading the opening Acknowledgments section and the Introduction. The authors' explanations of the book's four-section organization and the brief but useful section "about the language of this book" can equip the reader to deal more easily with the near-encyclopedic nature of the volume, and perhaps become more comfortably oriented to it.

Central to the many messages in this book is the explanation, on which chapter 6 focuses, of the sources of excellence that drive human performance. I predict that readers will be grateful for the guidance provided in this early chapter, and for explanations of how the sources for "wholeness" reside in the five states of mind that enable people to perform at their best: efficacy, flexibility, craftsmanship (on which point the Tiger Woods example is brilliantly useful), consciousness, and interdependence. These concepts are further developed in Part II of the book.

The early-on examination in chapter 8 of the knowledge base that undergirds teacher and learning would, in my judgment, provide a foundation not only for the readers of this book but also for students in other courses in schools or colleges of education. The same could well be said for the overall content of Part II, in which the seminal ideas are revisited and expanded.

Research-oriented readers will almost certainly be stimulated by the review of the studies, amazingly numbering 106, of cognitive coaching. In the rich concluding chapter, which aspires to define the "educational renaissance" that these authors hope to stimulate, is offered a vision that, we should well hope and pray, will come to be shared not only by all educators but by those persons in high places who, sometimes foolishly and sometimes wisely, seek to create an educationally stimulating world for children.

Robert H. Anderson
University of South Florida

Foreword

Years ago while overseas, I was struggling to gain support from teachers to begin a secondary school renewal process that would involve all stakeholders—students, parents, administrators, and faculty—in deciding about needed changes in teaching and learning to improve student achievement. Frankly, I was perplexed. I had done similar work with other schools and rarely received opposition from teachers. But, in this case, I knew little about the school or the community. I soon learned about the history of volatile teacher union and management issues and discovered that since the superintendent had invited me to the school, I was seen by teachers as a ploy of the administration to manipulate teachers. After two days of task-specific workshops and conferences with faculty, I realized that little could be accomplished, and it was time for me to go home.

Serendipitously, while moving through the buffet line for what I thought to be my last dinner at the school, I found myself standing next to the union head. We began polite small talk. I asked her where she had grown up and how she had come to teach overseas.

We found that we had a common history—my dad's furniture store had been located a few blocks from her childhood home, and some of the furniture in her home had probably been delivered by one of my brothers. Time passed quickly as we shared stories, and eventually, as the line of people wanting to eat grew, the two of us broke apart with mutual smiles and words of goodbye.

Upon arriving home a few days later, there was a message waiting for me that the school faculty, in my absence, had taken an overwhelmingly positive vote to become full partners in the two-year school renewal process. I later learned the vote was due to the influence of the union head I had met in the buffet line who argued before the vote that "he is an okay person".

It is lessons like this about developing trust as a prerequisite for later educational achievements that are the core of this revised edition of *Cognitive Coaching: A Foundation for Renaissance Schools*. Bob Garmston and Art Costa are to be thanked for detailing how trust can be built through shared experiences, communications, and mutual responsibilities. Trust opens our work and dreams to each other, and makes possible continuous improvement of how we teach and what our students learn. Bob and Art describe specifically the practices, formats, and structures that establish dialogue, inquiry, reflection, and purposeful action for improving classroom and school learning. They make clear that educators should not wait for a chance encounter, such as my "standing in line" event, in order to build openness, collegiality, and common purpose. Rather all leaders—whether peers, teachers, mentors, supervisors, or other—can create an inquiry-based school by using repertoires of behaviors that support and challenge teachers to become thoughtful and powerful about what they do in their classrooms.

The first edition of this book broke new ground in the field of supervision, leadership, and classroom practice in its emphasis on verbal and nonverbal interactions. This edition opens the field further with applications to coaching, mediation, dialogue, nonverbal behaviors, states of mind, knowledge of instruction, cognitive processes, navigating maps and use of standards. The book is reader friendly, full of case studies and examples, and research based. Bob and Art have a range of interdisciplinary expertise ranging from supervision, group dynamics, and counseling to cognitive processing, staff development, and school renewal that is rare to find. This book is an awesome array of help for arriving at a self-renewing "Renaissance" school. They are to be congratulated for once again showing how to make the continuous improvement of education a practical and richly rewarding reality.

Carl D. Glickman
Chairman, Program for School Improvement
The University of Georgia, Athens, Georgia

~ Acknowledgments

W e are indebted to scholars, practitioners, and researchers in many fields whose work has inspired and informed us, raised provocative questions, and guided our search.

The "gene pool" from which Cognitive Coaching emerges includes the work of Robert Anderson, Morris Cogan, and Robert Goldhammer (clinical supervision); Gregory Bateson (systems theory and psychology); Richard Bandler, Robert Dilts, and John Grinder (neurolinguistic programming); David Berliner (teacher "executive processes"); Reuven Feuerstein (mediated learning); Perc Marland (teacher decision making); Tom Sergiovanni (supervision theory); Richard Shavelson (basic behaviors of teaching); Norman Sprinthall and Lois Thies-Sprinthall (teacher as adult learner); Arthur Koestler (holonomy); Robert Keagan (adult development); Robert Sternberg (metacognition and intelligence); and Antonio Damasio and Candace Pert (neurosciences). For their pioneering work we are indeed grateful. Most notably we would like to thank Carl Glickman (developmental supervision) at the University of Georgia for his scholarship, inspiration, modeling, encouragement, and friendship.

Cognitive Coaching was conceived in the mid-1980s. From the beginning it was further enhanced by dedicated educators who shaped early forms of coaching practices and seminar design. We and countless educators will always be extremely grateful to these senior associates of the Institute for Intelligent Behavior for their influence on Cognitive Coaching. These pioneers are Bill Baker, John Dyer, Laura Lipton, Peg Luidens, Marilyn Tabor, Bruce Wellman, and Diane Zimmerman. We are appreciative, too, of the energies and rich contributions of many others associated with the Institute for Intelligent Behavior, especially members of the Institute's "Leather Apron Club." Of special mention are Jenny Edwards for her research contributions, Jane Ellison and Carolee Hayes for their integrity and leadership as co-directors of the Center for Cognitive Coaching, and all the training associates who continue to expand and apply these ideas through their work with the Center for Cognitive Coaching.

Particular thanks for special intellectual contributions from Linda Lambert, Bill Sommers, and Rosemarie Liebmann. For teaching us how Cognitive Coaching can impact school communities in international settings, our sincere thanks to Bill and Ochan Powell. We also wish to acknowledge and celebrate the growing numbers of dedicated people from whom we are learning as they infuse the principles and practices of Cognitive Coaching in their classrooms, schools, districts, and communities.

Sue Canavan and Hiram Howard of Christopher-Gordon Publishers have encouraged us and provided sound advice throughout both editions. Also at Christopher-Gordon, Kathryn Liston and Laurie Maker have given invaluable technical support. Our editor, René Bahrenfuss, saw us through several versions and gave untold hours of professional assistance in formatting, typing, and correcting numerous drafts of the manuscript. Michael Buckley loaned us his gifts to create illustrations. We are grateful for their patience and skills.

Undoubtedly, the two persons who have been the most patient with us, and have continuously extended their wisdom, support, and love, are our wives, Nancy and Sue.

Introduction

Can schools be better places, where more students succeed? Where satisfaction in learning and teaching prevail? Where increasing numbers of students and adults are empowered as self-directed learners? Where teachers continually construct more effective ways to reach students? We believe that all these are possible, and it is for these purposes that we have written this book.

We are pragmatic idealists. Significant advancements in educational knowledge and practice have occurred since the first edition of this book in 1994. In this new edition, we report the frontiers of our own learning and how new research and practice can support individuals and schools in reaching higher, more satisfying, and more holistic performance.

Through the work at the Center for Cognitive Coaching and the tireless efforts of many training associates, our knowledge of Cognitive Coaching has expanded over the past eight years. We have learned more about mediating learning. We have learned more about releasing the electrochemical energies of resourcefulness and what happens emotionally and cognitively as teachers creatively meet the daily challenges of classroom realities. We know more about how to teach people the mediational skills of Cognitive Coaching with greater efficiency and effectiveness. We also know more about supporting new teachers and applying Cognitive Coaching to work with students, parents, and groups of educators.

In this edition, we not only acquaint new readers with Cognitive Coaching but also offer experienced practitioners the benefits of recent developments, including information about advanced coaching skills never before in print.

A HISTORICAL PERSPECTIVE ON COGNITIVE COACHING

Cognitive Coaching has its source in the confluence of the authors' professional experiences. We both began our educational careers in the late 1950s, a time of great ferment in American education. In the early 1970s, Nabuo Watanabe, then director of curriculum services of the Office of the Contra Costa County Superintendent of Schools, convened a group of California educators to develop a strategy for helping school administrators understand and apply humanistic principles of teacher evaluation. Art was a member of that group. Using the clinical supervision model of Morris Cogan and Robert Goldhammer, the group outlined the basic structure of the preconference and the postconference. They also identified three goals of evaluation: trust, learning, and autonomy. These goals and processes foreshadowed key concepts in Cognitive Coaching.

At about the same time, Bob was a consultant and principal for the Arabian American Oil Company Schools in Saudi Arabia. He was implementing a systemwide innovation in computer-assisted individualized instruction, which cast the teacher in the roles of facilitator and mediator for student learning. Simultaneously, he and his colleagues were applying the pioneer work in clinical supervision developed by Cogan, Goldhammer, and Robert Anderson at the Harvard Graduate School of Education. Bob was also teaching communication courses in Parent and Teacher Effectiveness Training, developed by psychologist Thomas Gordon, a forerunner to some of the nonjudgmental verbal skills found in Cognitive Coaching today.

In his early career, Art was highly influenced by leaders in education and cognitive development. Art's doctoral work at the University of California, Berkeley, emphasized curriculum, instruction, and psychology. He conducted courses based on the curriculum and instructional theories of Jerome Bruner and Reuven Feuerstein.

Bob's early pedagogical mentors included an exceptional group of professors at San Francisco State University, Santa Rosa Center, who operated as an interdisciplinary team, and the national leaders in humanistic psychology, including Carl Rogers, Fritz Perls, and Abraham Maslow. After 20 years in the roles of teacher, principal, director of instruction, and district superintendent, Bob completed a doctorate at the University of Southern California with an emphasis on educational administration, sociology, and staff development.

About the same time that the emphases of cognition, instruction, and supervision were beginning to coalesce for Art, Bob was piecing together principles of counseling practices and strategies of group dynamics for school improvement. He joined the faculty at California State University as professor of educational administration, where he taught courses in curriculum development, school improvement, supervision, and neurolinguistics. Art was also teaching at California State University, and he and Bob were assigned to the same office. There they developed the first formal expression of Cognitive Coaching, and that December they tested their ideas with staff developers at a statewide conference. The enthusiastic reception led to further conceptual work and publications as well as invitations to present six-day "trainings" to educators.

By the summer of 1985, interest in Cognitive Coaching sparked the formation of the Institute for Intelligent Behavior, an association dedicated to enabling educational and corporate agencies to support their members' growth toward self-directed learning. Seven senior associates of the Institute have provided seminar programs in Cognitive Coaching to interested school districts and private-sector organizations throughout North America and the world.

As more people and agencies became intrigued with the power of Cognitive Coaching, numerous requests were received for a book to explain the concept. In 1994, the first edition of *Cognitive Coaching: A Foundation for Renaissance Schools* was published. The book came to be used as a basic text in university courses and as a reference to accompany the burgeoning seminars and leadership training.

To date, more than 200 organizational leaders have been trained to serve as resources to their own educational agencies to infuse, support, and study the effects of implementing the skills, maps, and principles of Cognitive Coaching. More than 30 consultants have been trained to provide foundation seminars to educational organizations such as schools, districts, and departments of education, as well as to professional organizations, businesses, and corporate agencies.

Coordinated by Carolee Hayes and Jane Ellison, the Center for Cognitive Coaching was established to provide leadership training and to serve as a resource to schools and districts that desire Cognitive Coaching services, information, and products.

In the eight years since the first book was published, much has happened on the educational scene. New research in the neurosciences has been found to support the assumptions and tools of Cognitive Coaching. Much experiential research has caused us to reexamine and refine the structure of Cognitive Coaching, and we now know better what works and what doesn't in the reality of school life.

With the current emphasis on standards for students, teachers, and administrators; with the political desire for "high stakes accountability"; and with increased knowledge about human learning, it is time for a renewal of our commitment to the ideals of Cognitive Coaching. The major purpose of this book, therefore, is to rejuvenate our focus on developing teachers and students as self-directed learners capable of coping with and living productively and harmoniously in an ambiguous, technological, and global future.[1]

THE STRUCTURE OF THIS BOOK

We invite readers to use this book as a personal resource, first reading chapters of immediate interest. Some groups may wish to use the book as a study guide or text for university work. This book will also be a valuable reference for those participating in Cognitive Coaching seminars and training. The book is organized into four sections.

Part I: Discovering the Meanings of Cognitive Coaching

This section describes Cognitive Coaching: its sources, its benefits, and the fresh vision that drives this work at Renaissance schools. A discussion of coaching basics includes new information on coaching maps, the processes and effects of mediation on the brain, and the mediator's role. We also explore new insights about when to advise and when to coach. Also included are descriptions of the basic tools of rapport, trust, mediative questioning, and other linguistic skills.

Part II: Sources of Excellence

This section addresses three major sources of teaching excellence: the five states of mind, research on instructional cognition, and the knowledge base of teaching. We define holonomy and present new information about the states of mind. The chapter on teacher cognition has been expanded to include recent research on complex thinking processes and findings from the neurosciences. The knowledge base of teaching explores six domains of inquiry and how Cognitive Coaching extends and integrates this knowledge. Advantages and cautions regarding teaching standards are also discussed.

Part III: Engaging in Coaching

This section is greatly expanded from the first edition. Fresh, detailed information is provided about the coaching map of pacing and leading, both in terms of neurological events and specific useful tools. How to flexibly navigate the three mental maps of planning, reflecting, and increasing resourcefulness in resolving problems is also explored. A new section on human variability in meaning making and its implications for coaching has been added. Another new chapter explores issues related to consulting and coaching—when to do which and how to do both and still maintain the integrity of mediational goals.

Part IV: Integrating Cognitive Coaching Throughout the System

In this section we give practical examples of how the ideals of Cognitive Coaching can be embedded in the curriculum, school culture, policies, and practices of the school. We review the most recent Cognitive Coaching research on the achievement of Cognitive Coaching goals, its effects on student learning, its impact on staff, and other dimensions. We close with our vision of an educational renaissance in schools, school systems, communities, and the world.

Appendixes and Glossary

The appendixes contain four useful elements: a transcript of a sample coaching cycle, a list of what teachers most want observed, an explanation of why coaches do what they do from a constructivist perspective, and sample mediative questions. A Glossary concludes the book.

ABOUT THE LANGUAGE IN THIS BOOK

To the extent possible, we have worked to eliminate gender bias in this text. For example, we alternate use of *he* and *she* in our examples, or we eliminate any need for gender reference by writing sentences with plural nouns (using a construction with *coaches/ their* instead of *coach/he* or *coach/she*).

However, some gender bias is unavoidable, as with the word *craftsmanship*. We searched for years for another word that would capture so precisely the attributes of this state of mind, but we could find no better alternative. "Craftspersonship" seems artificial and awkward, so we resigned ourselves to "craftsmanship." We hope readers will understand the dilemmas produced by the current limitations of the English language.

We also believe that it is important to recognize the value of Cognitive Coaching in a variety of professions, positions, life roles, and careers. However, for the purposes of this book, we have chosen to cast the coaching process in educational settings. Thus, most of our vignettes, descriptions, samples, and examples illustrate educational settings (especially with teachers and coaches). We hope that readers will read beyond this narrow focus to apply the mediative process to contexts beyond education: home, community, workplace, and congregations.

While the chapters ahead reflect developments in many areas, a companion book—Ellison, J. and Hayes C. (Eds.) (2002) *Applying Cognitive Coaching in a System.* Norwood, MA. Christopher-Gordon—provides explicit examples of how to use different applications of Cognitive Coaching to enhance self-directed learning in a variety to situations and settings. It is organized as a resource to individuals, schools, and districts who seek to develop more thoughtful and collaborative cultures integrating the practices and values of Cognitive Coaching into everyday work.

We fervently hope that this book supports you, the reader, in mediating self-directed learning in others—and in yourself—as you integrate the principles and values of Cognitive Coaching throughout your school programs and practice.

NOTE

1. While this book will provide immense knowledge about Cognitive Coaching, it can never take the place of training in Cognitive Coaching. We encourage readers to seek additional information about training seminars. For information concerning Cognitive Coaching seminars, leadership training, videotapes, manuals, and other products and services, contact The Center for Cognitive Coaching, 2916 Deer Creek Pl., Highlands Ranch, CO 80126; e-mail: CCClj@aol.com; phone: (303) 683-6146; website: www.cognitivecoaching.com.

Part I:

Discovering the Meanings of Cognitive Coaching

In this introductory section appear descriptions of Cognitive Coaching, including its sources, its benefits, and the vision that drives this work related to Renaissance schools. Information on coaching basics includes information on coaching maps, the processes and effects of mediation on the brain, and the mediator's role. Decisions about when to advise and when to coach are explored. Also included are discussions of the basic tools of rapport, trust, mediative questioning, and other linguistic skills.

1

Exploring the Meanings of Cognitive Coaching

To know what is important to you, to have a real sense of who you are and what would be deeply satisfying and archetypally true, is not enough. You must also have the courage to act. Courage is a willingness to act from the heart, to let your heart lead the way, not knowing what will be required of you next, or if you can do it.

—Jean Shinoda Bolen

After observing Cognitive Coaching for the first time, educators often make comments like these:

- The coach didn't make any value judgments; the other person had to judge for himself.

- There was a lot of silence after the coach's questions; she made the person think.

- The coach gave no advice or recommendations; instead she asked her partner to suggest what should be done.

- The coach seemed to have a strategy in mind, like he knew where he was going.

- The coach listened; she reflected back what the person said and clarified a lot.

- Cognitive Coaching seems to be like a Socratic dialogue in a form of inquiry.

People who have undergone Cognitive Coaching for the first time often reflect on the experience with comments such as these:

- I became much clearer about my plans and how to achieve them.

- I felt that the coach understood my problem and the goals I had in mind. I have a better handle on my problem now.

- The coach really made me think. She made my brain "sweat"!

- I want to know how I can learn to use this process in my work!

Although we agree with all of these comments, the essence of Cognitive Coaching is much more than these observations capture. In this chapter, we offer an overview of the model to serve as a basis for the detailed discussions of Cognitive Coaching theory and practice that follow.

A SNAPSHOT OF COGNITIVE COACHING

Research demonstrates that teachers with higher conceptual levels are more adaptive and flexible in their teaching style. They act in accordance with a disciplined commitment to human values,[1] and they produce higher achieving students who are more cooperative and involved in their work.[2] Cognitive Coaching increases the capacities for sound decision making and self-directedness, which helps to achieve goals like these.

At one level, Cognitive Coaching is a simple model for conversations about planning, reflecting, or problem resolving. At deeper levels, Cognitive Coaching serves as the nucleus for professional communities that honor autonomy, encourage interdependence, and produce high achievement.

Cognitive Coaching is a nonjudgmental, developmental, reflective model derived from a blend of the psychological orientations of cognitive theorists and the interpersonal bonding of humanists. The model is informed by current work in brain research, constructivist learning theory, and practices that best promote learning.

Fundamental to the model is the focus on a practitioner's cognitive development. This focus is based on the belief that growth is achieved through the development of intellectual functioning. Therefore, the coaching interaction focuses on mediating a practitioner's thinking, perceptions, beliefs, and assumptions toward the goals of self-directed learning and increased complexity of cognitive processing.

Cognitive Coaching strengthens professional performance by enhancing one's ability to examine familiar patterns of practice and reconsider underlying assumptions that guide and direct action. Cognitive Coaching's unique contribution is that it influences another person's thought processes. Cognitive Coaching is systematic, rigorous, and data-based. The initial purpose of this model is to enhance an individual's capacity for self-directed learning through self-management, self-monitoring, and self-modification.

We find a useful metaphor for the essence of Cognitive Coaching in the story of a boy watching a butterfly emerge from its chrysalis. The boy observed the chrysalis closely each day until the casing broke away and a small opening appeared. The boy could see the butterfly's head, and, as the butterfly began to emerge, an antenna appeared, then one leg.

The boy watched the butterfly for several hours as it struggled to force its body through the small aperture. Then the butterfly seemed to stop making any progress. It appeared as if the butterfly could go no farther. So the boy decided to help. He scratched away the remaining scales of the confining cocoon with his thumbnail, and the butterfly easily emerged. However, it had a swollen body, small shriveled wings, and bent legs.

The boy continued to watch the butterfly because he expected that, at any moment, the wings would expand to support the body, which would then contract. Neither happened! In fact, the butterfly spent the rest of its short life limping in circles with a swollen body and shriveled wings, never able to fly. The boy, in all his kindness and haste, did not understand that the struggle required for the butterfly to emerge from the confines of the chrysalis was nature's way of forcing fluids from the body into its wings so that it would be ready for flight once it achieved freedom.

The struggle for ultimate freedom is what makes a butterfly strong. So, too, the challenges and ultimate achievements of Cognitive Coaching make educators stronger and better equipped to fulfill their roles in schools today.

COMPONENTS OF THE COGNITIVE COACHING MODEL

Cognitive Coaching comprises a set of skills, capabilities, mental maps, beliefs, values, and commitments. All of these are practiced, tested over time, and assimilated into a person's day-to-day interactions. They also become part of the coach's identity as a facilitator of self-directed learning. Ultimately, Cognitive Coaching's values and beliefs become an outlook on life.

Cognitive Coaches are skilled at constructing and posing questions with the intention of engaging and transforming thought. They employ nonjudgmental response behaviors to establish and maintain trust and intellectual engagement. They use nonverbal behaviors to establish and maintain rapport. Cognitive Coaches know their own intentions and choose congruent behaviors. They set aside unproductive patterns of listening, responding, and inquiring. They adjust their own style preferences, and they navigate within and among several mental maps to guide their interactions.

Cognitive Coaches value self-directed learning. They delight in assisting others in becoming more self-managing, self-monitoring, and self-modifying. They cherish and work to enhance individual differences in styles, beliefs, modality preferences, developmental levels, culture, and gender.

Cognitive Coaches believe that all behavior is determined by a person's perceptions and that a change in perception and thought is prerequisite to a change in behavior. They also believe that human beings construct their own meaning through reflecting on experience and through interactions with others. They have faith that all human beings have the capacity to continue developing their intellect throughout their lifetimes.

Cognitive Coaches are committed to learning. They continually resist complacency, and they share both the humility and the pride of admitting that there is more to learn. They dedicate themselves to serving others, and they set aside their ego needs, devoting their energies to enhancing others' resourcefulness. They commit their time and energies to make a difference by enhancing interdependence, illuminating situations from varied perspectives, and striving to bring consciousness to intentions, thoughts, feelings, and behaviors and their effect on others and the environment.

FOUNDATIONS OF COGNITIVE COACHING

Humanistic psychological orientations such as empathy, unconditional positive regard, and personal congruence guide the coach's work with relationship building. Certain neurolinguistic principles are also applied to achieve rapport and access thinking. Rapport is essential to mediate cognitive processes, affecting brain chemistry and access to the neocortex. Thus, the Cognitive Coaching model links physiology and cognition, which increases the importance of deep relationship skills and nuance within interactions. Rapport is an important tool for building and maintaining trust in the moment, particularly when there is tension, miscommunication, or anticipated difficulty.

Cognitive Coaches are always alert to in-the-moment opportunities. Thus, they draw upon their tools, maps, and capabilities in many different situations. These include brief corridor conversations, casual planning conversations, more structured reflecting and problem-solving conversations, and formal planning or reflecting conferences, built around the observation of a lesson or event.

HISTORICAL BACKGROUND OF THE MODEL

Because educators are decision makers involved in context-specific practice, influencing their cognitive operations regarding instruction generically influences their specific instructional behaviors. Recognizing this fact, the authors and a powerful team of associates developed Cognitive Coaching for teacher supervision in 1984.[3] Over the years, the forms and uses of Cognitive Coaching have evolved to include applications in the business and corporate world, peer coaching, mentor services for teachers and administrators, peer assistance and review programs, and classrooms with students of all ages.

In the late 1960s, Morris Cogan, Robert Goldhammer, Robert Anderson, and a group of supervisors working in Harvard's Master of Arts in Teaching program found that traditional supervision placed the supervisor in an "expert" role superior to that of the teacher. Supervisors told the teacher what should be changed and how to do it. Supervisors offered solutions to problems that concerned them, which were not necessarily the problems that concerned teachers. All efforts to change the conference style in which the supervisor did the talking and the teacher did the listening had failed. The work of Cogan and his colleagues on this dilemma was the foundation for the clinical supervision model, and it is important to understand some of Cogan's work to appreciate the distinctive attributes of Cognitive Coaching.

Cogan[4] envisioned the purpose of clinical supervision as "the development of a professionally responsible teacher who is analytical of his own performance, open to help from others, and self-directing." Clinical supervision demanded a role change in which the teacher and the supervisor worked as colleagues, respecting each other's contributions. The intent of the process was to cultivate teacher self-appraisal, self-direction, and self-supervision.[5]

Cogan's clinical supervision was conceived as a cyclic, eight-phase process organized around planning and conferencing with a teacher before instruction, observing the lesson itself, and conducting a follow-up conference after the lesson. Cogan and his colleagues believed that the act of teaching is a collection of behaviors that can be understood and controlled. These behaviors can be observed singly and in interaction. Instructional improvement could be achieved by changing or modifying these instructional behaviors.

Cognitive Coaching is a modern expression of this orientation, built on the foundation laid by Cogan and Goldhammer.[6] There are, however, two significant departures. The first is in the conception of the teaching act. The second relates to the application of specific knowledge about teacher cognition, neurosciences, and psycholinguistics.

Although the traditional model of clinical supervision addresses overt teaching behaviors, we believe that these behaviors are the product and artifacts of inner thought processes and intellectual functions. Changing the overt behaviors of instruction requires the alteration and rearrangement of inner, invisible cognitive behaviors. The diagram of a tree and its roots in Figure 1-1 on page 10 displays the relationship and connections of the various philosophical, psychological, physiological, and historical concepts on which Cognitive Coaching is based.

DISTINCTIONS AMONG SUPPORT SERVICES

The many terms that are used in education to describe support services intended to improve instruction are often confusing: *consulting, mentoring, peer assistance, catalyst, supervision, coaching, evaluation.*

We distinguish four categories of functions intended to support teacher development: evaluating, collaborating, consulting, and Cognitive Coaching.[7] Table 1-1, on pages 14 and 15, elaborates these.

Three of these functions coaching, collaboration, and consulting, interact to improve instructional practice. For beginning teachers, the consulting and collaborating features prevail. Over time, coaching becomes the dominant function. These three functions, plus periodic evaluations of teacher performance based on adopted teaching standards, lead to increases in student learning. Each function plays a significantly different role, with very different mechanisms and intentions.

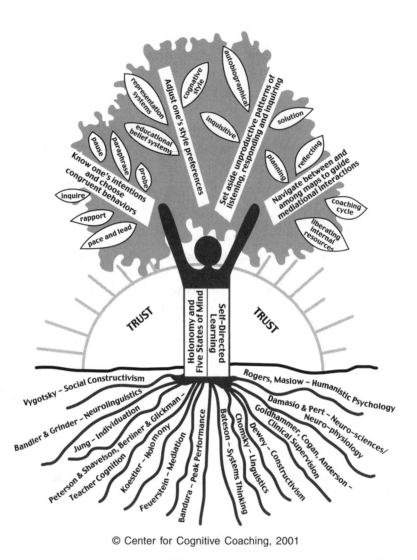

© Center for Cognitive Coaching, 2001

Figure 1-1.
The Roots of Cognitive Coaching^{SM}

Evaluation

Evaluation is the assessment and judgment of performance based on clearly defined external criteria or standards. In most systems, personnel authorized by their position as administrator, supervisor, or department chairperson conduct evaluations. According to Donald Haefele,[8] evaluation serves to do the following:

- Screen out unqualified persons from certification and selection processes

- Provide constructive feedback to individual educators

- Recognize and help to reinforce outstanding service

- Provide direction for staff development practices

- Provide evidence that will withstand professional and judicial scrutiny

- Aid institutions in terminating incompetent or unproductive personnel

- Unify teachers and administrators in their collective efforts to educate students

Consulting

To consult is to "inform regarding processes and protocols, advise based on well developed expertise, or advocate for particular choices and actions."[9] In most school districts, skillful teachers have been designated as consultants, mentors, or peer coaches. These role titles do not necessarily describe how they do their work, for they may employ consulting, collaborating, and coaching to achieve their aims. Mentoring in the educational setting is usually thought of as a relationship between a beginning teacher and a more experienced colleague; however, principals sometimes mentor new principals. If the evaluation process reveals concerns about an experienced teacher's work, a mentor may be assigned to suggest improved practices.

Consultants serve as information specialists about or advocates for content or processes based upon their greater experience, broader knowledge, and wider repertoire. A supporting teacher, working as a consultant, provides technical information to a more novice teacher or to peers about the content or skills being taught, the curriculum, teaching strategies, and child growth and development. As a process advocate, a consultant informs a teacher about alternative strategies and consequences associated with different choices of methodology and content. For beginning teachers, a consultant also provides information about school policies, procedures for obtaining special resources, protocols for parent conferences, and the like. Consulting skills include clarifying goals, modeling expert thinking and problem-solving processes, providing data, drawing on research about best practices, making suggestions based on experience, offering advice, and advocating.

To be successful, the consultant must have permission from the teacher to consult, which requires a high degree of credibility and trust. The consultant also must hold commonly defined goals and the client's desired outcomes in mind.

The true test of a consulting relationship is the transfer of skills, behaviors, and increased "coachability" over time. The support person who needs to be needed can trap the teacher and himself into a dependency relationship. Likewise, the support person whose identity is primarily about being an expert may also trap herself into dependency relationships with the teacher. Within the context of Cognitive Coaching, consulting functions consistently lead toward the ultimate goal of self-directedness.

Collaborating

Collaborate comes from "co-labor." Collaboration involves people with different resources working together as equals to achieve goals. Thus, teacher and support provider plan, reflect or problem-solve together. Both are learners, offering ideas, listening deeply to one another, and creating new approaches toward student-centered outcomes. Both bring information to the interaction. Goals may come from a coaching question or from the expert perspective of a consulting voice.

Cognitive Coaching

Cognitive Coaching is the nonjudgmental mediation of thinking. A Cognitive Coach can be anyone who is skillful in using the tools, maps, beliefs, and values of mediation described earlier in this chapter. Many of the tools of Cognitive Coaching can be used in consulting and collaboration. However, the greatest distinction of Cognitive Coaching is its focus on cognitive processes, on liberating internal resources, and on accessing five states of mind as the wellsprings of constructive thought and action. We discuss these in detail in Chapter 6.

Cognitive Coaching describes the assistance provided to support a teacher in self-directed learning while improving instruction. The following section of this chapter deals specifically with an expanded definition of Cognitive Coaching.

HOW COGNITIVE COACHING IS UNIQUE

Anyone planning to use Cognitive Coaching must be able to clearly distinguish the four functions of evaluation, consulting, collaboration, and Cognitive Coaching. These various forms of support are summarized in Table 1-1. No one cognitively coaches all the time, and it is important for a Cognitive Coach to know when it is appropriate and how each function differs from the others. Chapter 12 elaborates this dimension of a supervisor's or support provider's decision making.

Cognitive Coaching is a unique interactive strategy. It differs from other forms of coaching, mentoring, supervision, and peer review in that it mediates invisible, internal mental resources and intellectual functions, as represented in Figure 1-2. These resources and functions include perceptions, cognitive processes, values, and internal resources. Other forms of coaching may focus on the behaviors, the problem, the lesson, the topic, the meeting, or the activity.

Cognitive Coaching holds that a person's actions are influenced by internal forces rather than overt behaviors. Therefore, Cognitive Coaches focus on the thought processes, values, and beliefs that motivate, guide, influence, and give rise to the overt behaviors, as represented in Figure 1-3.

Only those charged with legal responsibilities can evaluate; but a principal, peer, mentor, department chairperson, curriculum specialist, or support teacher may serve as a Cognitive Coach. A Cognitive Coach helps another person to take action toward his or her goals while simultaneously helping that person to develop expertise in planning, reflecting, problem solving, and decision making. These are the invisible skills of being a professional, and they are the source of all teachers' choices and behaviors. The Cognitive Coach takes a nonjudgmental stance and uses tools of reflective questioning, pausing, paraphrasing, and probing for

TABLE 1-1.
DISTINCTIONS OF THE FOUR SUPPORT SERVICES*

Attribute	Cognitive Coaching	Collaborating	Consulting	Evaluating
Conversations focus on:	Metacognition, decision-making processes, perceptions, values, mental models.	Generating information, co-planning, co-teaching, problem solving. and action research.	Policies, procedures, behaviors, strategies, techniques, and events.	Professional criteria, expectations, standards, and rubics.
The intention is:	To transform the effectiveness of decision making, mental models, thoughts, and perceptions and habituate reflection.	To form ideas, approaches, solutions, and focus for inquiry.	To inform regarding student needs, pedagogy, cirriculum, policies, and procedures and to provide technical assistance. To apply teaching standards.	To conform to a set of standards and criteria adopted by the organization.
The purposes are:	To enhance and habituate self-directed learning: self-managing, self-monitoring, self modifying.	To solve instructional problems, to apply and test shared ideas, to learn together.	To increase pedagogical and content knowledge and skills. To institutionalize, accepted practices and policies.	To judge and rate performance according to understood externally produced standards.
The conversations are characterized by:	Mediation, listening, questioning, pausing, paraphrasing, probing, withholding advice, judgments, or interpretations.	Mutual brainstorming, clarifying, advocating, deciding, testing, assessing.	Rationale, advice, suggestions, demonstrations.	Judgments, encouragements, advice, direction, goal setting.
	"What might be some ways to approach this?"	"How should we approach this?"	"Here are several ways to approach this."	"Your approach to this was good. Here is why."
The support person's identity in relation to the teacher is:	Mediator of thinking.	Colleague.	Expert.	Boss.

TABLE 1-1. *(continued)*

Attribute	Cognitive Coaching	Collaborating	Consulting	Evaluating
The source of empowerment to perform this function stems from:	Trust. Competence in the maps, tools, and values of Cognitive Coaching.	Trust. Competence in forming partnerships. Knowledge and skills in the areas being explored.	Trust. Competence in consulting skills. Expertise in relevant areas.	Policy. Authority is by position, licensed, authorized by law, or a negotiated agreement to evaluate. Evaluators are held accountable for judgments and actions regarding work quality.
The source(s) of criteria and judgments about performance is (are):	The teacher. "How will you know that you are successful?"	The teacher and colleague. "How will we know that we are successful?"	The consultant. "Here's how you'll know that you are successful."	The evaluator in reference to established criteria. "Here's how I'll know that you are successful."

*We are grateful to Laura Lipton and Bruce Wellman for sharing their thinking about distinctions across the support services of coaching, collaborating, and consulting. Like Lipton and Wellman, we regard these as being listed in order of most to least effective in transforming teacher work and self-directedness; yet each, at times, contributes to this aim. Lipton, L. and Wellman, B. with C. Humbard. (2001) *Mentoring Matters: A Practical Guide to Learning-Focused Relationships.* Sherman, CT: MiraVia—www.miravia.com.

specificity. The successful coach focuses on the other person's perceptions, thinking, and decision-making processes to mediate resources for self-directed learning.

The Cognitive Coaching model, then, is predicated on a set of values, maps, and tools that, when combined with nonjudgmental ways of

Figure 1-2

Other forms of interaction focus on event or behavior.

A cognitive coach is concerned with the mental processes.

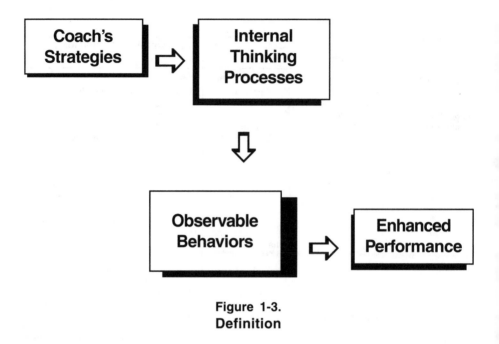

Figure 1-3.
Definition

being and working with others, invites the shaping and reshaping of thinking and problem-solving capacities. This shift happens for the person being coached and for the coach as well. Reciprocal learning is a critical component of the model.

Integral to Cognitive Coaching is the ability to work effectively with oneself and others across style differences and philosophical preferences. One fundamental element of a coach's effectiveness is the capacity to work within a colleague's worldview. As a result, the viewpoints of both participants are widened, which enables an exploration of new ideas along with existing beliefs and values.

THE MISSION

The mission of Cognitive Coaching is to produce self-directed persons with the cognitive capacity for high performance, both independently and as members of a community.

This ability to be self-directed in both independent and interdependent settings is related to holonomy—the study of interacting parts within a whole. These terms are defined below:

Self-Directedness

> *The foundational element in effective work systems is self-correcting, self-managing, self-accountable, self-governing behavior. Energy spent on monitoring and attempting to affect the behavior of team members or other entities from the outside is energy wasted and energy that could be better expended on improving the business and the capability of people. The critical element is to increasingly create self-governing capability.*
>
> —Carol Sanford

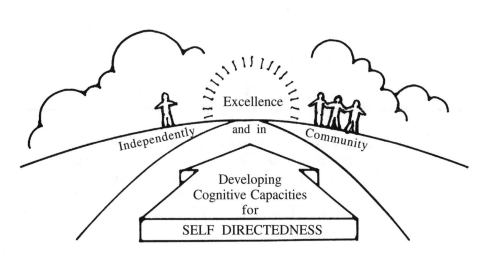

Figure 1-4.

A self-directed person can be described as being the following:

- *Self-Managing:* Approaches tasks with clarity of outcomes, a strategic plan, and necessary data, and then draws from past experiences, anticipates success indicators, and creates alternatives for accomplishment.

- *Self-Monitoring:* Establishes metacognitive strategies to alert the perceptions for in-the-moment indicators of whether the strategic plan is working and to assist in the decision-making processes of altering the plan when it is not.

- *Self-Modifying:* Reflects on, evaluates, analyzes, and constructs meaning from the experience and applies the learning to future activities, tasks, and challenges.

Self-directed people are resourceful. They tend to engage in cause-and-effect thinking, spend energy on tasks, set challenging goals, persevere in the face of barriers and occasional failure, and accurately forecast future performances. They proactively locate resources when perplexed. Seeking constant improvement, they are flexible in their perspectives and are optimistic and confident with self-knowledge. They feel good about themselves, control performance anxiety, and translate concepts into action.

Holonomy

> *It takes two to know one.*
>
> —Gregory Bateson

All beings exist within holonomous systems. That is, each person is part of several greater systems (e.g., families, teams, schools) yet maintains a unique identity and palette of choices, both as an independent agent and as the member of a group. Each system influences the individual, and, to a lesser degree, the individual influences the system.

Holonomous persons have an awareness of themselves in this somewhat oxymoronic state of being an independent entity while also part of and responsive to a larger system. They also have the cognitive capacity to exercise responsible self-directedness in both arenas.

When Arthur Koestler coined the word holon, he sought to describe something that has the characteristics of being both a part and a whole at the same time. Holonomy is the science or study of

The experience of the Chicago Bulls basketball team with Michael Jordan was an example of a merger of dualities. The Bulls were a great team, with a great star in Jordan. At times the team dominated; at times Jordan dominated. We need great teams, and we need great individuals. Teamwork can take us only so far; then we need individual greatness. Individual greatness can take us only so far; then we need team greatness. Team and individual are not separate and distinct concepts. They are in dynamic relationship, merged organically into one whole. The Chicago Bulls, as their success has demonstrated, optimized the interwoven strengths of teamwork and individual stardom, and they minimized the weakness of reliance solely on team or individual performance.[10]

wholeness. As such, holonomy considers both our integrative tendencies and our autonomous aspects.[11]

In a school, for example, teachers are autonomous decision makers. They are, however, part of a larger culture—the school—which influences and shapes their decisions. In turn, the school is an autonomous unit interacting within the influence of the district and community.

This dichotomous relationship, in which every human being exists, often gives rise to certain tensions, conflicts, and challenges. These stem from the internal drive for self-assertiveness, which conflicts with a yearning to be in harmony with others and the surrounding environment. A holonomous person, therefore, is one who possesses the capabilities to transcend this dichotomous relationship, maintaining self-directedness while acting both independently and interdependently. Holonomous people recognize their capacities to self-regulate and to be informed by the norms, values, and concerns of the larger system. Of equal importance, they recognize their capacity to influence the values, norms, and practices of the entire system.

> *We provide both irritation and inspiration for each other—*
> *the grist for each other's pearl making.*
> —Stephen Nachmonovitch

A holonomous person continually accesses and develops resources for further growth. One's goal is to become an integrated whole, capable of knowing and supporting the purposes and processes of the groups to which one belongs. A holonomous person is one who

- explores choices between self-assertion and integration.

- draws from prior knowledge, sensory data, and intuition to guide, hone, and refine actions.

- pursues ambiguities and possibilities to create new meanings.

- seeks balance between solitude-togetherness, action-reflection, and personal-professional goals.

- seeks perspectives beyond oneself and others to generate resourceful responses.

TWO GOALS

If I accept you as you are, I will make you worse; however, if I treat you as though you are what you are capable of becoming, I help you become that.

—Johann Wolfgang von Goethe

Cognitive Coaches work to achieve their mission by supporting people in becoming self-directed autonomous agents and self-directed members of a group. Toward this end, Cognitive Coaches regard all interactions as learning opportunities focused on self-directedness.

The goal of learning Cognitive Coaching is to develop the capacities and identity of a mediator, who can in turn help to develop the capacities for self-directedness in others. The skillful Cognitive Coach:

- establishes and maintains trust in oneself, relationships, processes, and the environment.

- interacts with the intention of producing self-directed learning.

- envisions, assesses, and mediates for states of mind.

- generates and applies a repertoire of strategies to enhance mind states.

- maintains faith in the ability to mediate one's own and others' capacity for continued growth.

The purpose of this book and the training provided by the Center for Cognitive Coaching is to support that learning.

METAPHORS FOR COACHING

You don't see something until you have the right metaphor to let you perceive it.

—Thomas Kuhn

Think of the term coaching, and you may envision an athletic coach. We like to use quite a different metaphor. To us, coaching is a means of conveyance, like a stagecoach (Figure 1-4). "To coach means to convey a valued colleague from where he or she is to where he or she wants to be."[12] Skillful Cognitive Coaches apply specific strategies to enhance another person's perceptions, decisions, and intellectual functions. The ultimate purpose is to enhance this person's self-directedness: the ability to be self-managing, self-monitoring, and self-modifying. Within this metaphor, the act of coaching itself, not the coach, is the conveyance.

WHY COACHING?

In a time when many schools are pressed for time and money, why is coaching so important? We have identified several compelling reasons.

1. **Teachers need and want support.** Studies tracked the implementation of state legislative mandates in 26 national sites. Among

Figure 1-5.
Stagecoach

the most significant findings was the importance of the support teacher. A cluster of studies found the support teacher-mentor to be the most powerful and cost-effective intervention in induction programs.[13] Schools and classrooms today are busy, active places where teachers and students are pressured by high-stakes testing to teach and learn faster and to be held accountable for demonstrating to others their achievement of specified standards and mastery of content. For that reason, classrooms are much more present- and future-oriented than they were in the past. Often it is easier to discard what has happened and simply move on.

Increasing evidence supports the link between student learning and staff learning. This means that as staff members learn and improve practices, students benefit and show learning increases.[14] Cognitive Coaching requires a deliberate pause, a purposeful slowing down of this fast-pace life for contemplation and reflection. Coaching serves as a foundation for continuous learning by mediating another's capacity to reflect before, during, and after practice. Kahn[15] emphasized the importance of "psychological presence" as a requisite for individual learning and high-quality performance.

2. Cognitive Coaching enhances the intellectual capacities of teachers, which in turn produces greater intellectual achievement in students. Professional development is a better predictor than age of growth in adult cognitive and conceptual development. Research shows that teachers with higher conceptual levels are more adaptive and flexible in their teaching style, and they have a greater ability to empathize, to symbolize human experience, and to act in accordance with a disciplined commitment to human values. These teachers choose new practices when classroom problems appear, vary their use of instructional strategies, elicit more conceptual responses from students,[16] give more corrective and positive feedback to students,[17] and produce higher achieving students who are more cooperative and involved in their work.

Witherall and Erickson[18] found that teachers at the highest levels of ego development demonstrated greater complexity and commitment to the individual student; greater generation and use of data in teaching; and greater understanding of practices related to rules, authority, and moral development than their counterparts. Teachers at higher stages of intellectual functioning demonstrate more flexibility, toleration for stress, and adaptability. They take multiple perspectives, use a variety of coping behaviors, and draw from a broader repertoire of teaching models.[19] High-concept teachers are more effective with a wider range of students, including students from diverse cultural backgrounds.

We know that adults continue to move through stages of cognitive, conceptual, and ego development and that their developmental levels have a direct relationship to student behavior and student performance. Supportive organizations with a norm for growth and change promote increased levels of intellectual, social, moral, and ego states for members. The complex challenge for coaches, of course, is to understand the diverse stages in which each staff member is currently operating; to assist people in understanding their own and others' differences and stages of development; to accept staff members at their present moral, social, cognitive, and ego state; and to act in a non- judgmental manner.

3. Few educational innovations achieve their full impact without a coaching component. Conventional approaches to staff development—workshops, lectures, and demonstrations—show little evidence of transfer to ongoing classroom practice. Several studies by Bruce Joyce and Beverly Showers[20] reveal that the level of classroom application hovers around only 5 percent, even after high-quality training that integrates theory and demonstration. This figure increases a bit when staff development includes time for practice and nonjudgmen-tal feedback and when the curriculum is adapted for the innovation. When staff development includes coaching in the training design, the level of application increases to 90 percent. With periodic review of both the teaching model and the coaching skills—and with continued coaching—classroom application of innovations remains at 90 percent.

4. Feedback is the energy source of self-renewal. However, feedback will improve practice only when it is given in a skillful way. Research by Carol Sanford[21] has found that value judgments or advice from others reduces the capacity for accurate self-assessment. Feedback that is data-driven, value-free, necessary, and relevant, however, activates self-evaluation, self-analysis, and self-modification.

5. Beginning teachers need mentors who employ Cognitive Coaching. At this time, massive numbers of educators are needed to lead the burgeoning number of classrooms and schools. As the Baby Boomers retire, the search for new teachers is accelerating to a fevered pitch. Incentives, bonuses, and special programs to lure qualified personnel to the education ranks illuminate the competitiveness of the times. Anyone entering a new profession needs help to get through the struggles and quandaries of their first years. Cognitive Coaching offers a valuable initiation into the education profession by providing a model of intellectual engagement and learning that promotes self-directed learning.

Cognitive Coaching also provides a leadership identity that endures in the minds of new teachers as they assume leadership roles throughout the organization. After three or four years of service, beginning teachers mentored with Cognitive Coaching in California schools gradually assumed significant teacher leader roles.[22]

6. Working effectively as a team member requires coaching. A harmonious collegial effort needs coordination. Consider a symphony orchestra. Its members are diversely talented individuals: an outstanding pianist, a virtuoso violinist, or an exquisite cellist. Together, they work diligently toward a common goal: producing beautiful music. Likewise, each member of a school staff is an extremely talented professional. Together, they work to produce a positive learning environment, challenging educational experiences, and self-actualized students.

In an orchestra, the musicians play, rehearse together, and come to a common vision of the entire score. Each musician understands how the part he or she plays contributes to the whole. They do not all play at the same time, but they do support each other in a coordinated effort. In the same way, members of the school community should support each other in creating and achieving the organization's vision. Teachers neither teach the same subjects at the same time, nor do they approach them in the same way. Cognitive Coaching provides a safe format for professional dialogue and develops the skills for reflection on practice, both of which are necessary for productive collaboration.[23]

7. Coaching develops positive interpersonal relationships that are the energy sources for adaptive school cultures and productive organizations. The pattern of adult interactions in a school strongly influences the climate of the learning environment and the instructional outcomes for students. Integral to the Cognitive Coaching model is the recognition that human beings operate with a rich variety of cultural, personal, and cognitive style differences, which can be resources for learning. Cognitive Coaching builds a knowledge of and appreciation for diversity. It also provides frameworks, skills, and tools for coaches to work with other adults and students in open and resourceful ways. Cognitive Coaching promotes cohesive school cultures in which norms of experimentation and open, honest communication enable everyone to work together in healthy, respectful ways.

Work by Susan Rosenholtz, Karen Seashore Louis, Milbrey Mclaughlin, and others document that "Workplace culture (i.e., the shared values, quality of relationships, and collaborative norms of the workplace)" has a greater influence on what people do than "the knowledge, skills or personal histories of either workers or supervisors."[24] Research by Gregory Moncada[25] reveals that conversation alters the nature of the social construction of reality. His work also reveals that change in schools is determined less by environmental influences than by modifications in the social construction of reality brought about by conversation.

8. Coaching supports and makes more successful school renewal programs. Numerous organizations that have adopted Cognitive Coaching find that self-directed learning becomes central to the organization's aims; curriculum standards become broadened and organized around self-directed learning; and evaluation of teachers, students, and organizational effectiveness changes from performance reviews to mechanisms for continuous spirals of growth and learning. Schools that have adopted Cognitive Coaching have skills and values with which to accelerate growth into collaborative learning communities. Furthermore, reflection becomes habituated throughout the organization.[26] (The integration of Cognitive Coaching principles and ideals is elaborated in chapter 13).

A MODERN RENAISSANCE

A quiet revolution continues in corporate offices and industrial settings across the United States. Writings by Peter Senge, Peter Block, Alvin Toffler, Perry Pascarella, Steven Covey, W. Edwards Deming, Margaret Wheatley, Gerald Bracey, Tom Sergiovanni, and many others have highlighted a need for greater caring for the personal growth of each individual. We see a growing desire to enhance individual creativity, to stimulate collaborative efforts, and to continue learning how to learn. The new paradigm of industrial management emphasizes a trusting environment in which growth and empowerment of the individual are the keys to corporate success.

We are witnessing a corresponding revolution in schools as well. For many years, supervisors were expected to instill, redirect, and reinforce overt behaviors of workers. Teaching was viewed as labor. Management set the standards, directed how the work was to be done, monitored and reviewed for compliance, and then evaluated and rewarded the completed work. Now we see a revolution of relationships and a revolution of the intellect, placing a premium on our greatest resource: our human minds in relationship with one another.

The relationship presumed by Cognitive Coaching is that teaching is a professional act and that Coaches support teachers in becoming more resourceful, informed, and skillful professionals. Cognitive Coaches do not work to change overt behaviors, but rather attend to the internal thought processes of teaching as a way to improve instruction. Behaviors change as a result of refined perceptions and cognitive processes.

We believe that a new philosophy is emerging. We call it the *Renaissance school.* The Renaissance school we envision is defined by capturing some of the spirit we associate with the historical Renaissance. For us, Renaissance represents a rebirth into wholeness, rejoining the mind and the soul, the emotions and the intellect. The Renaissance school forges new practices and dreams new potentials for all humans. The Renaissance school also celebrates learning at all ages for all persons in all disciplines. Schools today are being influenced by a variety of new perspectives that challenge our notions of learning and relationships. A modern Renaissance view holds the following:

- The human mind has no limits except those in which we choose to believe.

- Humans are makers of meaning, and knowledge is constructed, both consciously and unconsciously, from experience.

- All people at all ages can continue to develop intellectually.

- All members of the school community are continual and active learners.

- Leadership is the mediation of both the individual's and the organization's capacity for self-renewal.

The Renaissance school acknowledges interdependent communities of autonomous human beings bound by core values, common goals, caring, respect for diversity, and the ability to struggle together. Its members are reflective, examining their products and processes in a continuing climate of self-renewal. The Renaissance school allows for the development and contribution of each person's unique personal and professional identity. The celebration, valuing, and utilization for diversity of personal history, culture, gender, race, and interests are all important to continued growth and change.

Renaissance schools are wellsprings of growth and self-renewal for all who dwell there. Clearly, many of the attributes of the Renaissance school are reflected in the principles of Cognitive Coaching and vice versa. Reflection, respect for diversity, and ongoing renewal are all-important principles of the Cognitive Coaching process and the Renaissance school. We discuss our vision of the Renaissance school further in chapter 14, but we introduce it here because the vision has guided us through many of the chapters that follow. Schools and agencies that have adopted Cognitive Coaching have begun to profit from its effects not only in the United States but also increasingly throughout the world. Ultimately, we believe, Cognitive Coaching will significantly contribute to the creation of Renaissance schools worldwide.

CONCLUSION

In a personal correspondence from Bill Powell, formerly director of the American School of Tanganyika in Dar es Salaam, Tanzania, he stated the following:

> We interviewed internal candidates for the High School Vice-Principal's position. During the course of the interviews, I asked each of them what was the most important learning experience of their lives. Without hesitation, one candidate responded, "Cognitive Coaching! It changed the way I think about teaching, about learning . . . in fact; it changed the way I think about myself."

All who wish to continually improve their craft—be they teachers, entrepreneurs, ballerinas, musicians, auto mechanics, or potters—never lose the need to be coached. Cognitive Coaching is a model of interaction that helps others to take action toward goals that are important to them while simultaneously developing their capacities for self-directedness. As the following chapters illustrate, Cognitive Coaching consists of a composite of linguistic tools, beyond verbal tools and mental maps, which, when applied to interactions over time, are intended to enhance self-directed learning in oneself and others.

Cognitive Coaching is rooted in dispositions, beliefs, and values that honor the human drive for continuous learning and the spirit of collaboration. Cognitive Coaching is not giving advice solving other people's problems, as with the boy and the butterfly chrysalis. Cognitive Coaching is a nonjudgmental process of mediation applied to those human life encounters, events, and circumstances that can be seized as opportunities to enhance one's own and another's resourcefulness.

NOTES

1. Sprinthall, N., and Theis-Sprinthall, L. (1982). The teacher as an adult learner: Cognitive developmental view. In G. Griffin (Ed.), *Staff development: 1982 yearbook of the National Society for the Study of Education, Part II.* Chicago: University of Chicago Press.

2. Harvey, O. J. (1967). *Conceptual systems and attitude change: Attitude, ego involvement, and change* (p. 17). New York: Wiley.

3. See the Introduction for additional information about the evolution of the concepts and processes of Cognitive Coaching. We are especially grateful to the senior associates of the Institute for Intelligent Behavior: Bill Baker, John Dyer, Laura Lipton, Peg Luidens, Marilyn Tabor, Bruce Wellman, and Diane Zimmerman.

4. Cogan, M. (1973). *Clinical supervision.* Boston: Houghton Mifflin.

5. For a more detailed description of clinical supervision, see R. H. Anderson, Clinical supervision: Its history and current context, in *Clinical supervision: Coaching for higher performance.* Lancaster,

PA: Technomic. See also Pajak, E. (2000). *Approaches to clinical supervision*, Norwood, MA: Christopher-Gordon.

6. Cogan, Clinical Supervision; Goldhammer, R. (1969). *Clinical supervision: Special method for the supervision of teachers.* New York: Holt, Rinehart, and Winston.

7. Lipton, L., and Wellman, B., with Carlette Humbard (2001). *Mentoring matters: A practical guide to learning-focused relationships.* Sherman, CT: MiraVia.

8. Haefele, D. (1993). Evaluating teachers: A call for change. *Journal of Personal Evaluation in Education, 7,* 21–31.

9. Lipton and Wellman, *Mentoring Matters*, p. 20.

10. Heurman, T., and Olson, D. (1998). *Beyond dualism.* www.amorenaturalway.com.

11. Koestler, A. (1972). *The roots of coincidence.* New York: Vintage Books.

12. Evered, R., and Selman, J. (Autumn 1989) Coaching and the art of management. *Organizational Dynamics, 18,* 116–32.

13. Oja, S., and Reiman, A. (1998). Supervision for teacher development across the career span. In G. Firth and E. Pajak (Eds.), *Handbook on research on school supervision* (pp. 463–487). New York: Simon and Schuster Macmillan.

14. Richardson, J. (1998). Putting student learning first put these schools ahead. *Journal of Staff Development, 18* (2), 42–47; and Richardson, J. (1998). We're all here to learn. *Journal of Staff Development, 19* (4), 49–55.

15. Kahn, W. A. (1992). To be fully there: Psychological presence at work. *Human Relations, 45* (4), 321–349.

16. Hunt, D. E. (1980). *Teachers' adaptation: Reading and flexing to students' flexibility in teaching.* New York: Longman Press.

17. Calhoun, E. F. (1985). *Relationship of teachers' conceptual level to the utilization of supervisory services and to a description of the classroom instructional improvement.* Paper presented at the Annual Meeting of the American Educational Research Association. Chicago, Illinois, April.

18. Witherall, C. S., and Erickson, V. L. (June 1978). Teacher education as adult development. *Theory into Practice*, p. 17.

19. Hunt, D. C. (1977–78). Conceptual level theory and research as guides to educational practice. *Interchange, 8,* 78–80; McNerney, R. F., and Carrier, C. A. (1981) *Teacher development.* New York: Macmillan; Glickman, C. (1985). *Supervision of instruction: A developmental approach* (p. 18). Newton, MA: Allyn and Bacon.

20. Joyce, B., and Showers, B. (1995). *Student achievement through staff development* (2nd ed.) New York: Longman.

21. Sanford, C. (1995). *Myths of organizational effectiveness at work.* Battle Ground, WA: Springhill.

22. Riley, S. (2000). Personal communication. Educational Consultant. Professional Development Unit. California State Department of Education.

23. Costa, A., and Kallick, B. (2000). *Discovering and exploring habits of mind* (pp. 81–86). Alexandria, VA: Association for Supervision and Curriculum Development.

24. Garmston, R., and Lipton, L. (1998). The psychology of supervision. In G. Firth and E. Pajak, *Handbook research,* p. 279.

25. Moncada, G. (1998). A model for conversation and change within interdisciplinary teams. Unpublished dissertation, University of Minnesota.

26. York-Barr, J., Sommers, W., Ghere, G., and Montie, J. (2001). *Reflective practice to improve schools: An action guide for educators.* Thousand Oaks, CA: Corwin Press.

2

Coaching Basics

The finest gift you can give anyone is encouragement. Yet almost no one gets the encouragement they need to grow to their full potential. If everyone received the encouragement they need to grow, the genius in almost everyone would blossom and the world would produce abundance beyond our wildest dreams.

—Sidney Madwed

In this chapter we describe the basic structures and variations of Cognitive Coaching processes and elaborate on two of the three mental maps that guide the coach's interactions. Examples of dialogues are presented to illustrate the process in action. We also offer suggestions on how to get started and how to find time to implement the coaching process.

THE MENTAL MAPS OF COGNITIVE COACHING

One of the most important capabilities a mediator possesses is the ability to navigate among and within coaching maps and across support functions as described in chapter 1 to guide mediational interactions. A map can be thought of as an internal representation, or scaffold, that displays the territory involved in a goal-oriented conversation. Knowing the territory, in this sense, allows the coach to make a conscious choice from the various routes that may be taken. Three mental maps, and their variations, guide the Cognitive Coach. They are as follows:

1. *The Planning Conversation* occurs before a colleague conducts or participates in an event, resolves a challenge, or attempts a task. The coach may or may not be present during the event or available for a follow-up conversation.

2. *The Reflecting Conversation* occurs after colleague conducts or participates in an event, resolves a challenge, or completes a task. The coach may or may not have been present at or participated in the event.

3. *The Problem-Resolving Conversation* occurs when a colleague feels stuck, helpless, unclear, or lacking in resourcefulness; experiences a crisis; or requests external assistance from a mediator.

The coaching cycle is a combination of these first two maps, with some slight variations. It is conducted both before and after an event for which the coach will be present and gather data. In the context of the coaching cycle, we describe the planning and reflecting interactions as *conferences* to distinguish them from conversations, which do not necessarily include observing the event or engaging the teacher both before and after the event. (The coaching cycle is discussed later in this chapter, and in chapter 10. A complete transcript of a sample cycle appears in Appendix A.)

These mental maps are not recipes, prescriptions, or step-by-step instructions. As maps, they simply display the territory, and travelers choose which route they want to take to reach their destination. Skilled Cognitive Coaches know these maps backwards and forwards. They use them spontaneously and know exactly where in the map they are during the coaching processes.

Alert to cues, the coach decides to shift from one map to another depending on the needs of the person being coached, the time available, and the context. For example, toward the end of a reflecting conversation, a colleague may begin talking about plans for future activities. The coach might decide to shift into the planning map as a conversational guide. Or, during a planning or reflecting conversation, the colleague may seem frustrated, confused, or vague. The coach may decide to use the third map to amplify and liberate the colleague's internal resources in relation to a problem that seems overwhelming to the colleague. Coaches may vary from the maps or embellish them, but these maps are always the basic structure of the coaching process.

THE PLANNING CONVERSATION

Before a colleague participates in an event or attempts a task, the Cognitive Coach "mediates" by illuminating and facilitating the refinement of the colleague's cognitive processes of planning. Holding the planning map in mind, the coach engages the colleague's cognitive processes that will maximize the significance, success, and meaning of the event. A map of the planning conversation is displayed in Figure 2-1.

This first mental map displays the territory of a planning conversation, the regions within it, and the possible routes to reach a destination. Within the territory of planning, there are five dominant regions, which the coach mediates by having the planner do the following:

- Clarify goals.
- Specify success indicators and a plan for collecting evidence.
- Anticipate approaches, strategies, decisions, and how to monitor them.
- Establish personal learning focuses and processes for self-assessment.
- Reflect on the coaching process and explore refinements.

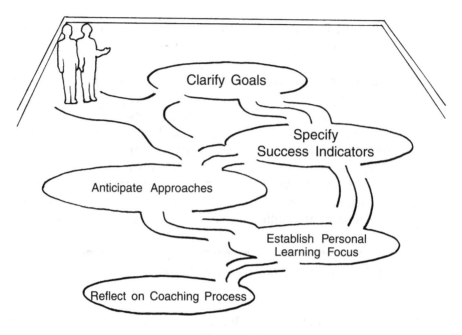

Figure 2-1.
Planning Conversation

Many relationships exist among territories in a reflecting conversation and many paths connect them. The pathways of most frequent use by coaches are shown with a center line in pathways between territories. The most essential territories are shown in a larger font.

The regions of a planning conversation exist in the coach's mind in the above, logical order. However, the regions may be visited in any sequence, depending on the interests and thinking processes of the colleague. At any time during a planning conversation, either the coach or the colleague may decide to revisit a region for more specificity or to examine its influence on other regions.

The coach and the colleague visit each of the regions of the map with specific intentions. In the region of "clarify goals," the intent is to decide what purposes or outcomes one wants for the event that is being planned. Within the "anticipate approaches" region, the intent is to describe those strategies or activities that are intended to achieve the outcomes. In "specify success indicators," the intent is to envision and specify those observable indicators of success: what would participants in the event be doing or saying that would indicate that the approach is achieving its purposes? Also in this region, the coach and the colleague devise a plan for monitoring (recording and/or collecting evidence) for specific success indicators. Because Cognitive Coaches consider each event as an opportunity for meaning-making, the intent of the "establish personal learnings" region is for the partner to establish a basis for self-directed learning.

Finally, the coach may invite the partner to reflect on the entire coaching conversation, to explore its effects on thinking and decision making, and to recommend modifications that could enhance future planning conversations.

Following is an example of a planning conversation between Angie, a reading resource teacher, and Cheryl, the school principal.

All five regions of the map were visited in this planning conversation: clear goals, success indicators, approaches, personal learnings, and an opportunity to reflect on the entire process.[1]

TABLE 2-1.
Planning Conversation

	Dialogue	Regions of the Planning Map
Angie	Cheryl, I'd like to get your reactions to my plan for the kindergarten and first-grade in-service meeting that I'm planning for tomorrow. Do you have a few minutes?	
Cheryl	Sure. Sit down. What do you have in mind?	
Angie	Well, the district has given us a set of reading standards, and the primary teachers are feeling a little, well, resistant to them. They feel that what they have been doing is quite satisfactory. They feel confident in their existing reading program, and now the district is going to "hold them accountable" for meeting these standards. I think they feel that they are going to have to give up what they've been doing to adopt these new standards.	
Cheryl	Yes, we have a group of very dedicated and experienced K–1 teachers who have been working together as a team for quite some time. What do you hope to accomplish in your meeting?	Clarify goals.

continued on next page

TABLE 2-1. (continued)

	Dialogue	Regions of the Planning Map
Angie	Well, mainly to overcome resistance and to have them at least consider the standards to see which of them they are already using and which of them they might stretch to learn more about.	
Cheryl	So you want them to feel comfortable with these new standards and to consider what can be learned from them. What will your approach be?	Anticipate approaches, strategies, decisions, and how to monitor them.
Angie	Well, I think I'll start by having them describe the accomplishments of their children when they leave first grade, what they see in their children that pleases them most. We'll make a list of those achievements. Then I was thinking of duplicating a set of standards and cutting them into strips so that there is one standard on each strip. Then I thought I'd have them match the standards they have with their accomplishments. In other words, which of the standards are they already meeting? They can tape the standard to the chart of their accomplishments.	
Cheryl	So, you're starting from their positive feelings about their accomplishments.	
Angie	Yes, but I don't want them to feel too complacent. I want them to stretch to consider that there is room for improvement too.	
Cheryl	So how would you know that they have met this challenge to consider some additional standards?	Specify success and a plan for collecting evidence.
Angie	Well, after posting those standards they feel comfortable with, I think I might have them take each of the standards they have "left over" and have them define them operationally. What would they see or hear children doing if they were accomplishing that standard? For example, one K–1 standard is: "Reads narrative and informative texts." I'd say that standard may be a stretch for our kindergartners, particularly those who come from homes where reading may not be valued.	
Cheryl	So you're helping them build a vision of what children would be doing if they were successful with that standard and contrasting that with what they are currently doing.	
Angie	Exactly.	
Cheryl	What do you hope to learn from this experiment?	Establish personal learning focus

continued on next page

TABLE 2-1. *(continued)*

	Dialogue	Regions of the Planning Map
Angie	Well, we pride ourselves at this school on being flexible in our thinking. I hope I can be flexible and see this problem from the teacher's point of view. I also hope they can be flexible and see these standards from the district's point of view. In fact, that's gives me an idea.I think I'll start with our school's statement about thinking flexibly as one of our general learningoutcomes and ask them to monitor our own flexibilityof thinking as we approach these standards that they think are kind of an imposition on them. Hmm. Why didn't I think of that before?	
Cheryl	So, you're going to make this meeting kind of a learning laboratory to practice and reflect on our school's mission?	
Angie	Yes.	
Cheryl	As you reflect on our conversation, Angie, how did this help you in planning your grade-level meeting?	Reflect on the coaching process and explore refinements.
Angie	It helped me to think through my plan and to become a lot clearer about my outcomes. I raised my sights from standards for students to practicing standards for ourselves.Thanks!	

THE REFLECTING CONVERSATION

Self-discovery is a process of reflection that is built into coaching as a learning habit. Self-discovery is a process that reaches the colleague on both an affective level and a cognitive level. It is designed around a set of questions that the person must think through and react to with concrete responses.[2]

Sometimes, only the opportunity of engaging in reflection is available, even though the coach was not present during the event. After the colleague participates in an event, resolves a challenge, or completes some task, the Cognitive Coach may seize this opportunity to mediate the cognitive processes of reflection. Holding the reflecting conversation map in mind, the coach engages the colleague's cognitive processes of reflection so as to maximize the construction of significant meanings from the experience and to apply those insights to other settings and events. Figure 2-2 displays a map of the reflecting conversation.

There are five regions in the reflecting conversation.[3]

The coach mediates by inviting the reflector to:

- Summarize impressions and recall supporting information.
- Analyze causal factors; compare, analyze, infer, and determine cause-and-effect relationships.
- Construct new learning and applications.
- Commit to applications.
- Reflect on the coaching process and explore refinements.

They may be visited in any order, although exploring the "summarize impressions" region is usually a first destination and committing to action is often the last, before reflecting on the coaching process. The coach and the colleague visit each of the regions of the map with specific intentions. In "summarizing impressions," the intent is to revisit the experience or event. Because sensitive coaches realize that there is a tremendous emotional investment in any event for which a person has had the responsibility of planning and conducting, the summarize region provides an opportunity to summon those feelings and to recollect the events, conditions, or actions that produced them. The intent of the "analyze" region is to compare the planned event with what actually happened, to identify and interpret causal factors that produced the results, to explain and give reasons for the "in action" decisions that were made, and to make inferences from the information that has been recalled. The intent of the "construct" region is to make meaning from the analysis, to draw insights, and to synthesize the personal learnings that were described in the planning conference. Because Cognitive Coaches value self-directed learning, the purpose of the "commit" region is to make applications of the learnings to future events, to bridge to other life situations, to transfer such learnings, and to self-prescribe modifications in personal behaviors.

Upon completion of the learning journey, the coach invites the partner to reflect on the entire conversation, to explore its effects on thinking and decision making, and to recommend modifications that could enhance future reflecting conversations.

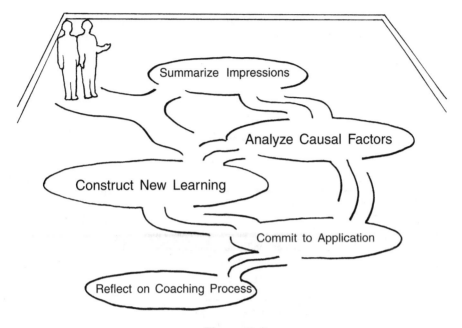

Figure 2-2.
Reflecting Conversation

Many relationships exist among territories in a reflecting conversation, and many paths connect them. The pathways of most frequent use by coaches are shown with a center line in pathways between territories. The territories most essential to self-directed learning are shown in a larger font.

An example of a reflecting conversation is shown in Table 2-2.

Even in a brief conversation, the coach can stimulate reflection in each of the five reflecting conversation themes.

THE COACHING CYCLE

If time permits, coaches may find the opportunity to engage in a full coaching cycle. This is a combination of the planning and the reflecting maps, and it is conducted before, during, and after some goal-directed event or while attempting some task. Figure 2-3 presents a diagram of a coaching cycle. It depicts a continuous process of learning in which goals are set, actions are taken, and data is monitored, collected, and interpreted, leading to a revision in actions from which new goals are set. It is intended to illustrate that coaching is a continual process and, though mediated by a coach, is intended to help another internalize this cycle of learning and become self-coaching.

TABLE 2-2.
Sample Reflecting Conversation

	Dialogue	Regions of the Reflecting Map
Coach	Hey, Raul! So how was the curriculum meeting? I'm sorry I wasn't there. Tell me about it.	Summarize impressions . . .
Raul	Well, it went pretty well. Our task was to review and adopt standards of learning for our primary grade social studies curriculum. We made a lot of progress.	
Coach	What exactly did the group accomplish?	. . . and recall supporting information.
Raul	We didn't adopt the standards yet, only reviewed them. We argued a lot about what primary kids could accomplish in a project-based curriculum. I must say, I've had to revise my thinking about my youngsters' abilities.	
Coach	What contributed to your change of heart?	Analyze causal factors, compare, infer, and determine cause-and-effect relationships.
Raul	Well, some of the teachers brought in samples of their kids' extended projects. I was amazed at how much those second and third graders knew about Australia and the problems the Australians were having with conservation efforts.	
Coach	So what insights are you gaining?	Construct new learnings and commit to applications.
Raul	Well, two things. One, I'm going to go back and review those standards to see if they are too simple for primary students. And second, I'm going to expect more from my kids. I think this project stuff is the way to go.	
Coach	So you've been resisting project-based learning for your primary students because you thought they couldn't handle those types of assignments, and now you are seeing things differently?	
Raul	Yeah. Thanks for asking. This conversation helped me realize I've got some expectations to change!	Reflect on process.

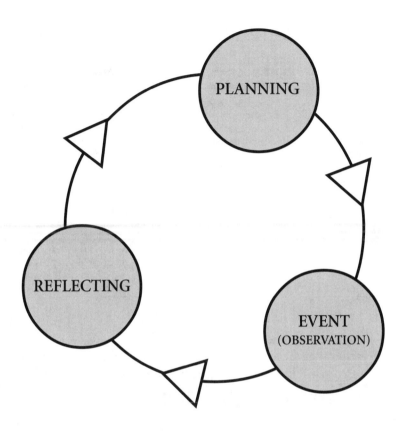

Figure 2-3.
A Coaching Cycle

Table 2-3 is a basic map of the steps in a typical Coaching Cycle: the planning conference, observation of the event, and the reflecting conference. A planning conference—when the coach will be present for the event—differs slightly from the planning conversation, when the coach will not be present for the event. The coach may serve as a data collector for the planner by sharing the task of monitoring the performance of either the participants in the event or the planner. The coach may collect data and mediate the planner by establishing mental mechanisms for self-observation or self-monitoring as well.

TABLE 2-3.

Four Phases of Thought in a Coaching Cycle

Planning	Monitoring	Reflecting
I. Planning Coaches mediate by having the planner: • Clarify goals • Specify success indicators and a plan for collecting evidence • Anticipate approaches, strategies, decisions, and how to monitor them. • Establish personal learning focus and processes for self-assessment	**II. The teacher and the coach observe for:** • Indicators of student success • Approaches, strategies, and decisions	**III. Analyzing:** Coaches mediate by having the reflector: • Summarize impressions and recall supporting information • Analyze casual factors; compare, infer, and determine cause-and-effect relationships **IV. Applying:** Coaches mediate by having the reflector: • Construct new learning • Commit to application • Reflect on the coaching process

For example, the coach might say, "Okay. Now, you mentioned earlier that there was something you'd like me to look for. What is it that you'd like me to observe today when I'm in your classroom? How would you like me to collect and record that data?"

As in the planning conversation, the goal is to have the planner identify a personal learning focus and processes for self-assessment. The coach might ask, "In addition to paying attention to evidence of student learning, how might you use this lesson for your own growth? What might you focus on, and gather data about, to support your own continuing growth as a teacher?"

The Planning Conference

The planning conference is both powerful and essential to the coaching process for six reasons.

1. It is a trust-building opportunity. Learning cannot occur without a foundation of trust, and establishing and maintaining this trust is one of the coach's primary goals. To this end, the colleague, or teacher, controls the planning conference agenda. In the planning conference, the teacher suggests the time for a classroom visit, specifies which data should be collected during the observation, describes how the data should be recorded, and even chooses where the coach will sit, stand, or move about in the classroom. These specifics are especially important in the early stages of a coaching relationship. (The significance and skills of trust building will be expanded in chapter 5.)

2.   It focuses the coach's attention on the teacher's goals. Art was once leaving a school when he peeked into a classroom where the students were being especially loud. He saw children jumping on the desks, running around the room, and yelling and screaming. Alarmed, he hurried to the principal's office: "You'd better get down to Room 14! Those kids are going wild and the teacher has lost control!" The principal calmly assured him, "Don't worry. They're practicing the school play. That's the riot scene." Without knowing a teacher's objectives or plan, an observer can make entirely incorrect inferences. Coaches cannot know what to look for in an observation unless they have met with the teacher before a classroom visit.

3.   It provides for a detailed mental rehearsal of the lesson. As teachers talk with coaches about their lessons, they refine strategies, discover potential flaws in their original thinking, and anticipate decisions they may need to make in the heat of the moment. Specific questions in the planning conference can spark this mental rehearsal, promote metacognition, and prepare teachers with a repertoire of strategies for the lesson ahead. For example, "How will you know that your strategy is working?" or "How will you know when it is time to move into the activity portion of the lesson?"

4.   It establishes the parameters of the reflecting conference. Agreements in the planning conference establish the coach's role and the data to be collected during the lesson. The teacher sets this agenda, and it provides the context for the reflecting conference.

Without a planning conference, teachers can evaluate their lesson only in terms of what happened rather than in terms of what their intentions were. You don't want to be in the situation of the rifleman whose targets Art and his wife saw as they traveled through Nevada. Every shot had hit the bull's-eye! When Art and his wife stopped at a local general store, Art approached a couple of old gentlemen sitting on the porch. "Somebody around here is a really good marksman," Art observed. "I see all of these targets, and in the center of every one there's a bull's-eye!" The men laughed and slapped their knees, and one of them explained, "Let me tell you about that guy. He shoots first and draws the circles afterwards!"

5.   It promotes self-coaching. The planning conference may ultimately be the most important, as it relates to a long-range goal of teacher automaticity in instructional thought. The coaching map represents a way of thinking about all instruction—in fact, all goal-directed activities. After experiencing a number of planning conferences, teachers adopt this way of thinking about most lessons. They internalize the conference questions, automatically asking themselves, "What are my objectives? What are my plans? How will I know students are learning?" They are activating the first step in self-coaching.

In meeting with the teacher before the lesson, the coach is seeking several kinds of information: the goals and objectives the teacher envisions, including the lesson plan and what the teacher wants to accomplish. We have discovered that as the coach probes and clarifies in an attempt to better understand the teacher's plan, the teacher also becomes clearer about the lesson. The coach engages the teacher in a process of mental rehearsal similar to what athletes do before their games.

6.   It accelerates sophisticated instructional thinking in teachers. Novice teachers tend to focus on the event. More skillful teachers focus on goals and success indicators. Beginning teachers in one California school integrated this pattern so well that during an evaluation conference with their principal, they wanted to know what indicators supported her conclusions about their performance.

The coach also invites the teacher to describe which strategies will be used to accomplish the goals. The coach leads the teacher to anticipate what students will be doing if they are, indeed, successfully performing the goals and objectives of the lesson. The coach helps the teacher to specify what will be seen or heard within or by the end of the lesson to indicate student learning. Throughout the discussion, the coach clarifies her role in the process, the kind of data she is to collect, and the format of data collection.

We have found that in addition to the items previously listed for a planning conservation, there are two other areas of a planning conference that are most frequently useful to a coach or a teacher: (1) information regarding the relationship of this lesson to the broader curriculum picture for the class, and (2) information about teacher concerns. The coach may ask the teacher, "Any concerns?" This artfully vague question allows teachers to say no or to discuss anything that might be troubling them.

When we've asked teachers what information they would like observers to have about their class prior to an observation, we have gotten an extensive list of requests. These are situational, of course, and depend on many environmental and personal factors. However, teachers often want coaches to know the following:

- Where this lesson fits into the teacher's overall, long-range plan for the students, and what has happened previously on this topic
- Information about the social dynamics of the class
- Behavioral information about specific students
- Aspects of the lesson about which the teacher is unclear
- Concerns about student behavior
- Concerns related to trying a new teaching technique
- Why this lesson concept is important to students
- Events beyond the classroom experience affecting students

While the teacher or the coach might introduce any of the above topics into a planning conference, the planning conference items presented earlier represent the five cornerstones of any and all Cognitive Coaching planning conferences or conversations.

Even though the description of the planning conference described above appears to be focused on the lesson, the Cognitive Coach is actually focused on more long-range outcomes: developing and automating these intellectual patterns of effective instruction. A tip: Don't ask teachers to bring a written response to planning conference questions. For busy teachers, this often feels like one more burden, and it robs both of you of the spontaneity related to deepening thought as you talk.

Monitoring the Event

Coaches do not specify data-gathering instruments for their observations. Instead, they assist the planner in designing the instrument in the planning conference and in evaluating the instrument's usefulness in the reflecting conference. The intent is to cast the colleague in the role of experimenter and researcher, and the coach in the role of data collector. (A list of those teacher and student verbal and nonverbal behaviors that teachers most often request to be observed appears in Appendix B.)

It is important for the coach to strive for specificity of what should be recorded. Data gathering during coaching is not the place for subjective judgments. Pursuing definitions and observable indicators of what behavior will look like or sound like will determine the objectivity and therefore the usefulness of the data. For example, the coach might say, "You want me to determine if students are on task as they are working on their projects. What will you hear them saying and see them doing when they are on task?" Or the coach might say, "So your goal is to have the students comprehend the symbolism of this story. What are some examples of comments students might make if they have comprehended the symbolism?"

It is also important that the coach invite the planner to construct the system for collecting the data. Data must make sense to the teacher during the reflecting conference, which is the time when meaning will be constructed from the data. The coach might say, "So my job is to collect evidence of students' on-task behavior. How could I record that for you? (For example: "When during the lesson should I record it? How often should I collect the data? Do you want me to record it on a seating chart? A checklist? Are there specific students you want me to observe?") Or the coach might say, "In what form might I collect evidence of the students' understanding the symbolism of the story? Should I record all their comments? At what point in the lesson should I start recording? Do you want me to specify which student made which comment?"

Having clarified the instructional goals and how the teacher and coach will collect evidence of their achievement—and having determined with the teacher exactly what data should be collected for teacher growth and how it should be recorded—the coach is now prepared for the observation. During the classroom observation, the coach simply monitors for and collects data regarding the teaching behaviors and student learning as discussed in the planning conference. The coach may employ a variety of data-collection strategies, including classroom maps of teacher movement, audio and video recordings, verbal interaction patterns, verbatim recording of what teachers say, student participation, on-task counts, or frequency counts of certain teacher behaviors. Of more importance, however, is the teacher's perception of the data and the format in which it is collected. Both must be meaningful and relevant to the teachers' self-improvement efforts.

The Reflecting Conference

While the planning conference is best done just before instruction, when teachers are clearest about their objectives, we have found that the reflecting conference is most profitable after a period of time has elapsed since the lesson. This intervening time allows for reflection on the event before participating in the reflecting conference, and it encourages deeper processing and self-analysis.

The coach can also use this time to organize the data and plan the reflecting coaching strategy. The coach may wish to review the data collected and organize the rough notes in a more presentable form to give to the teacher. She may wish to reflect on the quality of trust with that teacher to decide which outcomes are paramount at this stage of their relationship and which coaching tools should be selected to achieve those conditions (establishing trust in the coaching process, for example). The coach may wish to plan and construct questions at an appropriate depth and level of complexity for the teacher at his present stage of professional development.

As the reflecting conference begins, the coach encourages the teacher to share his impressions of the lesson and to recall specific events that support those impressions. We have found that it is important for teachers to summarize their own impressions at the

outset of a conference. This way, the teacher is the only participant who is judging his own performance or effectiveness.

The coach also invites the teacher to make comparisons between
what he remembers from the lesson and what was desired (as determined in the planning phase). The coach facilitates the teacher's
analysis of the lesson goals by using reflective questioning. The
coach also shares the data collected during the observation and
invites the teacher to make inferences for the data. The aim is to
support the teacher's ability to draw causal relationships between
his actions and student outcomes. Drawing forth specific data and
employing a variety of linguistic tools are important coaching
skills in supporting the teacher as he makes inferences regarding
instructional decisions, teaching behaviors, and the success of the
lesson.

As the reflecting conference continues, the coach will encourage
the teacher to project how future lessons might be rearranged
based on new learnings, discoveries, and insights. The coach also
invites the teacher to reflect on what has been learned from the
coaching experience itself. The coach invites the teacher to give
feedback about the coaching process and to suggest any refinements or changes that will make the relationship more productive.

NAVIGATING WITHIN AND AMONG THE COACHING MAPS

The mental maps of cognitive coaching are not necessarily intended to be used separately. As the coach interacts with a colleague, the coach may detect that it is an opportunity to switch
from a reflecting mode to a planning conversation. For example,
in the reflecting conversation with Raul, the coach might seize the
opportunity to begin planning: "So, Raul, you'd like to implement
project-based learning with your primary students. What might
you do to get started?" Or, during a planning conversation, the
vigilant coach might, based on the comments of the planner, find
it profitable to switch to a reflecting conversation: "What was it
about some of those projects you saw that you might use in your
planning for your students?"

By knowing these mental maps deeply, skillful coaches have the flexibility to maneuver within each map and to draw forth components of each of the maps as the situation demands. Chapter 10 specifically discusses navigation within and among the three maps for various types of situations.

GETTING COACHING STARTED

We are often asked questions like the following:

- How do I get started?
- Where do I begin?
- How do I find the time to coach?
- How much time should I allow?
- How long will it take to implement Cognitive Coaching?
- What should I do about reluctant teachers?

Although we have no prescriptions for each reader's unique situation, we have some general suggestions gleaned from working with numerous educators and school districts.

Deepening Skills

Skillfulness in Cognitive Coaching takes time and practice beyond reading this book. Other opportunities can help coaches to acquire the skills and understanding of this complex process. Several visual aids are available as an introduction to Cognitive Coaching and in skill refinement. The Center for Cognitive Coaching has two helpful videotapes, one showing a planning conversation and another displaying a reflecting conversation. These programs are annotated and come with a training manual.[4] The Association for Supervision and Curriculum Development (ASCD) videotape inservice program, *Another Set of Eyes: Conferencing Skills*[5] may be also be used in skills training sessions for coaching. The co-directors and associates of the Center conduct training sessions in Cognitive Coaching in many locations throughout the world.

Getting Started

As a novice Cognitive Coach, begin with a colleague who is relatively secure and with whom you already have a trusting relationship. Preview your intentions and procedures. As your skills become more automatic, you may wish to become more venturesome with new acquaintances and less experienced teachers.

For administrators whose staff has experienced a more traditional evaluative form of supervision, a demonstration in which staff members observe the differences between Cognitive Coaching and their previous experiences is a highly successful strategy. Communicate clearly at the outset that the purpose of Cognitive Coaching is to refine and make automatic the intellectual skills associated with effective instruction. Be equally clear that the coaching process is not an evaluation. Explain that your coaching behaviors will include questioning, paraphrasing, and probing. Explain why you remain nonjudgmental and do not give advice. The Video Journal's videotape *Cognitive Coaching*[6] provides an overview and would be helpful to acquaint the staff with Cognitive Coaching purposes and strategies.

Some Cognitive Coaches have begun by switching roles: having the uninitiated teacher follow the planning conversation map. While the coach teaches a lesson or conducts a meeting, the colleague observes. Thus, the teacher becomes acquainted with the process by actually coaching the coach. Variations of this process have been used with student teachers and first-year teachers to model for them the basics of instructional thought.

Scheduling Time

Time, that precious and rare commodity, must be allocated for conducting the coaching cycle. Teachers engaged in peer coaching, often establish times for the segments of the full conference cycle before or after school, during planning periods, or even over lunch. Often, substitutes are hired, or other resource teachers and administrators take the coach's class to free the teacher to conference and observe other teachers. Hiring a substitute teacher for a day, to spend one hour in each grade level to free each teacher, is a powerful and inexpensive way to make some time for coaching.

The planning conference, observation, and reflecting conference may consume extra time initially, because both parties are learning the process. However, that time diminishes as the expectations of the teacher are better understood and the coach becomes more skillful. It has been found that highly proficient coaches working with teachers experienced in the process can conduct a planning conference in about 8 to 12 minutes. This does not mean that speed is valued, however. It only points out that as experiences are gained, there is a greater economy of time for coaching.

Administrators and supervisors find time for coaching by incorporating it into their regular duties. They block out time on their calendars and inform their secretaries, staff, central office, and community that they will be in classrooms during these hours.

Arranging for coaching by peers is most often done informally, with teachers agreeing to meet at times convenient to them. Sometimes, however, substitutes have to be hired and teachers released. One school keeps a sign-up sheet in the faculty lounge to arrange for the substitute to take a class at a certain time. Often, the school administrator initially sets up a coaching session with the teacher, both of them suggesting and agreeing on a suitable time. As trust develops, the teacher will request the conference with the administrator or other resourceful colleague.

Planning and reflecting conversations can be conducted in informal, unscheduled settings: in the teacher's lounge, in the car while driving, in the hallway on the way to or from a class or meeting, and even on the telephone or over the Internet.

CONCLUSION

This chapter introduced the basic structures and variations of the Cognitive Coaching model. Two of the three mental maps that guide a coach's interactions, along with examples of dialogues intended to illustrate the process in action, were presented. Suggestions for how to get started and find time to implement the coaching process were also given.

The following chapters describe the specific kinds of knowledge, techniques, and skills that coaches need to achieve the goals described in this chapter. At this point we recommend that you examine the example of an actual coaching conference in Appendix A. As you proceed through the subsequent chapters, you may want to return to these interactions to see how the principles of Cognitive Coaching are applied.

NOTES

1. Lipton, L., and Garmston, R. (1997). *The Planning Conversation.* Cognitive Coaching Seminar Series *The Journey to Mastery.* Video and Manual. Highlands Ranch CO: Center for Cognitive Coaching. www.cognitivecoaching.cc

2. For an extensive discussion of the need for and value of reflection, see: York-Barr, J., Sommers, W., Ghere, G., and Montie, J. (2001). *Reflective Practice to Improve Schools: An Action Guide for Educators.* Thousand Oaks, CA: Corwin Press. Sanford, C. (1995). *Feedback and Self Accountability: A Collision Course.* Battleground, WA: Springhill.

3. Costa, A., and Wellman, B. (2002). *The Reflecting Conversation.* Cognitive Coaching Seminar Series *The Journey to Mastery.* Video and Manual. Highlands Ranch, CO: Center for Cognitive Coaching. www.cognitivecoaching.cc

4. Lipton and Garmston, *The Planning Conversation*; Costa, and Wellman, *The Reflecting Conversation.*

5. This videotape is available from the Association for Supervision and Curriculum Development, 1703 N. Beauregard St., Alexandria, VA 22311-1714; (703) 933-ASCD; www.ascd.org.

6. This videotape is available from TeachStream, Inc., 8686 S. 1300 E. Sandy, UT 84094; (877) 350-6500; fax (888) 566-6888. www.schoolimprovement.net

3

Coaching as Mediation

The self is not a thing, but a point of view that unifies the flow of experience into a coherent narrative—a narrative striving to connect with other narratives and become richer.
—Jerome Bruner

The ultimate goal of Cognitive Coaching is self-directed learning, which means to self-manage, self-monitor, and self-modify. With Cognitive Coaching, the mediator helps to engage and enhance a colleague's cognitive and emotional capacities to develop self-directed learning. Ultimately, mediators work to modify another person's capacity to become self-coaching.

THE PROCESSES AND ROLE OF MEDIATION

The word *mediate* is derived from the word *middle*. Therefore, mediators interpose themselves between a person and some event, problem, conflict, challenge, or other perplexing situation. The mediator intervenes in such a way as to enhance another person's self-directed learning.

Human learning is a matter of strengthening internal knowledge structures. Planning for and reflecting on experience activates these knowledge structures. With mediation, existing knowledge structures can be made more complex through more connections. The structures can also be altered to accommodate new understandings, or they can be made obsolete because some new experience has caused the creation of a new knowledge structure. This sifting and winnowing of prior knowledge structures constitutes learning. (See Appendix C for a more detailed description of constructivism and its relationship to coaching.)

Reuven Feuerstein states the following in "Mediated Learning Experience":

> Mediated learning is an experience that the learner has that entails not just seeing something, not just doing something, not just understanding something, but also experiencing that thing at deeper levels of cognitive, emotional, attitudinal, energetic, and affective impact through the interposition of the mediator between the learner and the experienced object or event (stimuli). In such a context, learning becomes a deeply structured and often a pervasive and generalizable change.[1]

Figure 3-1 illustrates how the mediator may intervene at two points: between a person and a task and between a person and meaning.

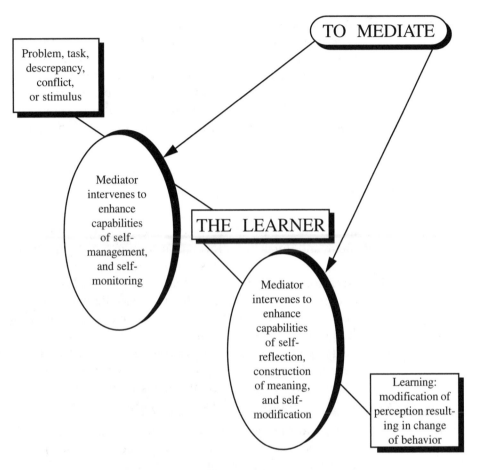

**Figure 3-1.
A Mediator Intervenes**

Intervening Between a Person and a Task

When a person encounters some task, problem, or obstacle that involves planning, the mediator intervenes by helping to think through a strategic, deliberate approach. This means establishing clear goals and planning to gather as much data as possible. Mediating in this case also means drawing out past successes with similar problems and considering alternate strategies. What will the end product be like? How can the colleague monitor steps in the strategy and collect indicators of success along the way? The question "What will be your indicators of success?" is a simple expression of this form of mediation.

Intervening Between a Person and Meaning

This type of mediation involves helping the other person to reflect on the experience to maximize meaning-making. Meaning is made by analyzing feelings and data, comparing results with expectations, finding causal factors, and projecting ahead to how the meaning may apply to future situations. "How else might you explain that?" illustrates an intervention at this level.

THE MEDIATOR'S ROLE

Mediators influence the intensity, flow, directionality, importance, excitement, and impact of information coming to the person being coached. According to Feuerstein, the mediated learning experience transforms the information that impinges on a learner and enters his repertoire in a totally different way. Rather than give advice to or solve problems for another person, a mediator helps the colleague to analyze a problem and develop her own problem-solving strategies. A mediator helps a colleague to set up strategies for self-monitoring during the problem-solving process. Acting as a sounding board, a skilled mediator helps another person to become more self-directed with learning. A mediator also:

- is alert to the mediational moment—usually when a colleague is faced with a complex task, dilemma, discrepancy, or conflict. Often, the colleague exhibits tension and anxiety, the resolution of which is not immediately apparent.

- facilitates mental processes for others as they solve their own problems, make their own decisions, and generate their own creative capacities.

- invites the colleague to reflect on and learn from the problem-solving process to find applications in future problem situations.

- helps others to become continuous learners.

- maintains faith in the human capacity for continued intellectual, social, and emotional growth.

- possesses a belief in his or her own capacity to serve as an empowering catalyst for others' growth.

HOW MEDIATION AFFECTS THE BRAIN

> *[The] talking cure can physically change the brain and . . . any-time you have a change in behavior you have a change in the brain.*
>
> —Lewis Baxter

Feuerstein believes that mediation produces new connections in the brain. He states:

> One of the most interesting and exciting aspects of mediated learning . . . is that the quality of interaction not only changes the structure of behavior of the individual, not only changes the amount and quality of his repertoire, but—according to increasingly powerful sources of evidence from fields of neurophysiology and biochemistry—changes the structure and functioning of the brain itself in very meaningful ways.

This idea finds support from many quarters. Neuroscientist Gerald Edelman proposes that the brain reconstructs itself from experience. One commonly understood example of this is the neural pruning that occurs within the first two years of life, cauterizing neural capacities for distinguishing sounds outside one's own language group.[2] Ornstein claims, "To make a personal change, we have to be able to observe the automatic workings inside ourselves."[3] This requires the kind of consciousness evoked by mediation. He describes the brain as having a neural selection system that wires up the nervous system differently, depending on the demands on the organism. Managing and developing the mind is to bring automatic processes into consciousness.

THREE RESOURCES OF MEDIATION

Three resources are constantly monitored and sustained in the mediation process: reciprocity, clear intentions, and vision.

Reciprocity refers to how skillful mediators maintain mutually cooperative, trusting relationships. The mediator holds and demonstrates the utmost respect for the individual's feelings, ideas, and perspectives.

When assuming the identity of a mediator, one must also be very clear about intentions. Mediators monitor their own values and realize that although it might be tempting to solve a problem, evaluate, or give advice, they must hold those thoughts in abeyance in order to allow the other person to resolve the situation. Mediators are not "fixers." Instead, they have faith that others can solve their own problems. Trying to "fix" others detracts from a trusting relationship.

The mediator and the individual also need a clear vision of a more desirable state for the individual. For example:

- If the person is experiencing a feeling of helplessness, the vision would be to help him achieve a feeling of efficacy.

- If the person were struggling with vagueness or a lack of clarity, the vision would be for her to become clear about goals, outcomes, strategies, or definitions.

- If the person is unaware of his actions and values and their effects on others, the vision would be to build greater self-awareness.

- If the person is holding on to a rigid stance or narrow perspective, the vision could be for her to think more flexibly or more broadly.

- If the person is experiencing a feeling of isolation, the vision would be for him to develop interdependent relationships, connectedness, and a sense of affiliation and belonging.

WHY MEDIATION WORKS

Knowledge is a rediscovery of our own insights.

—Plato

Four theorems guide the Cognitive Coach's beliefs and actions and explain why mediation works:

1. The sum of an individual's constructed meanings resides internally at conscious and unconscious levels and serves as the criterion for perceptions, decisions, and behavior.

2. When these meanings are given form in language, they become accessible to both parties in a verbal transaction.

3. Through verbal transaction (mediation), these meanings and the perceptions, decisions, and behaviors related to them can be refined, enriched, and modified.

4. Through Cognitive Coaching, not only are an individual's meanings, decisions, and behaviors refined and modified, with related results in improved performance, but also refined is the individual's capacity to self-mediate and to become more proactive in continuing self-directedness.[4]

WHO CAN BE A MEDIATOR?

Anyone can assume the role of mediator for another's self-directed learning. Thus, mediation can occur between two students, two teachers, two administrators, a leader and a group member, or a teacher and a student.

When a coaching relationship is established between two professionals with similar roles, or peers, it may be referred to as peer coaching. Cognitive Coaching has a more specific meaning; it refers to the identity that mediators assume, the coaching maps and tools with which they work, the desire for enhancing other's self-directedness that they embrace, and the faith in the human capacity for meaning-making that they cherish. Peer coaching describes with whom you coach; Cognitive Coaching defines how you coach.

In an increasing number of educational communities, custodians, school secretaries, bus drivers, parents, students, and cafeteria workers are learning the skills of Cognitive Coaching. In one Michigan school district, the director of maintenance coaches an elementary principal, who in turn coaches a teacher. In a California school district, a superintendent receives monthly coaching from a mentor teacher. In an international school in Malaysia, the head of schools is coached by a special education teacher.

THE MEDIATIONAL MOMENT

We all have many opportunities to engage others in problem solving. The challenge, however, is in deciding among these three questions:

- Can I, do I wish to, and should I provide someone with solutions?

- Can I, do I wish to, and should I collaborate and assist others with ideas or information?

- Can I, do I wish to, and should I assist others in learning how to solve their problems themselves?

For example, if a teacher has a problem with a leak in the classroom ceiling, then the principal should arrange for the appropriate maintenance personnel to take care of the problem. If the teacher's challenge has to do with implementing a new teaching strategy, determining a more effective behavior management technique, devising an innovative way to deal with student diversity, or optimizing the use of a new technological tool, mediation would be a better way to help the teacher generate ideas for planning, implementing, and resolving the challenge.

Many people are not accustomed to seeing themselves as mediators. They may try to solve others' problems instead of facilitating the problem-solving process. They may give advice instead of helping others to self-prescribe. They may evaluate rather than help a person to self-evaluate.

There are advantages and disadvantages to performing as an advisor for others. Some advantages are the following:

- The problem will be solved (or appear to be solved) swiftly and efficiently.

- The solution will be congruent with your beliefs and values.

- You may feel satisfaction for having been of help.

- Others may perceive you as an effective leader.

- You will learn more about the process of problem solving.

There are also some disadvantages to acting as an advisor:

- The problem you have "solved" may be a surface manifestation of deeper issues that have not been resolved.

- The other person may become dependent on you to solve future problems or blame you if a satisfactory resolution is not achieved.

- The other person will have learned little about problem-solving processes.

- The other person may not take your suggestions for solving the problem.

- The other person may build resentment because he views himself as inadequate and helpless.

- You will miss the opportunity for developing another's capacities for self-directedness.

CAPABILITIES OF A MEDIATOR

The settings in which Cognitive Coaching may occur range from informal, spontaneous conversations to more formal, planned conferences. Sometimes opportunities for mediation present themselves spontaneously and informally in day-to-day life, such as during a conversation in the faculty room or in the hall on the way to class. More formal, planned events are also opportunities for mediation, such as a formal classroom observation of teaching and learning or a scheduled department or faculty meeting.

A coach seizes all these opportunities to use specific mediational skills to engage and develop the other person's thinking processes. Mediators need certain skills, attitudes, and capabilities to perform their role well. For example, a mediator uses language with the intent of causing a change in the other person's reality. These linguistic tools include the following: posing questions intended to engage and transform the mind, creating conditions of trust, envisioning a desired state of mind, remaining nonjudgmental, and resisting the tendency to solve the problem for the learner. (A description of these specific tools can be found in chapter 4.) Following are descriptions of four specific capabilities, or metacognitive attributes, of a mediator.

Knowing One's Own Intentions and Choosing Congruent Behaviors

Behaviors can be either reactive or proactive. Proactive behaviors are based on intention or goal awareness. The ultimate goal of mediation is to help an individual become self-mediating. With that end in mind, mediators are clear about their intentions in the moment. Perhaps they want to reflect understanding, clarify a communication, help the colleague to feel comfort, or cause self-examination. Choosing behaviors that support intentions like these requires the following:

- Being conscious of one's intention in the moment and how that intention serves a greater goal

- Being alert to a colleague's verbal and nonverbal cues

- Having a repertoire of mediational tools

- Knowing how a particular tool may serve a specific intention

- Being able to use that tool with a great degree of craftsmanship

- Anticipating and searching for the effects a tool produces in a colleague

Setting Aside Unproductive Patterns of Listening, Responding, and Inquiring

> *In trying to really listen, I have often been inspired by the Zen Master Suzuki-roshi, who said: "If your mind is empty, it is always ready for anything; it is open to everything. In the beginner's mind there are many possibilities."*
>
> —Sogyal Rinpoche

Mediators monitor and manage their own listening skills by devoting their mental energies to the other person's verbal and nonverbal communications. To listen with such intensity requires holding in abeyance certain normal, tempting, but unproductive behaviors, which may interfere with the ability to hear and understand a colleague.

For example, *autobiographical listening* occurs when the brain exercises its associative powers and the colleague's story stimulates the coach to think of her own experiences. (If a colleague mentions recent automobile repairs, that reminds you of your car's most recent breakdown.) Coaches set this type of listening aside as soon as they become aware that their attention has drifted into their own story. Besides being distracting, autobiographical listening may stimulate judgment in which negative or positive experiences prejudice listening. Autobiographical listening may also stimulate comparison, in which the coach is further distracted by comparing the situations. Finally, autobiographical listening may spark immersion, in which we are lost in attentiveness to our own story.

Inquisitive listening occurs when we begin to get curious about portions of the story that are not relevant to the problem at hand. Knowing what information is important is one critical distinction between consulting and coaching. As a consultant, a person needs lots of information in order to "solve the problem." As a coach, a person needs only to understand the colleague's perspective, feelings, and goals and how to pose questions that support self-directed learning.

Mind reading is sometimes a byproduct of inquisitive listening. With mind reading, we try to figure out what someone is really thinking and feeling. Mind reading does not allow us to pay sufficient attention to what a partner is saying. Scrutinizing is also a by-product of inquisitive listening. With scrutinizing, curiosity about that which is not relevant to the mediational moment sinks the conversation into a hole of analytical minutiae that may cause a coach and colleague to lose sight of the larger issue.

Solution listening is what we have a tendency to do when we serve as a problem solver for another. Because we may view ourselves as great problem solvers, ready with help and eager to give suggestions, we immediately begin searching for the right solution to a problem. When coaching, however, thinking of solution approaches as your colleague speaks interferes with understanding the situation from the colleague's perspective. It also interferes with formulating mediational moves.

Filtering is often a by-product of solution listening in which we listen to some things and not to others, paying attention only to those ideas that support the solution approach we are developing. This is a common problem for physicians, who must work hard to stay open to possibilities during the early stages of diagnostic visits with a patient. Rehearsing, too, can be a by-product of solution listening, as our attention gets focused on preparing and crafting the way that we are going to present a solution.

Adjusting One's Own Style Preferences

Mediators understand a fundamental and common principle: humans differ. Distinct patterns of perceiving and processing information are neither good nor bad. They transcend race and culture, characterize males and females equally, and are observable at all age levels.

Conscious of these differences, Cognitive Coaches strive to be flexible communicators. They recognize their own style preferences and seek to overcome these habits when interacting with someone who operates from a different style.

Setting aside their own style preferences, coaches observe, respect, appreciate, are open, inquire, let go of judgment, are authentic, are collaborative, are caring, and are compassionate.[5] To achieve this, coaches constantly sense, search for, and detect cues about the person with whom they are working. They constantly expand their repertoire so they can match their style to a variety of situations and individuals. Style flexibility is elaborated in chapter 12.

Navigating Through the Coaching Maps and Support Functions

Three basic coaching maps provide the coach with information about the mental territories of planning, reflecting, and problem resolving. Similar to a road map, mental maps provide the coach with directions to destinations as well as options for alternate routes. Humans reference many maps to guide their interactions in different settings. Problem-solving steps, brainstorming rules, algorithms, and other procedural knowledge that adults accumulate are all forms of mental maps. We consciously use some of these daily; other maps, with practice and habituation, are used unconsciously. Bloom's Taxonomy and Marzano's Taxonomy[6] are examples of mental maps that teachers hold in their heads as guides for questioning, sequencing a lesson, and composing test items.

Coaches make decisions within coaching maps (such as the sequence with which items in the planning map are discussed). Coaches also make decisions across coaching maps; that is, they are alert to a moment during a reflecting conversation when it might be appropriate to switch to a problem-solving map to guide an interaction. Coaches also decide when to coach, when to collaborate and when to consult.

SEARCHING FOR OUR IDENTITY AS MEDIATORS

The circumstances in life, the events in life, the people around me in life do not make me the person I am, but reveal the way I am.

—Jim St. John

Throughout our lifetimes we play out a variety of roles. We are parent or child, husband or wife, brother or sister, friend or student, boss or employee. The archetype of each of these roles carries certain presuppositions, orientations, and goals, which are manifested verbally and with our entire being. Communicating from any one these orientations casts us into a response loop with others. For example, if I sound, feel, and look like a parent to you, you are likely to respond to me as a child.[7]

Assuming the stance of the expert establishes one's responsibility to share one's greater knowledge and experience and to help others develop correct and appropriate performance. The friend values the relationship and will be loath to jeopardize it. The boss, in the traditional sense, wants compliance and feels responsible for the other person's success or failure.

Contrast these orientations with the identity of mediator. In this chapter we have described a mediator's mission as helping individuals to develop their own resources for problem solving. A mediator is a co-learner, engaging another person with the intent of transforming his capacities to become more self-directed: self-managing, self-monitoring, and self-modifying.

Being aware of these orientations helps us to recognize these recurring patterns of our own behavior as we play out our many life roles. The "default position" as a mediator, however, may be manifest in many situations across many relationships, such as between parent and child, husband and wife, or administrator and teacher. The mediator's overriding intention is always present: as a result of this interaction, the other person will become more capable of solving the problem for herself and will have the capacity to solve future problems with greater efficacy. Thus, mediators evaluate their own performance based on the degree to which they have helped others to become more autonomous and interdependent.

The Neuropsychological Origins of Identity

Neuroscientist Antonio Damasio helps us to understand the neuropsychological origins of identity. He explains that for some aspects of consciousness there is an anatomy, or an involvement, of specific brain regions and systems. He notes that wheras emotion and consciousness are not separable in humans, consciousness "can be separated into simple and complex kinds. The neurological evidence makes the separation transparent."[9] Damasio calls the simplest kind of consciousness core consciousness. "It provides the person with a sense of self about one moment—now and about one place—here." There is also an *extended consciousness* that provides the person with a sense of self and places "me" into a historical frame, richly aware of the lived past, the anticipated future, and the world beside oneself.

Extended consciousness reaches its highest peak in humans. It is a complex biological phenomenon and depends on conventional

---

Identity and Sense of Self

Wheatley and Kellner-Rogers observe, "Every living thing acts to develop and preserve itself. Identity is the filter that every organism or system uses to make sense of the world. New information, new relationships, changing environments—all are interpreted through a sense of self. This tendency toward self-creation is so strong that it creates a seeming paradox. An organism will change to maintain its identity."[8]

---

memory, working memory, reasoning, and language. The sense of self, which emerges in core consciousness, is a transient entity, ceaselessly re-created for each and every object with which the brain interacts. Our traditional sense of self, however, corresponds to a nontransient collection of unique facts and ways of being that characterize a person. Damasio calls this the autobiographical self. The thoughts, feelings, inferences, and interpretations of the experiences available to the autobiographical self constitute one's identity. Identity is the story we tell ourselves of who we are.

The Social Origins of Identity

Identity, then, is constructed from the meaning we make of our interactions with others and with the environment. Identity emerges from a web of relationships constructed within a community. It is not only how I see myself, but also the meanings I make from how others see me as a result of my interactions over time. There is no identity in isolation from each other.

One's identity is not fixed but, rather, is in a constant and imperceptibly gradual transformation. It is the temporary result of a struggle for authenticity, striving to align ourselves more congruently from within (our ego ideals, our sense of self) and with reciprocal relationships (between the external world and internal self). It is a struggle for authenticity to our autobiographical self as we understand and envision it.

A new identity may not be something that we build but rather something that we dissolve. As Michelangelo carved his sculptures by chipping away the excess stone to reveal the figure that was already inside the marble, our identity may go through a gradual "morphing" process to form new dimensions of itself. Through Cognitive Coaching, we have seen these transformations countless times as people "discover" powers they have through the processes of mediation.

Identity organizes our beliefs and values; these provide structures for capabilities that drive the selection, shaping, and use of knowledge and skill.[10] Identity drives perception, choice, and behavior; thus, reciprocally, actions to some degree reinforce identity. Our identity evolves from preexisting patterns through meanings we make from a history of reciprocal interactions. In a similar manner, our words and labels allow us to see new realities, and our seeing new realities affects our words. Our identity defines our reality, and our subjective reality helps to shape our identity.

Cognitive Coaching requires refining and habituating new maps and patterns of thinking and increasing sensitivity to how those patterns affect our relationships with others. Students of Cognitive Coaching may experience dissolution of the old thoughts that held their identity as they develop new identities that constitute new thoughts.

CONCLUSION

In asking, "Who am I?", it is useful to reflect on the following questions:[11]

- How do I see myself?

- How do I want to see myself?

- How do I think others see me?

- How do I see others?

- How do I want others to see me?

As a format for identity building, these questions allow mediators to assess how they see themselves as individuals as well as in relationship to others. This exploration can set the groundwork for personal goals that the coach can develop for himself. They also provide a vehicle for coaches to learn more about their client's identity, her affiliations, and the references to which she makes connections and which she thus values.

For some people, the role of mediator may fit immediately into their desired identity, and the behaviors may follow "naturally." For others it will take a psychological shift. Transforming one's identity implies foraging in the unknown—opening oneself to the psychological risks of a new venture, the physically unknown demands on time and energy, and the intellectually unknown requirements for new skills and knowledge. Adopting an identity as a mediator requires a shift away from obsolete beliefs about learning, teaching, achievement, and talent.

The concepts in this chapter invite a shift from the present paradigms. For many educators, a dominant sense of satisfaction has come from their expertise as problem solvers. The shift to a mediational identity creates a feeling of being rewarded by facilitating others to solve their own problems. The shift is from teaching others to helping others learn from situations; from holding power to empowering others; from telling to inquiring; and from finding strength in holding on to finding strength in letting go. Changing one's identity requires patience, stamina, and courage.

NOTES

1. Feuerstein, R. (2000). Mediated learning experience. In A. Costa (Ed.), *Teaching for intelligence II: A collection of articles* (p. 275). Arlington Heights, IL: Skylights.

2. Edelman, G. (1987). *Neural Darwinism: The theory of neuronal group selection.* New York: Basic Books.

3. Ornstein, R. (1991). *The evolution of consciousness: Of Darwin, Freud, and cranial fire—The origins of the way we think* (p. 224). New York: Prentice-Hall Press.

4. Kegan, R., and Lahey, L. (2001). *How the way we talk can change the way we work: Seven languages for transformation.* San Francisco: Jossey-Bass.

5. Seagal, S., and Horn, D. (1997). *Human dynamics.* Cambridge, MA: Pegasus Communications.

6. Bloom, B. S., Engelhart, M. D., Furst, E. J., Hill, W. H., and Krathwohl, D. R. (Eds.). (1956). *Taxonomy of educational objectives: The classification of educational goals. Handbook I: Cognitive domain.* New York: David McKay. Marzano, R. (2001). A new taxonomy of educational objectives, in A. Costa (Ed.), *Developing Minds.*

7. Costa, A., and Garmston, R. (1999). *Cognitive coaching: A foundation for renaissance schools syllabus* (p. 9). Norwood, MA: Christopher-Gordon.

8. Wheatley, M. and, Kellner-Rogers, M. (1996) *A simpler way.* (p. 14). San Francisco: Barrett-Kohler.

9. Damasio, A. (1999). *The feeling of what happens: Body and emotion in the making of consciousness* (p. 16). New York: Harcourt Brace.

10. Dilts, R. (1994). *Effective presentation skills.* Capitola, CA: Meta.

11. Jackson, Y. (2001). Reversing underachievement in culturally different urban students: Pedagogy of confidence. In A. Costa (Ed.), *Developing minds: A resource book for teaching thinking* (pp. 222–228). Alexandria, VA: Association for Supervision and Curriculum Development.

4

The Mediator's Toolbox

A skillful coach uses certain well-crafted verbal and nonverbal tools to facilitate others' cognitive growth. All are used without judgment; all are intended to sustain a colleague's access to the highest possible neocortical intellectual functions and body-mind intelligence. These tools can be catalogued into four groups: paralanguage, response behaviors, structuring, and mediative questioning.

Paralanguage refers to vocal qualities, body gestures, and other verbal and nonverbal behaviors that exist alongside the words we speak. (The prefix para means "alongside.") When confronted with conflicting verbal and nonverbal messages, humans inevitably choose the meaning behind the nonverbal behavior. We are just beginning to increase our appreciation of the body in thinking. Distinguished neurologist Antonio Damasio conjectures that mental activity, from its simplest aspects to its most sublime, requires both brain and body.[1]

Response behaviors refers to verbal responses to another person's communications. Five types of verbal responses are helpful in mediating thinking:

- Silence, through wait time and listening
- Acknowledging, both nonverbally and verbally
- Paraphrasing, such as summarizing, organizing, shifting levels, and empathizing
- Clarifying, by probing for meanings and specificity
- Providing data and resources, thus facilitating the acquisition of information through primary and secondary sources

Structuring establishes the parameters of time, space, and purposes.

Mediative questioning helps coaches to construct and pose questions intended to engage thinking.

This chapter examines each of these coaching tools and describes their positive effects on intellectual growth.

PARALANGUAGE

On the average, adults find more meaning in nonverbal cues than in verbal ones. A recent summary of communication literature supports the theory that nearly two-thirds of meaning in any social situation is derived from nonverbal cues.[2] In addition to posture, gesture, and use of space, the intonation, rhythms, pacing, and volume of a person's voice all contribute important information about the communication.

Vocal cues affect attention. In a classic book, top nonverbal-behavior scholars Burgoon, Buller, and Goodall report studies that demonstrate that "Vocal variety, which includes variation in pitch, tempo, intensity and tonal quality, has been shown to result in increased comprehension."[3] In classroom work, Michael Grinder, observing in more than 5,000 classrooms, found that teachers tend to use one of two voices that elicit student attention in order to achieve comprehension.[4] One is a credible voice, with which the teacher gains attention and gives direction. This voice is characterized by a limited range of modulation and a tendency to go down in intonation at the end of a sentence. (Imagine a newscaster reporting news.) The second voice, and the one used in coaching, is an approachable voice. This has a wider range of modulation and a tendency, at times, to rise in inflection at the end of a sentence. When delivered in an approachable voice, questions like "Can you say more?" or "What are your goals?" signal safety and inquiry. The same questions offered in the credible voice feel like interrogation and lead to shutdowns in thinking.

Recently, the neuropsychologist Giacomo Rizzolatti found neurons in monkeys that fire both when the monkey carries out certain specific hand motions and when it views those specific motions being carried out by someone else. The existence of "mirror neurons" indicates that we are built to respond to what others in our environment do. We believe that these "mirror neurons" will also be found for other gestures, including facial movements.[5]

Humans gesture when they talk. The observant coach will notice that colleagues place people, events, time periods, and concepts in space. "On the one hand . . . and then on the other hand" is a verbal equivalent of this physical talk. Understanding is communicated and rapport is enhanced when the coach points to the space assigned to a concept when verbally responding. A verbal paraphrase is a reflection of what the colleague is thinking and feeling. Repeating a colleague's gesture adds a visual component to the reflection.

Even laughter, as a paralanguage, is valuable in coaching. Researchers at Stanford University and the Loma Linda Medical School found an increase in white blood cell activity while subjects listened to a comedian. This change in blood chemistry may boost the production of the neurotransmitters required for alertness and memory.[6]

During the early 1970s, Richard Bandler and John Grinder conducted a series of investigations to learn why some therapists were almost magically effective, in contrast to others who simply did a good job. They initially studied Fritz Perls, the founder of Gestalt therapy; Virgina Satir, noted for her results in family therapy; and Milton Erickson, generally acknowledged to be the world's leading practitioner of medical hypnosis.[7]

The researchers discovered that Perls, Satir, and Erickson constantly mirrored their clients. For example, if the client had his legs crossed, the therapist crossed his legs. If the client leaned forward on her elbows, so did the therapist. When the client spoke rapidly, the therapist did, too.

Whether they were conscious of it or not, Perls, Satir, and Erickson were modeling the theory of entrainment, which was formulated in 1665 after a Dutch scientist noted that two pendulum clocks mounted side by side on a wall would swing together in a precise rhythm. It was discovered that the clocks were synchronized by a slight impulse through the wall. Figure 4-1 shows other manifestations of this kind of rapport.

When two people "oscillate" at nearly the same rates, we observe entrainment. Human beings seek this kind of synchronization. George Leonard reports that human beings pulse at frequencies of oscillation, as do the simplest single-celled organisms at the atomic, molecular, subcellular, and cellular levels.[8]

At the Boston University School of Medicine, William Condon studied films of many sets of two people talking. Not only were the bodies of the speakers matched, but another "very startling phenomenon" was observed: entrainment existed between the speaker's words and the listener's movements. As one person would talk, the second person would make tiny corresponding movements. As Condon expressed it:

> Listeners were observed to move in precise shared synchrony with the speaker's speech. This appears to be a form of entrainment since there is no discernible lag even at 1/48 second. It also appears to be a universal characteristic of human communication, and perhaps characterizes much of animal behavior in general. Thus, communication is like a dance, with everyone engaged in intricate and shared movements across many subtle dimensions, yet all strangely oblivious that they are doing so.[9]

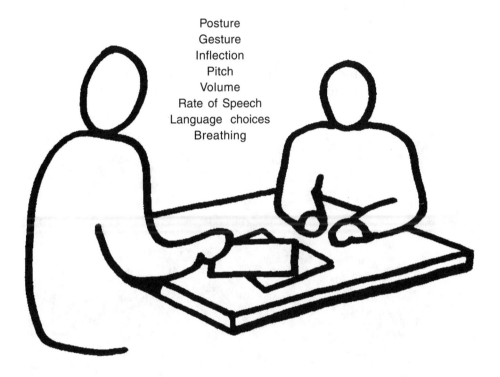

Posture
Gesture
Inflection
Pitch
Volume
Rate of Speech
Language choices
Breathing

Figure 4-1.
Rapport

When entrainment (matching) of several of these processing and communication systems is present, people can be said to be in rapport.

An example of entrainment in a school setting might be the following: Lee says, "Fran, I've got some teachers on my staff doing things I am really excited about. I'm trying to figure out how I can get them to share some of their good ideas with other faculty." While Lee is speaking, she gestures broadly with her hands and arms. Then she shrugs her shoulders as she notes her predicament. Now Fran says, "Lee, tell me a little bit about what's so special about these teachers." As Fran speaks, she mirrors Lee's gestures and body movements.

Because Lee's nonverbal behaviors are congruent with her feelings and thoughts, each particular movement and gesture conveys specific meanings. When Fran borrows these same nonverbal cues, Lee subconsciously senses that Fran knows exactly what she's talking about. Figure 4-2 shows another example of matching body positions and gestures as a manifestation of rapport.

Photo by Bruce Wellman, Mira Via, Guilford, CT

Figure 4-2.
Matching Posture and Gesture

RESPONSE BEHAVIORS

The effective Cognitive Coach draws on several response behaviors, depending on the colleague and the setting. These behaviors are silence, acknowledging, paraphrasing, clarifying, and providing data and resources.

Silence

Some coaches may wait only one or two seconds after having asked a question before they ask another question or give an answer to the question themselves. It is easy to feel that unless someone is talking, no one is learning. In actuality, however, silence is an indicator of a productive conference. If the coach waits after asking a question, or after the partner gives an answer, the silence (1) communicates respect for the other's reflection and processing time, and (2) results in a positive effect on higher level cognitive processing.

If the coach waits only a short time—one or two seconds—then a brief, one-word type of response will typically result. On the other hand, if the coach waits for a longer period, teachers tend to respond in whole sentences and complete thoughts. There is a perceptible increase in the creativity of the response as shown by greater use of descriptive and modifying words and an increase in speculative thinking.[10] There is also an increased feeling of being valued and respected by the coach.

Coaches can communicate expectation through the use of silence. When the coach asks a question and then waits for an answer, it demonstrates that the coach not only expects an answer but also has faith in the other person's ability to perform the complex cognitive task, given enough time. If the coach asks a question, waits only a short time, and then gives the answer or gives hints, it subconsciously communicates that the colleague is inadequate and can't really reason through to an appropriate answer.[11]

When the coach waits after the other person gives an answer, it causes the continuation of thinking about the task or question. Furthermore, when a coach waits after the partner asks a question or gives an answer, it models the same thoughtfulness, reflectiveness, and restraint of impulsivity that are desirable behaviors for others to use.[12]

Acknowledging

Acknowledging without making judgments is a response that simply receives and recognizes what the speaker says without making any value judgments. It communicates that the other person's ideas have been heard. The following are examples of this type of response:

- Verbal: "Um-hmm," "That's one possibility," "Could be," or "I understand."

- Nonverbal: Nodding the head or recording the speaker's verbatim statement on a note pad.

Paraphrasing

Paraphrasing is one of the most valuable and least used tools in human interaction. A well-crafted paraphrase communicates, "I am trying to understand you and therefore I value what you have to say." A paraphrase also establishes a relationship between people and ideas. Paraphrasing aligns the parties and creates a safe environment for thinking.

Mediational paraphrases reflect the speaker's content and emotions about the content. They frame the logical level for holding the content. Questions by themselves, no matter how artfully constructed, put a degree of psychological distance between the asker and the person being asked. Questions preceded by paraphrases gain permission to probe for details and elaboration. Without the paraphrase, probing and questioning may be perceived as interrogation.

To structure an effective paraphrase, begin by carefully listening and observing to calibrate the content and emotions of the speaker. Signal your intention to paraphrase by modulating intonation and using of an approachable voice. Don't use the pronoun I. (For example, "What I think I hear you saying . . .") The pronoun I signals that the speaker's thoughts no longer matter and that the paraphraser is now going to insert his own ideas into the conversation.

Open with a reflective stem. This language structure puts the focus and emphasis on the speaker's ideas, not on the paraphraser's interpretation of those ideas. For example, these stems signal that a paraphrase is coming:

- You're suggesting . . .
- You're proposing . . .
- So you're wondering about . . .
- Your hunch is that . . .

Choose a logical level with which to respond. There are at least three broad categories of logical levels:

1. *Acknowledge and clarify* content and emotion. If the paraphrase is not completely accurate, the speaker will offer corrections. For example, "So, you're concerned about the district-adopted standards and how to influence them."

2. *Summarize and organize* by offering themes and categories that relate several extensive topics. For example, "So you are concerned about several issues here. One is the effects of testing on students' higher level thinking. Another is making inferences about school effectiveness based upon test scores alone. And yet another is how they influence teachers' instructional practices."

3. *Shift focus* to a higher or lower logical level. Paraphrases move to a higher logical level when they name concepts, goals, values, and assumptions: "So, a major goal here is to define what constitutes effective learning and to design authentic ways to gather indicators of achievement." Paraphrases move to a lower logical level when abstractions and concepts require operational definitions: "So authentic assessments might include portfolios, performances, and exhibitions."

Clarifying

We are prepared to see, and we see easily, things for which our language and culture hand us ready-made labels. When those labels are lacking, even though the phenomena may be all around us, we may quite easily fail to see them at all. The perceptual attractors that we each possess (some coming from without, some coming from within, some on the scale of mere words, some on a much grander scale) are the filters

> *through which we scan and sort reality, and thereby they de-*
> *termine what we perceive on high and low levels.*
> —D. Hofstadter[13]

The brain and central nervous system filters an enormous amount of sensory input. A million bits of information per minute come pouring into the brain—and we certainly can't attend to it all. Instead we generalize, fitting information into already stored patterns and categories. Sometimes we delete, or literally stop data from coming in. (For example, we see bugs and dirt on a windshield but look through them to focus on the road and other cars.) At other times we distort, shaping information to fit our preconceived structures and beliefs. There is a story about a man who thought he was a corpse. After six months, his psychiatrist asked him if corpses could bleed. The patient said, "Of course not!" The doctor pricked the patient's finger and squeezed out some blood. The patient stared at it and exclaimed, "What do you know? Corpses do bleed!"

Because our brains easily filter and distort information, it's important to understand some of the cognitive reasons that probing and clarifying are essential. The skillful coach looks for the speech patterns described below.

Vague nouns or pronouns. When the teacher talks about "the textbooks," she has deleted information about which textbooks she's referring to. The coach can ask, "Which textbooks, specifically?" Clarifying vague nouns and pronouns supplies missing data and provides more precise information. When the teacher says "the girls in the class," the coach can get a better understanding by asking, "Which girls?"

Vague action words. These refer to unspecified verbs, such as *think* and *understand,* and they also signal deleted information. When the coach hears, "I want students to understand," he can ask, "Understand how, specifically?" to clarify the performance. "Which students?" will clarify the audience. "What will you see them doing when they are understanding?" tells the coach exactly what the teacher is looking for.

Comparisons. Distortions or generalities will sometimes be masked by comparisons. Often, the teacher will not elaborate to whom or to what she is comparing students. For example, if the teacher says, "The class is much brighter," the coach can probe, "Brighter than what?" Or if the teacher says, "Rebecca's getting along much better," the coach can ask, "Better than what?"

Rule words. Phrases like "I can't," "We shouldn't," "It happens all the time," or "Nobody does that" should alert the coach that the teacher is limiting his thinking and possibly working with distorted perceptions. Skillful coaches challenge this mindset. When a teacher says, "I can't," the coach can respond, "What's stopping you?" When the teacher says, "We shouldn't," one response is "What would happen if we did? Who made up that rule?"

Universal quantifiers. Terms such as *everybody, all the time, nobody, never,* and *always* also limit thinking. Statements employing these terms can be challenged with intonation. If the teacher says, "Nobody around here does that," the coach may simply respond, "Nobody?" Most people will recognize that they have overgeneralized. Or the coach can ask for exception: "Nobody around here does that? Can you think of someone who does?" This, too, leads the teacher to see that she has generalized. If the relationship permits it, the coach can use a gentle exaggeration: "Nobody ever does that? Never in the history of this school has anyone done that?"

Clarifying and probing are effective skills to call on when the speaker uses a vague concept or a vocabulary that the listener doesn't understand. The purpose of clarifying is to invite the speaker to illuminate, elaborate, and become more precise in his meaning. Clarifying helps the listener to better understand the speaker. Some examples of clarifying and probing include the following:

- Help me to understand what you mean by . . .

- What will students be doing if they are comprehending the story?

- Which students, specifically?

- When you say this class is better, better than what?

- When you say "the administrators," which administrators do you mean?

- What do you mean by "appreciate"?

Providing Data and Resources

While data may be provided during collaborating or consulting, one of the main objectives of Cognitive Coaching is to mediate the other person's capacities for processing information by comparing, inferring, or deducing causal relationships. For coaching to be data driven, therefore, data must be richly and readily available for the colleague to process. Providing data nonjudgmentally means that the coach makes it possible for the colleague to acquire the data she needs to deduce these relationships. There are several ways to facilitate this process.

During a planning conference or a coaching cycle, the coach invites the teacher to identify what information is desired, when it should be collected, and in what format the data will be recorded. Examples might include the following:

- Tell me what you want me to record about student responses that will be of help to your understanding of their higher level thinking.

- So, my job is to keep a tally on this seating chart of which students are on task and which students are off task.

- When in the lesson do you want me to record your directions? Just at the beginning when you outline their assignment, or throughout the entire lesson whenever you give a direction?

During the lesson, the coach observes and records information, data, and facts that the teacher requested during the planning conference. For example, a coach can record data with videotapes, audiotapes, classroom maps, time-on-task charts, and verbatim scripts of teachers' or students' statements.

During the reflecting conference, the coach provides the teacher with the data nonjudgmentally. Examples include the following:

- You asked three questions within the first five minutes of your lesson.

- Of the six students you wanted me to observe, Eric spoke four times, Sarah spoke two times, Shaun spoke once, and the remaining three did not speak at all.

- Here is a map of your classroom showing where you moved. Each circle indicates where you stopped and interacted with students. During the group work, you stopped and interacted with group 1 five times, group 2 three times, and group 3 two times.

Because the ultimate goal of the coach is to mediate another's capacity for self-coaching and self-modification, the coach may also mediate the colleague's gathering of data. For example, during a planning conversation the coach might say the following:

- What information do you have about these students that will guide your lesson design?

- What indicators will you be aware of to let you know you are achieving the meeting's goals?

- How will you monitor your own pacing to accomplish your agenda within the time constraints?

During a reflecting conversation, the coach mediates the acquisition of data by drawing forth and focusing on the information gathered by the colleague during the event:

- How much time did you spend explaining the task?

- What indicators were you aware of that let you know the group understood its task?

- What data were you collecting during the meeting that informed your decision to change the agenda?

STRUCTURING

Structuring is defined as the many ways in which a coach clearly communicates expectations about purposes and the use of such resources as time, space, and materials. Structuring should be clear, conscious, and deliberate. It should be based on a common understanding of the purposes for the coaching, the roles the coach should play, the time allotments, the most desirable location for the conversation, and the placement of the coach during the observation.

Examples of verbal structuring behavior include the following:

- Since you want me to observe the group members' participation, I'll need to sit in a place in the room where I can see them all during the meeting. Where would that be?

- It will take us about 15 minutes for a planning conference. Let's set a time that would be convenient for both of us.

- Here is a copy of the map of the coaching cycle. During the planning conference, I'll be asking you to share with me your goals and objectives, which instructional behaviors you'll use to achieve those goals, and by what indicators you'll know your students achieved your purposes. I'll also be asking you to give me directions for what to look for during the lesson that will be of assistance to you.

ATTRIBUTES OF MEDIATIVE QUESTIONING

It's not the answers that enlighten us, but the questions.
—Descouvertes

Mediative questioning is intentionally designed to engage and transform the other person's thinking and perspective. These kinds of questions meet at least three criteria:

- They are invitational in intonation and form.

- They engage specific complex cognitive operations.

- They address content that is either external or internal to the other person.

Invitational

An approachable voice is used with invitational questions. There is a lilt and a melody in the questioner's voice rather than a flat, even tenor. Plurals are used to invite multiple rather than singular concepts:

- What are your *goals* for this project?

- What *ideas* do you have?

- What *outcomes* do you seek?

- What *alternatives* are you considering?

Words also are selected to express tentativeness:

- What conclusions *might* you draw?

- What *may* indicate his acceptance?

- What *hunches* do you have to explain this situation?

Invitational stems (dependent clauses and prepositional phrases) are used to enable the behavior to be performed:

- As you think about . . .

- As you consider . . .

- As you reflect on . . .

- Given what you know about the children's developmental levels . . .

Both invitational stems and the paraphrase that precedes the question often employ positive presuppositions. Positive presuppositions assume capability and empowerment. A presupposition is something that a native speaker of a language knows is part of the meaning, even if it is not overtly present in the linguistic structure of the communication. We sometimes receive these deeper meanings unconsciously because they are not communicated by the surface structure of the words and syntax. Subtle- and not-so-subtle-presuppositions embedded in our statements carry meanings that can either hurt or support others.

For example, the statement, "Even Bill could pass that class!" conveys the ideas that (1) Bill is not a great student, and (2) the class is not challenging. Neither of these pieces of information is present in the surface structure of the sentence. Still, the sentence communicates, "Even Bill [who is not a great student] could pass that class [so therefore the class can't be that challenging]!". The two unstated pieces of information are inferred by the listener as presuppositions, or assumptions underlying the sentence.[14]

By paying attention to the presuppositions we use and choosing our words with care, we more positively influence the thinking and feelings of others with whom we communicate. For example, consider the positive presuppositions in the following sentences:

- "What are some of the benefits you will derive from this activity?" (Presuppositions: You can anticipate outcomes; you will derive benefits; your thoughts are more important than my own ideas.)

- "As you anticipate your project, what are some indicators that you are progressing and succeeding?" (Presuppositions: You are someone who plans and anticipates; you will progress and succeed; your indicators are more important than anything I might suggest; you are alert to cues and are self-monitoring.)

- "Given your experience and knowledge of learning styles, what are some of your ideas about this?" (Presuppositions: You are experienced, your experience has value because you have reflected on and grown from it, you know about learning styles, you can generate ideas; your ideas have great value.) The phrase "your experience and knowledge of learning styles" tends to pull into short-term memory content with which to process the question.

Specific Cognitive Operations

Questions invite different levels of complexity of thinking. Embedded in questions are certain syntactical cues that signal and invite behavior or thinking processes. Skillful coaches deliberately use these linguistic tools to engage and challenge complex thinking. Table 4-1 illustrates this process. In the first column, Input, are the

TABLE 4-1.
Cognitive Operations

Input	Process	Output
Recall	Compare/Contrast	Predict
Define	Infer	Evaluate
Describe	Analyze	Speculate
Identify	Sequence	Imagine
Name	Synthesize	Envision
List	Summarize	Hypothese

data-gathering cognitive operations. In the second column, Process, are the cognitive operations by which meaning is made of the data. The third column, Output, invites speculation, elaboration, and application of concepts in new and hypothetical situations.

Table 4-2 shows some examples of questions intended to engage certain cognitive operations.

External or Internal Content

External content is what is going on in the environment around, and thus outside, the person. Internal content is what is going on inside the other person's mind and heart: satisfaction, puzzlement, frustration, thinking processes (metacognition), values, intentions, or decisions. Questions that most effectively mediate thinking link internal content with external content.

APPLYING QUESTIONING CRITERIA TO MENTAL MAPS

To learn new habits is everything, for it is to reach the substance of life. Life is but a tissue of habits.

—Henri Fredric Amiel

TABLE 4-2.
Cognitive Operation Questions

Cognitive Operation	Question
Identify	Who, specifically . . .?
Values/Beliefs	What do you believe about . . . ?
Relevance/Justification	How is this important to . . . ?
Intentionality	For what purposes . . . ? Toward what ends . . . ?
Metacognition	What were you thinking when . . . ?
Behavior	What will you be doing when . . . ?
Temporality:	
Simultaneity	While . . . ?
Synchronicity	During . . . ?
Duration	How long . . . ? For what period of time . . . ?
Rhythm	How often? How frequently?
Sequence	What came before? What comes after? What comes first, second, third?
Flexibility:	
Perspective	How would you feel if . . . ?
Alternatives	How else might you . . . ?
Evidence	How will you know if . . . ? What evidence supports . . . ?
Predictions	If you were to . . . , what do you predict would happen?
Causality	What did you do to cause . . . ? What produced . . . ?
Data Use	Of what use will you make of these data? What would that information tell you?
Applications	What will you take from this? How will you apply this elsewhere?
Evaluative Criteria	What criteria will you use to . . . ? By what standards will you judge . . . ?

Drawing on the mental maps of the planning and reflecting conversations and on the characteristics of effective questions, Table 4-3 provides some examples of questions that a coach might ask with the intention of eliciting and evoking each of the goals in the coaching cycle. (Additional examples are found in Appendix D.)

TABLE 4-3.

QUESTIONS TO ELICIT GOALS OF THE PLANNING CONVERSATION

Intention	Sample Questions
PLANNING:	
1. Clarify goals.	What are some of the goals you have in mind for this lesson?
2. Determine success indicators.	As you envision the lesson progressing, what will you be alert to as indicators that you are achieving your goals?
3. Anticipate approaches, strategies, decisions, and how to monitor them.	Given your previous experiences with these students and this content, what strategies will you use to help them. How will you know they are learning?
4. Identify personal learning focus, data to be collected,and a plan for collecting evidence.	As you experiment with your instructional strategies, skills are you interested in perfecting? What will you pay attention to in your own and your students' behavior to let you know that your strategies are working?
REFLECTING:	
Analyzing	
Summarize impressions.	As you reflect on your lesson, how do you feel it went?
Recall supporting information.	What did you notice in your student's behavior that indicated success?
Compare, analyze, infer, and determine cause-and-effect relationships.	What are some of your hypotheses about the factors that contributed to the success of the lesson?
Applying	
Construct new learnings and applications.	What new insights will you carry forth in your work? How might you apply them?
Reflect on the coaching process and explore refinements.	As you reflect on this coaching session, what did it do for you? As you consider my role, what suggestions do you have to increase my effectiveness as a coach?

CONCLUSION

Mediators are clear about their purposes and intentionally employ certain verbal and nonverbal tools with others to help transform and empower their cognitive functioning. In this chapter we have presented the verbal and nonverbal tools that serve a mediator in achieving the goals of helping others to become increasingly more self-directed. Although these skills are presented in the context of Cognitive Coaching, they are useful in any dialogue between two human beings desiring to grow together, to plan, to reflect, to solve problems together, and to create deeper meaning and understanding.

For some, the behaviors described in this chapter come naturally. For others, it will take time and practice to become proficient and comfortable using these tools. We recommend that coaches isolate certain skills and consciously practice them rather than attempt to learn them all at once.

If we choose to intentionally employ, over time, the Cognitive Coaching values described in chapter 1, the mental maps described in chapter 2, the capabilities described in chapter 3, and the tools described in chapter 4, we can become increasingly skillful in facilitating the self-actualization of others. As our colleagues assume greater responsibility for coaching themselves, others will come to identify us as mediators of self-directed learning.

NOTES

1. Damasio, A. (1994). *Descartes' error: Emotion, reason and the human brain.* New York: Avon Books.

2. Swanson, L. J. (1995). *Learning styles: A review of the literature.* ERIC Document No. ED 387 067; and Jenson, E. (1996). *Brain based learning.* Del Mar, CA: Turning Point.

3. Burgoon, J., Buller D., and Woodall, W. (1996). *Nonverbal communication: The unspoken dialogue* (p. 174). New York: McGraw-Hill.

4. Grinder, M. (1991). *Righting the educational conveyor belt.* Portland, OR: Metamorphous Press.

5. Caine, G., and Caine, R. (2001). *The brain, education and the competitive edge.* Lanham, MD: Scarecow Press.

6. Jenson, E. (1995). *Brain-based learning* (p. 112). Del Mar, CA: The Brain Store.

7. Bandler, R., and Grinder, J. (1975). *The structure of magic.* Palo Alto, CA: Science and Behavior Books; Lankton, S. (1980). *Practical magic: A translation of basic neurolinguistic programming into clinical psychotherapy* (p. 38). Cupertino, CA: Meta.

8. Leonard, G. (1978). *The silent pulse: A search for the perfect rhythm that exists in each of us.* New York: Bantam Books.

9. Condon, W. S. (1975). Multiple response to sound in dysfunctional children. *Journal of Autism and Childhood Schizophrenia, 5* (1), 43.

10. See Rowe, M. B. (1996). *Science, silence and sanctions: Science and children*; and, Rowe, M. B. (1974). Wait time and rewards as instructional variables: Their influence on language, logic and fate control. *Journal of Research in Science Teaching, 11,* 81–94.

11. Good, T. L., and Brophy, J. (1973). *Looking in classrooms.* New York: Harper & Row.

12. Rowe, M. B. (January-February, 1986). Wait time: Slowing down may be a way of speeding up! *Journal of Teacher Education,* 42–49.

13. Hofstadter, D. R. (2000). Analogy as the core of cognition. In J. Gleick, (Ed.), *The best American science writing 2000.* New York: Ecco Press.

14. Elgin, S. (1980). *The gentle verbal art of self-defense.* New York: Dorset Press.

5

Developing and Maintaining Trust

In the preceding chapter we described a mediator's eight tools, which we clustered in four groups: paralanguage, response behaviors, structuring, and mediational questioning. In this chapter, we describe how these tools contribute to one of the essential elements of Cognitive Coaching: developing and maintaining trust.

Marilyn Tabor tells a story that poignantly illustrates the need to develop and maintain trust. As a new mentor teacher, she called a meeting at her school. Because she was inexperienced in the process, she expected everyone to attend. That wasn't necessarily the case.

Gwen was one teacher who didn't come to the meeting, and she didn't attend a second one, either. Marilyn decided to talk to Gwen privately. Because she was apprehensive, Marilyn rehearsed exactly what she would say.

Marilyn went into Gwen's classroom one day when no students were there. Gwen looked up from her desk, crossed her arms, and said, "What do you want?" Her unexpectedly cool reaction destroyed Marilyn's prepared speech.

Marilyn searched for something else to talk about, and she saw a photograph of a young girl on Gwen's desk. When Marilyn asked who she was, Gwen answered, "That's my daughter."

"What's her name?" Marilyn asked, and they began to talk about the teacher's child. Marilyn discovered that Gwen was a single parent and her daughter was the most important person on earth to her. They talked for quite a while, and although Marilyn remembered her speech, she was too embarrassed to say it. Instead she closed with "Well, I'll see you later," and she left.

The next morning, something remarkable happened. Gwen usually kept to herself in the faculty room, but instead she called across the crowd, "Hi, Marilyn!" Over the next few weeks, Marilyn noticed that she and Gwen talked more, especially about Gwen's daughter. As their relationship changed, Gwen started to attend Marilyn's meetings without being asked. She even took a leadership role in certain activities.

In this situation, getting to know Gwen and being interested in what was important to her allowed the development of interpersonal trust. Trust is a vital element in all sorts of relationships, but it is especially important in Cognitive Coaching, in which colleagues are encouraged to inquire, speculate, construct meanings, self-evaluate, and self-prescribe. These kinds of activities occur only when the coach helps to create a low-stress environment in which the colleague feels comfortable enough to create, experiment, reason, and problem solve. Building trust in four areas is one of the coach's most important tasks: trust in the self, trust between individuals, trust in the coaching process, and trust in the environment.

CHARACTERISTICS OF TRUST

We've asked hundreds of people to describe how they develop trusting relationships. They report behaviors that are strongly consistent with research on the subject. Among the factors mentioned are maintaining confidentiality, being visible and accessible, behaving consistently, keeping commitments, sharing personal information about out-of-school activities, revealing feelings, expressing personal interest in other people, acting nonjudgmentally, listening reflectively, admitting mistakes, and demonstrating professional knowledge and skills. Trust grows stronger as long as these behaviors continue, but a relationship can be seriously damaged when someone is discourteous or disrespectful, makes value judgments, overreacts, acts arbitrarily, threatens, or is personally insensitive to another person.

Because Cognitive Coaching relies on trust, any manipulation by the coach is incompatible with the goals of trust and learning. Should an employer have performance concerns about a staff member, those concerns are best communicated directly outside the coaching process. Coaching should never be about "fixing" another person. Inevitably, that person perceives the motivation to "fix" and becomes defensive. For example, if you believe that your job is to fix Naseem, she will accurately read your real intention, no matter how many pleasant conversations you share. Naseem clearly detects that you think something is deficient about her, or that she is not cared for.

To coach without manipulation, you must change the way in which you see a problem employee. This may be difficult, but it is even more necessary when you have been working over time with someone whose performance is problematic, who seems to be making limited growth, who isn't making any effort toward growth, or who is resisting your assistance. In these cases, coaching without manipulation is even more important because a natural outgrowth of these processes over time is frustration for the coach. Sometimes the coach will even unconsciously blame the colleagues being coached for remaining so resistant to change and rendering the coach so incompetent.

At times like that, coaches must remind themselves that all behavior is motivated by what are positive intentions, in the other person's point of view. Each person consistently, and often unconsciously, makes choices to maintain psychological benefits from existing actions and to protect ego states. Knowing this helps the coach to reframe the interpretation of events. Thus, the coach is free from negative and debilitating emotions and better able to work empathically and rationally with the other person.

Now, setting aside this discussion of maintaining trust in the face of performance concerns, let's focus on what hundreds of educators and the literature[1] have to say about the practical realities of creating trust.

TRUST IN SELF

To do good things in the world, first you must know who you are and what gives meaning to your life.

—Paula Brownlee

Self-trust is prerequisite to developing trusting relationships with others. The best coaches we've seen are conscious and clear about their own values and beliefs in areas such as pedagogy, philosophy, and spirituality. They manage their behaviors to be congruent with those core values. They experience a well-defined sense of personal identity, which comes, in part, from their ability to articulate their beliefs with precision and passion. They function at a high stage of affective development,[2] characterized by a strong sense of values. They maintain the belief that no matter what the situation, they will remain true to themselves. We would say that they have integrity.

Ultimately, these personal core values shape a coach's perceptions about leadership responsibilities, the meaning of learning, the potential for a school or community, and what motivates people. Trusting yourself also means being conscious of the ways in which you process and make meaning of experiences.

For example, we relate easily to those with similar cognitive styles, but it requires great effort to withhold value judgments about other people's attitudes and perceptions when their style differs from ours. Although we use all of our senses all the time, we often pay attention to one sense more than another. One of the capabilities of a skillful coach is being able to adjust one's own style preferences. This requires knowing your own modality strengths and being conscious of how you understand your experiences through visual, kinesthetic, and auditory channels.

We like the notion of "learnable" intelligence. Although each person has a disposition for certain ways of knowing and learning because of genetics and experience, we would avoid saying that a person is field independent or *is* auditory or *has* interpersonal intelligence. Rather, we should be aware of our dispositions and hold them as starting points for learning, not limitations.

Many researchers have mapped the structure of intelligence from various perspectives.[3] Howard Gardner, for example, has proposed a schema of at least eight intelligences: verbal-linguistic, logical-mathematical, visual-spatial, bodily-kinesthetic, musical-rhythmic, interpersonal, naturalistic, and intrapersonal.[4] Effective coaches become aware of how they are employing their own intelligences at that moment; they also know how to work effectively with those who are stronger in different areas. Effective coaches are not only aware of their own intelligences, they also know how to work effectively with others who possess different forms of intelligence.

Gender, culture, race, religion, geographical region, childhood experiences, and family history also predispose us to draw certain inferences and to attend to certain stimuli while blocking out others. None of us leaves our emotions on the doorstep when we go to work. At times we function at less than our best for a variety of spiritual or emotional reasons. Flexible coaches know when they're being negatively influenced by their emotions, and they respect the fact that colleagues also experience emotional shifts that sap energy and distract attention. Coaches who trust themselves are more capable of building trust with others.

TRUST BETWEEN INDIVIDUALS
The most important thing we can do is to trust and love one another.

—George Land and Beth Jarman[5]

Before you can successfully cognitively coach a person, you have to be credible in that person's eyes. We trust those who are believable, of good character, and sensitive to our interests and styles.[6] Peg, a kindergarten teacher, once told us the story of how she tried to develop trust with another teacher on the staff. "It seems the more I tried to express interest in her, reach out to her, let her know I cared for her, the more she put distance between us."

As Peg elaborated on the situation, it became clear that she had an image of how two people behave in a trusting relationship, and *she presumed that the other teacher held the same vision.* As it turned out, Peg's image of trust included far more intimacy than the other teacher expected. Peg's colleague believed that emotional reserve and only a certain amount of self-disclosure characterized a comfortable, trusting relationship.

To see things from another person's point of view requires cognitive flexibility and is essential to any healthy relationship. Seeking to understand is one of the more important ways in which a coach can communicate that another person is valued. Apart from understanding how the other person processes information, we should attend to four areas.

- What is it that is trustworthy about me? Qualities like dependability, authenticity, honesty, kindness, courtesy, and integrity are found on this list. Keeping people fully informed also generates trust.[7] Maureen, a new personnel director in a California district, met with teacher representatives for contract negotiations. The district laid all its fiscal data on the table. Mistrustful, the teacher representatives kept saying, "The district has not done this before. This must be some kind of trick!" Undaunted, Maureen repeatedly paraphrased these comments. In time, the mood of the entire meeting shifted, and teachers began to believe that the district might be telling the truth, so they started to work collaboratively with district representatives on understanding the figures.

- What is important to the person in the long term—what values, goals, ideals, interests, passions, and hobbies?

- What are the information-processing patterns the person displays, such as cognitive style, perceptual filters, and modality preferences? In settings where tension exists because people perceive one another as different, they must find a shared language and common reference points in order to value one another and build a common work culture.[8]

- What are the person's current reactions, concerns, thoughts, and theories?

An expression of personal regard is also important to interpersonal trust building, especially in a Cognitive Coaching relationship in which praise is withheld because it interferes with thinking.

Praise communicates a value judgment about another person or the person's performance. It infers an unconscious entitlement to evaluate another. At some level we often feel uncomfortable about receiving praise. Even on occasions when it might feel good to hear "You did a great job," the praise removes any need for one to apply her own criteria to self-assessment.

When we ask supervisors why they use praise, they often report two reasons. One is to reinforce behavior. This is contrary to the tenants of Cognitive Coaching. A second is to communicate positive regard. Robert Kegan and Lisa Lahey implore us to move from the language of prizes and praising to the language of ongoing regard. One attribute of this language is to replace "you" statements with "I" statements. "Abdulla, I appreciate the way you took time to bring me up to date. It made a real difference to me." Kegan and Lahey say, "By characterizing our own experience, positive or negative, leaves the other informed (not formed) by our words."

Kegan, R., and Lahey L. (2001). *How the way we talk can change the way we work: Seven languages for transformation* (p. 100). San Francisco: Jossey-Bass.

Coaches signal personal regard by the following behaviors:

- Spending time with the other person in activities not related to the coaching task.

- Making inquiries or statements related to the other person's personal interests or experiences.

- Practicing all the fundamental behaviors of courtesy and respect revealed in the research on trust building: proximity, touch, courteous language, and personal compliments (I like that tie).[9] Sometimes the workplace gets so busy and task oriented that these little personal connections are abandoned, and the day-to-day workplace becomes an emotional wasteland.

Excessive reliance on personal trust without regard to the goals of the organization can lead to paternalism and parochialism. Andy Hargreaves notes that trust in expertise and in a process that helps to solve problems on a continuing basis maximizes the organization's collective expertise.[10]

TRUST IN THE COACHING RELATIONSHIP
The work will teach you how to do it.

—Estonian proverb

Nearly all relationship difficulties are rooted in conflicting or ambiguous expectations surrounding roles and goals. Whether we are assigning tasks at work or choosing a decision-making process for a meeting, we can be certain that unclear expectations will lead to misunderstanding, disappointment, and decreased trust.

Skillful coaches maintain trust by signaling the purpose of their communications:

- I'm not going to give you advice. Let's explore some alternatives together.

- My job is not to evaluate you but to help you reflect on your teaching.

Clear expectations are most important in dealing with the purposes and forms of classroom observations. Where principals perform the two supervisory functions of coaching and evaluation, it's important to be clear about the goals of a classroom visit. Confusion, suspicion, and even hostility arise when a teacher isn't certain which activity is occurring, coaching or evaluation.

When mentor teachers are responsible for the dual functions of consulting and coaching, it is important to be clear about the intention of each conversation. Peer assistance and other ongoing staff development efforts send a signal that this is a learning community for all teachers. Within that context, peer assistance may be seen as an expression of continuous learning, with a recognition that teachers, too, are individuals. Some may be at different stages in their development and require different types of support.

Strategically, we would recommend that peer assistance programs, in which teachers are mentoring and coaching each other, be part of an ongoing, well-developed staff development system.[11] This allows time for collective learning about how to give and receive support without the threat of evaluation.

TRUST IN THE ENVIRONMENT

Just as a picture is drawn by an artist, surroundings are created by the activities of the mind.

—Buddha

We believe that the people in an organization will trust each other to the degree that they find indicators of trust throughout the entire environment. The culture of the workplace often signals norms and values that are more influential on staff performance than are skills, knowledge, training, staff development, or coaching.[12] Subtle signals from the environment, culture, and climate of the organization influence co-workers' thoughts, behaviors, and perceptions. Employees are quick to perceive the congruity between a learning organization's stated core values and its day-to-day practices. If there is consistency, greater trust will exist; the organization "walks its talk." If there is inconsistency, suspicion and mistrust will arise.

"Walking the Talk"

Joe Saban, superintendent of the Crystal Lake High School District in Illinois, describes how teachers learned the process of using portfolios with students by first keeping their own portfolios. Soon they decided that if portfolios were useful for teachers and students, then they would also be beneficial for school administrators. Thus, the building principals began keeping school portfolios. Soon the practice spread, and now Joe also keeps portfolios to demonstrate his accomplishments to the Board of Education.

The effective coach also works to create, monitor, and maintain a stimulating, mediational, and cooperative environment deliberately designed to sustain and enhance trust. Wheatley[13] theorizes that the movement toward participation in organizations is rooted, perhaps subconsciously, in our changing perceptions of the universe. Knowing how to network, how to draw on the diverse resources of others, and how to value each person's expertise, diverse views, perceptions, and knowledge base is increasingly essential to survival. We might view this as a new form of interlocking intelligences: collaboratively melding perceptions, modalities, skills, capacities, and expertise into a unified whole that is more efficient than any one of its parts.

Cognitive Coaches, being aware of this, strive to behave consistently in regard to these core values and beliefs. Because life in school is often fragmented, idiosyncratic, fast-paced, and unpredictable,[14] coaches' long-term impact on a school occurs through the consistency with which they handle day-to-day interactions.

Researchers at Rutgers University studied teachers' perspectives on what makes principals trustworthy.[15] Three characteristics emerged. First, principals took responsibility for their own behaviors. They admitted mistakes and did not blame others. Second, principals acted as people rather than as "roles." Trusted principals revealed personal information about themselves—their likes and dislikes, their emotions, their history—so others had a sense of who they were away from the job. Third, trusted principals were nonmanipulative. They influenced directly, not covertly, and they had no hidden agendas.

This research also found links between interpersonal trust and trust in the environment. Teachers who had faith in the principal often trusted each other and the central office personnel.

We sometimes hear the complaint "But there is no trust here," as if that settled the matter about being able to move forward on any venture. When you are told this, ask what kind of behaviors would people be seeing and hearing if trust were present. With a behavioral description of a desired state, one has targets to work toward rather than wallowing in despair.

TRUST-BUILDING TOOLS

In chapter 4, we described eight behaviors that contribute to the intellectual growth and the engagement of cognition in others. Many of these same nonjudgmental behaviors contribute to a trusting relationship as well. In fact, we know that the neocortex of the brain shuts down by degrees under stress. The greater the stress, the greater the shutdown.[16] Generally, human males will move toward fight or flight; females tend and befriend. Under great stress, we lash out, run away in terror, or freeze up. Physical rapport, subtleties of body language, voice tone, implied value judgments, and embedded presuppositions in our language all have an effect on the comfort and thinking of others. To communicate with skill and grace, we must communicate with the total body-brain system. The systems that process nonverbal signals and feelings are as important to thinking processes as they are to establishing a trusting relationship.

Rapport and Trust

Trust is about the whole of a relationship; rapport is about the moment. Trust is belief in and reliance on another person developed over time. Rapport is comfort with and confidence in someone during a specific interaction. Rapport may be naturally present or you may consciously seek it, even when you are meeting a parent, student, or colleague for the first time. You cannot manipulate someone into a relationship of trust and rapport, but you can draw on specific verbal and nonverbal behaviors to nurture the relationship.

Many studies have found that doctors' and therapists' nonverbal behaviors are important in conveying empathy and trustworthiness. For example, leaning forward, making direct eye contact, and having a concerned voice and facial expression are better at conveying empathy than words are.[17] In addition, the research reviewed in chapter 4 revealed that the coach's matching of gestures, postures, or voice qualities contributes to rapport. Some scientists refer to this form of alignment as mental state resonance. These behaviors have an enormous impact on feelings of connectedness and rapport. Such an alignment permits a nonverbal form of communication that the other person is being "understood" in the deepest sense, is "feeling felt" by another person.[18] Under these conditions, permission is being tacitly given for coaching. The coach recognizes this permission by observing full, rather than shallow, breathing patterns.[19]

What explains these phenomena? Recent explorations in cognitive neurology characterize the body as the theatre of the mind. What we see on the outside is an accurate reflection of what is occurring internally. Peptides, neurotransmitters, and steroids rush information through every cell in the body. Neuron activity is affected by emotion and oxygen as well as by blood chemistry. The mind-body operates as one unit. Emotion and consciousness are inseparable neurologically. Somatic knowing (body or "gut" knowledge) serves as a filtering mechanism for decision making. Humans gesture in order to think. Unconsciously, humans interpret degrees of safety and connectedness by witnessing what is played out physically. The safer one feels, the greater the access to neocortical functioning.[20]

When people experience stress, there is an altered blood flow and changes in activity patterns in the brain. The body-mind functioning is minimized. The person is less flexible and more predictable, and survival patterns override pattern detection and problem solving. People lose their train of thought and their resourcefulness. States of even mild stress show up in the body. Coaches use this information to modify their own behavior. Noticing nervousness, they may scan body systems—their own and the colleague's—looking for areas of congruence. Where mis-matching occurs, the coach will come into paralanguage align-ment to help the colleague.

Don't imagine that you can trick someone into a trusting relation-ship. Babad, Bernieri, and Rosenthal conducted a study in which five groups of judges viewed 10-second film clips of teachers talking to or about students. The judges, who ranged from fourth graders to expe-rienced teachers, were asked to rate the students' scholastic excellence and the teacher's love for each student. In some cases, the judges heard teachers talking about students; in other cases they simply watched, with no sound, as the teacher talked to a student (who was not vis-ible). In each case, one was a good student of high potential and one was a weak student of poor potential.

None of the judges had difficulty detecting students' excellence and teachers' love. The negative affect that teachers tried to conceal was detected by observers through "leaks" in communication channels that are not under as much conscious control as what the teachers were saying to the students.[21]

The teachers' words gave them away when they talked *about* stu-dents; their actions alone gave them away when they talked *to* stu-dents. We can consciously take action to nurture trust and rapport, but we can't mask our true feelings.

Listening From Your Mission
There is no effective communication without listening. Listening is the tool that turns words into communication. Right now, you could be reading this chapter and no matter how clever or useful the words may be, they will not enter your brain if you are thinking of something else and not "listening."

Physiologically, a part of your brain, the thalamus, decides where to send incoming signals. The thalamus is like a great receptionist in the office of your brain. It looks at the "phone" in your brain, sees three lights on, and says, "No way that brain is going to take another call. I'll just get rid of at least one of those calls." Like a good receptionist, the thalamus is highly sensitive to what's going on in the office, sees how tense people are, and evaluates incoming traffic.

continued on next page

You cannot fool your thalamus. You say, "I am ready to take the call," but you mean, "I can't believe I've got another call now! This is totally insane!" At that point, your thalamus doesn't let any more real content into the decision-making parts of your brain because they are already busy.

If you actually listen, you have to go beyond the outward steps of "active listening" that we all learned as a rote procedure for dealing with conflict. You actually have to care. You might not truly care about the person, you might not care about the conversation or the issue, but at least you should care that your behavior helps you to meet your real goals and objectives. For many people, that personal mission includes some kind of problem solving, learning, personal accountability, or sense of making the world better. Chances are, if you cannot summon one of these commitments, then your communication is doomed to mediocrity.

People who are able to bring their hearts "online" are able to listen to the message beyond the words. They turn conflict into a learning experience. They persevere in spite of the complexity, the messiness, and the frustration.

Response Behaviors

Nonverbal communications may convey much of the meaning in an exchange, but the words we choose—and how we state them—also have a strong effect. Through the Cognitive Coaching process, coaches must seek a nonjudgmental environment in which others feel safe to experiment and risk. This environment can be partially created through the response behaviors of silence, acknowledging, paraphrasing, clarifying, providing data and resources, and structuring.

Silence. Sometimes periods of silence seem interminably long. However, if trust is the goal, teachers must have the opportunity to do their own thinking and problem solving. A coach's silence after asking a question communicates "I regard you as sufficient; I trust your processes and knowledge; also I trust that you know best the time you need to formulate a response."

Acknowledging. The noted psychologist and medical hypapist Milton Erickson began his work with patients by acedging their existing states. To acknowledge is not to agree signal "I got your communication" or "I got your communica, and am understanding it from your viewpoint." In North Ame. can cultures, this is accomplished by nodding the head or using "subverbals" like "uh huh." Not all cultures use these cues, however.

An Israeli colleague once told of his experience visiting California. He spent quite a bit of time trying to figure out what Americans were doing when they kept saying, "Uh huh. Uh huh." He finally came to understand that Americans were using this phrase to confirm that they had received another's communication. This was a new behavior for him. Acknowledging another's presence and interpretation of experience may be one of the strongest bonding elements between humans.

Paraphrasing. One function of a paraphrase is to acknowledge another person's communication. In this sense, paraphrasing is a strong trust builder. When people feel understood, they breathe deeper. Deeper breathing provides more oxygen to the brain. Oxygen is an essential resource for thinking. At another level, we believe that empathic paraphrasing changes blood chemistry and helps to maintain a resourceful state in the person being coached.

Clarifying. Clarifying signals that the coach cares enough to want to understand what a colleague is saying. It is not meant to be a devious way of redirecting what a person is thinking or feeling, nor is it a subtle way of expressing criticism of something the colleague has done. The intent of clarifying is to help the coach to better understand the colleague's ideas, feelings, and thought processes.

Clarifying that is proceeded by a paraphrase helps to make clear that the probe for more detail is for understanding, not for judgment or interrogation. Clarifying contributes to trust because it communicates to a colleague that his or her ideas are worthy of exploration and consideration even if their full meaning is not yet understood.

Providing data and resources. The sense of being trusted is a potent stimulus to motivation and self-directed learning. Carol Sanford writes, "The ability to be self-correcting or self-governing is dependent on the capability to be self-reflecting [and] to see one's own processes as they play out.[22] To support this aim, processes for feedback must be conducted within a system that the person being coached has helped to create. Sanford adds that feedback should be done based only on a previously arranged agreement that specifies the principles and arenas to be covered. This is, in fact, the model for the Cognitive Coaching cycle.

As one of the main objectives of Cognitive Coaching is to nurture the teacher's capacities for processing information by comparing, inferring, or drawing causal relationships, data must be rich and readily available for the teacher to process. To contribute to the maintenance of trust, data should meet several criteria:

- It must be requested.

- It must be stated in observable terms.

- It must be relevant.

- It must allow for interpretation by the colleague, not the coach.

During a reflecting conference, the data must be about what was agreed upon during the planning conference. Information also must be presented in a nonjudgmental, behaviorally descriptive fashion and after the teacher has recalled as much as possible. "During the first five minutes of the lesson, five students shared their recollection of yesterday's lesson." Or, "Of the six students you wanted me to observe, Natasha spoke four times, Tyrone spoke two times, Nuyen spoke once, and the remaining three not at all. What do you make of that?" Having offered data, the coach does not interpret but rather asks the teacher to construct meaning. Providing data is in itself rewarding[23] and is the source of energy for self-improvement.[24]

Observers are sometimes tempted to share all the information collected during an observation. Our first tip in managing trust is this: don't dump the data by reporting all the information you collected. To be relevant, the data must be about information that the colleague does not know. Therefore, ask colleagues to share the data they recall, then fill in the gaps.

We have stated the following premise before, but it bears repeating. To nurture trust and contribute to the goal of self-directedness, the colleague, not the coach, must make meaning of the data. According to Sanford, the best form of feedback is questions.

Structuring. A safe, trusting relationship exists when you know what the other person expects of you. When expectations are unclear, you spend your energy and mental resources interpreting cues about what the other person wants and detecting any hidden agendas. With structuring, the coach clearly and deliberately communicates expectations about the purposes and use of resources such as time, space, and materials. Structuring generates a common understanding of the purposes of an observation, the roles the coach should play, time allotments, the most desirable location for the conference, and the placement of the coach during the observation.

Criticism and Praise

We'd expect a statement like "Can you give me a *better* answer?" to weaken someone's trust. However, what about saying, "Your lesson was *excellent!*" Surprisingly, praise can be as damaging to trust as criticism and other put-downs.

We define criticism as negative value judgments. A coach who responds to a teacher's ideas or actions with such negative words as *poor, incorrect,* or *wrong* is signaling inadequacy and disapproval. This terminates the teacher's thinking about the task. Negative responses can be subtle statements, such as "You're *almost* right," or "You're getting *close.*" Sometimes the intonation of the voice conveys sarcasm or a negative impression: "Why would you want to do it *that* way?" or "Where on earth did you get *that* idea?" However it occurs, criticism leaves the teacher with a feeling of failure, cognitive inadequacy, and poor self-concept.

When we praise, we use positive value judgments such as *good, excellent,* and *great.* Some peer coaching and supervisory strategies advocate the use of praise to reinforce behaviors and build trust, but research on

continued on next page

praise indicates that the opposite often happens instead. While most of us enjoy rewarding and praising others, Jere Brophy[25] found that the one person for whom praise has the most beneficial effects is the praise giver. When praise and rewards are given, experimentation is inhibited.[26] Teachers tend to acquire or exercise skills that the coach values rather than their own skills.[27] A skillful coach will avoid phrases like the following:

- That was an *outstanding* strategy you used today, Linda.
- You're doing a *great* job, Leo.
- Yours was the *best* lesson plan that anybody shared.
- Your students are progressing *well* and certainly did a good job today.

Praise and criticism actually detract from the trusting relationship and should be avoided.[28] More powerful alternatives are to paraphrase, acknowledge, empathize, convey positive regard or just use silence!

TRUST IN THE COACHING PROCESS

Trust building begins with the first encounter, when the colleague realizes that the coach is interested, that the coach is an empathic listener, and that the relationship is nonevaluative. Increasingly, as the coach and the teacher work together in a nonthreatening relationship, they both place greater value on the coaching process. They realize that the intent of the process is to grow intellectually, to learn more about learning, and to mutually increase their capacity for self-improvement. They realize that the process is not one that the "superior" does to the "inferior"; rather, they are two dedicated professionals striving to solve problems, improve learning, and make the curriculum more vibrant. Furthermore, the teacher soon realizes that the coach is working at the coaching processes as hard as the teacher is working at the teaching process.

In time, we find that teachers begin to request the coaching process with phrases like the following:

- That felt good.

- You really made me think.

- Could you come back?

- Would you teach me how to coach like that?

Soon the process begins to spread. Word gets around through the school grapevine. Principals call each other, requesting to be cognitively coached through an upcoming parent conference. The director of staff development calls a principal, asking to be coached through a forthcoming inservice presentation. Teachers in grade-level or department meetings soon find that they are coaching each other spontaneously, beyond the classroom situation.

CONCLUSION

Now that we have described the tools of the mediator as they contribute to both cognitive development and trust, you may wish to turn to Appendix A to examine a sample interaction between a coach and a colleague. In the end, trust is cemented when the coach asks the teacher to evaluate the coaching process and recommend refinements. This specifically signals that the exchange was a coaching situation, not an evaluation, and it shows the teacher that the coach is working to refine her own behaviors, too. This kind of ending question also communicates that the teacher is the authority about which coaching behaviors are most appropriate and useful.

Ken Blanchard, who wrote *The One-Minute Manager,* was in San Diego, California, visiting Sea World, which trains whales and porpoises. Talking to some of the trainers, Ken said, "I understand that you are using some of my techniques; that you catch the animals doing something right and then you reward them."

The trainers replied, "yes." Blanchard was very pleased because this is what he recommended in his book about working with employees.

"However," the trainers added, "we do something first."

"What is that?" Ken asked.

"When we first get the animal here to Sea World, we get into the water and play with them to convince them."

Puzzled, Ken pursued, "I'm not sure I understand what you mean.

What do you do in the water and what do you convince them of?"

The trainers replied, "We get in the water and we play with them to convince them that we intend them no harm." They added, "If we don't do that, the animals don't learn anything!"

The Sea World trainers obviously knew what we want all Cognitive Coaches to know: learning requires trust. With trust, the brain can function at its highest neocortical level and engage in experimentation, problem finding, and creativity. One of the first intentional considerations of a coach, therefore, is to establish and then to maintain trust. Hargreaves states, "Trust in people remains important, but trust in expertise and processes precedes it."[29] Trust is a fragile commodity that must be constantly nurtured and tended. Once lost, trust is even more difficult to cultivate.

NOTES

1. Many authors have described the essential nature of trust and the operation of trust in productive working relationships. See for example: Louis, K., and Kruse, S. (1995). *Professionalism and community: Perspectives on reforming urban schools.* Thousand Oaks, CA: Corwin Press. Arrien, A. (Ed.). (1995). *Working together: Producing synergy by honoring diversity.* Pleasanton, CA: New Leaders Press. Deal, T. E., and Kennedy, A. A. (1982). *Corporate culture: The rites and rituals of corporate life.* Menlo Park, CA: Addison-Wesley. Likert, R. (1967). *The human organization: Its management and value.* New York: McGraw-Hill. Ouchi, W. (1981). *Theory Z: How American business can meet the Japanese challenge.* Menlo Park, CA: Addison-Wesley. Bennis, W., and Nanus, B. (1985). *Leaders: The strategies for taking charge.* New York: Harper & Row. Rosenholtz, S. J. (1989). *Teachers' workplace: The social organization of schools.* White Plains, New York: Longman. Schmuck, R., and Runkel, P. (1985). *The handbook of organization development in schools.* (3rd ed.). Prospect Heights, IL: Waveland Press. Senge, P. (1990). *The fifth discipline: The art and practice of the learning organization.* New York: Doubleday. Covey, S. (1989). *The seven habits of highly effective people: Powerful lessons in personal change.* New York: Simon & Schuster. Bracey, H., Rosenblum, J., Aubrey, S., and Trueblood, R., (1990). *Managing from the heart.* New York: Delacorte Press.

2. Krathwohl, D. R. (1956). *Taxonomy of educational objectives: The classification of educational goals. Book 2: Affective domain.* New York: Longman.

3. Perkins, D. (1995). *Outsmarting IQ: The emerging science of learnable intelligence.* New York: Simon & Schuster.

4. Gardner, H. (1983). *Frames of mind: The theory of multiple intelligences.* New York: Basic Books.

5. Land, G., and Jarman, B. (1992). *Breakpoint and beyond: Mastering the future today.* New York: Harper.

6. Tice, L. (1997). *Personal coaching for results: How to mentor and inspire others to amazing growth.* Nashville: Pacific Institute.

7. Freiberg, K., and Freiberg, J. (1996). *Nuts! Southwest Airlines' crazy recipe for business and personal success.* Austin: Bard Press.

8. LaFair, S. (1998). The inside out project: Diversity and the human psyche. In A. Arrien (Ed.), *Working together: Producing synergy by honoring diversity* (pp. 162–176). Pleasanton, CA: New Leaders Press.

9. Good, T. L., and Brophy, J. (1973). *Looking in classrooms.* New York: Harper & Row.

10. Hargreaves, A. (1994). *Changing teachers, changing times: Teachers' work and culture in the postmodern age.* New York: Teachers College Press.

11. Woods, F. (1997). Staff development: A process approach. In A. Costa & R. Liebmann (Eds.), *The Process-centered school: Sustaining a renaissance community* (pp. 70–85). Thousand Oaks, CA: Corwin Press. See also Costa, A., Lipton, L., and Wellman, B. (1996). Shifting rules, shifting roles: Transforming the work evironment to support learning. In S. Caldwell (Ed.), *New directions in staff development* (pp. 92–115). Oxford, OH: National Staff Development Council.

12. Louis, K., Marks, H., and Kruse, S. (1996). "Teachers' professional community in restructuring schools." *American Educational Research Journal, 33* (4), 757–798. Frymier, J. (September 1987) Bureaucracy and the neutering of teachers. *Phi Delta Kappan,* 10. Rosenholtz, S. (1989). *Teacher's workplace: the social organization of schools.* White Plains: Longman.

13. Wheatley, M. J. (1992). *Leadership and the new science.* San Francisco: Berrett-Koehler.

14. Peterson, K. (1985). The principal as instructional leader. *The Peabody Journal of Education, 63,* 1. This is also expressed as the highest form of affective attainment. Krathwohl labeled it "characterization by a value or a value complex." This means the principal maintains consistency in action expression of a set of core values in a variety of settings over time.

15. Kupersmith, W., and Hoy, W. (1989). *The concept of trust: An empirical assessment.* Presentation at the American Educational Research Association Annual Meeting, New Orleans.

16. Closing down of the neocortex is described by many authors. See for example: Goleman, D. (1995). *Emotional intelligence: Why it can matter more than IQ.* New York: Bantam Books. Damasio, A. R. (1994). *Descartes' error: Emotion, reason, and the human brain.* New York: Putnam. Kotulak, R. (1997). *Inside the brain: Revolutionary discoveries of how the mind works.* Kansas City, MO: Andrew McMeel.

17. Burgoon, J., Buller, D. and Woodall, W. (1996). *Nonverbal communication: The unspoken dialogue* (p. 138). New York: McGraw-Hill.

18. Caine, G., and Caine, R. (2001). *The brain, education and the competitive edge.* Lanham, MD: Scarecow Press.

19. Grinder, M. (2001). Private communication. Michael Grinder is national director of Neuro-Linguistic Programming in Education and an expert in nonverbal communication. See www.michaelgrinder.com.

20. Damasio, A. (1994) *Descartes' error: Emotion, reason and the human brain.* New York: Avon Books. See also Csikszentmihalyi, M. (1993). *The evolving self: A psychology for the third millennium.* New York: HarperCollins. Pert, C. (1997). *Molecules of emotion: The science behind mind-body medicine.* New York: Simon & Schuster. Damasio, A. (2000). *The feeling of what happens: Body and emotion in the making of consciousness.* Orlando, FL: Harcourt.

21. Babad, E., Bernieri, F., and Rosenthal, R. (1991). Students as judges of teachers' verbal and non-verbal behavior. *American Educational Research Journal, 28* (1), 211–234.

22. Sanford, C. (1995). *Feedback and self-accountability: A collision course* (p. 3). Battle Ground, WA: Springhill.

23. Bandura, A. (1997). *Cognitive functioning in self-efficacy: The exercise of control* (pp. 212–258). New York: Freeman.

24. Garmston, R., and Wellman, B. (1999). *The adaptive school: A sourcebook for developing collaborative groups.* Norwood, MA: Christopher-Gordon.

25. Rowe, M. B. (January-February, 1986). Wait time: Slowing down may be a way of speeding up! *Journal of Teacher Education,* 42–49. See also Kohn, A. (1994). *Punished by rewards: The trouble with gold stars, incentive plans, A's, praise and other bribes.* Boston: Houghton Mifflin.

26. Kohn, *Punished by rewards.*

27. Lepper, M., and Greene, D. (1978). *The hidden cost of rewards: New perspectives on the psychology of human motivation.* New York: Erlbaum.

28. Kohn, *Punished by rewards;* Deci, E. (1995). *Why we do what we do.* New York: Grosset Putnam.

29. Hargreaves, *Changing teachers,* p. 254.

Part II

Sources of Excellence

This section addresses three major sources of teaching excellence: five states of mind, research on instructional cognition, and the knowledge base of teaching. We define holonomy and describe the five states of mind that drive human resourcefulness. The chapter on teacher cognition includes recent research on complex thinking processes and findings from the neurosciences. The knowledge base of teaching explores six domains of inquiry and how Cognitive Coaching extends and integrates this knowledge. Advantages and cautions regarding teaching standards are also discussed.

6

States of Mind

As we develop soul in our work we need to recognize our dual identity: we are both individuals and members of a group. Indeed, finding the soul of work involves the balance and integration of apparent opposites, such as head and heart, intellect and intuition, and self and group. This process is not so much based on the "shoulds" but upon "what is." It is my belief that as we attend to the soul of work we will find we feel more complete.

—Daryl Paulson[1]

In this chapter we look beyond surface behaviors of thinking and teaching to discover the sources of excellence that drive human performance. Our aim is to focus the coach's capacities on mediating the energy sources that fuel self-directed learning, behavior, and, ultimately, the development of capacities for effective action in holonomous settings. The five states of mind we describe are the wellsprings that nurture all high-performing individuals, groups, and organizations. They are beacons guiding us toward increasingly authentic, congruent, and ethical behavior.[2]

First, we revisit the concept of holonomy (the state of being simultaneously a part and a whole) and the tensions that the paradox of holonomy produces. Next, we explore five states of mind that people draw upon to perform at their best and to resolve such tensions. Finally, we offer ideas for mediating these states of mind.

THE SEARCH FOR WHOLENESS

If we represent knowledge as a tree, we know that things are divided and yet connected. We know that to observe the division and ignore the connections is to destroy the tree.

—Wendell Berry

Every person's story is about moving toward wholeness.

Forward-looking professional development programs know and support this. Carl Jung, one of the 20th century's most influential psychologists, describes this as the joining of opposites, which can be depicted by a snake eating its tail or the joining of poles to make a single whole. Others describe the development toward wholeness as an evolving journey of deepening complexity—cognitively, morally, and in ego states.[3]

Holonomy, the study of wholeness, was described in chapter 1. Each person strives to resolve a duality; to develop and preserve a unique, separate, and personal identity and at the same time, to strive for affiliation and reciprocity with others.

Recognizing people as holonomous beings reveals the polarity that drives much of their emotive behavior. Self-assertion finds an outlet in ambition, competitiveness, and aggressive or defensive behaviors. On the other hand, the integrative potential finds fulfillment through *authenticity* identification with family, community, or other social groups. This simultaneous drive for self-assertion and affiliation is a continuing source of tension among individuals and within groups.[4] Living holonomously requires a person to continually engage in the process of growing toward wholeness while seeking balance with individuality. Table 6-1 demonstrates how these tensions can be resolved.

TABLE 6-1.

RESOLVING TENSIONS BETWEEN . . .

Self-Assertion and Integration	Our striving to become an autonomous, self-initiating, unique individual and at the same time hold membership in and allegiance to the larger community.
Knowledge and Action	Our striving for congruence between what we know and believe and how we behave.
Egocentricity and Allocentricity	The amelioration of our own perspective with another's perspective.
Ambiguity and Certainty	Our human passion for certainty and the simultaneous need for doubt.
Inner and Outer Lives	What we are feeling inside and what we are presenting as our behavior on the outside.
Solitude and Interconnectedness	Our desire to be alone and introspective and our need to be interactive and in reciprocity with others.

One goal of Cognitive Coaching is to develop each individual's capability to accept and then work to realize that he or she is simultaneously a whole and a part (whole in terms of self and yet subordinate to a larger system). Effective teachers, for example, are autonomous individuals: self-asserting, self-motivating, and self-modifying. However, they are also parts of larger wholes: a department, a school, a district. They are influenced by the norms, attitudes, values, and behaviors of the collective. The school, in turn, is an autonomous unit interacting within the influence of the district and the community. Holonomy is both a goal and an ideal: a vision toward which humans and organizations forever strive.

By resolving these dichotomies, we can develop intellectual, moral, and ego resourcefulness. Russian psycholinguist Lev Vygotsky[5] suggests that intelligence grows in two ways: through our own experiences and through our interactions with others. Our intelligence actually increases as we justify reasons, resolve differences, listen to another person's point of view, achieve consensus, and receive feedback.

With repeated opportunities to resolve these conflicts, and with purposeful reflection, we develop resourcefulness in coping with future conflicts and tensions. To effectively balance and resolve these challenges, we must develop and draw upon certain internal resources. We describe these internal capacities as five states of mind.

FIVE STATES OF MIND

We all have the extraordinary coded within us, waiting to be released.

—Jean Houston

Five states of mind inform human perception and are the resources that human beings access as they resolve the tensions inherent in holonomous settings. They are the tools of disciplined choice making and the primary vehicles in a lifelong journey toward integration. These basic human forces drive, influence, motivate, and inspire our intellectual capacities, emotional responsiveness, high performance, and productive human action. We categorize and define them as shown in Figure 6-1: efficacy, flexibility, craftsmanship, consciousness, and interdependence.

Although some of the states of mind may periodically be more dominant than others, we propose that these five distinctly human forces unite the expression of wholeness in an individual. The capacity to access and channel these forces provides the continuing sources of excellence in all of life's endeavors, both professional and personal.

Just as gravity is invisible, the states of mind cannot be seen, but we know them by their effects. They are recognizable in our language and actions, and they are at once dispositional and cognitive. The states of mind inform and make possible the application

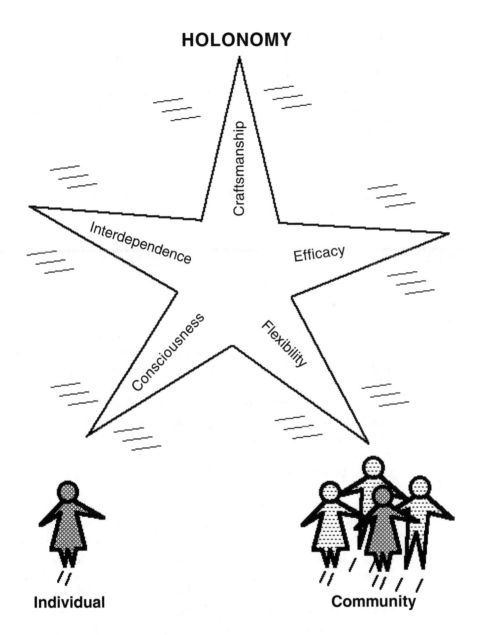

Figure 6-1.
Five States of Mind

of strategies and the selection of thinking processes appropriate to a situation. Unlike cognitive style, these five states of mind are developmental. They exist within the dimensions that Robert

Marzano calls linguistic, nonlinguistic, and affective ways of knowing as elaborated in chapter 7. The five states of mind can be developed over a person's lifetime. They contribute to increased accomplishment and satisfaction. Cognitive Coaching strengthens and makes these resources more accessible in the moment and over time.

Efficacy

Self-development of personal efficacy requires mastery of knowledge and skills attainable only through long hours of arduous work.

—Albert Bandura

Efficacious people are resourceful. They engage in cause-and-effect thinking, devote energy to challenging tasks, set challenging goals, and persevere in the face of barriers and occasional failure. People with efficacy accurately forecast future performances. They are optimistic and confident, and they feel good about themselves. They have sound self-knowledge, and they control performance anxiety. They implement curriculum in collegial environments and translate concepts into action. Consider the state of mind of efficacy in the following example.

Schools A and B serve low-income, minority children. Teachers in each school have similar years of teaching and academic preparation. Both work in old buildings with the same instructional materials. School A's teachers are upbeat. School B's teachers are frustrated and stressed. They believe that if parents would be more supportive and students better motivated, reading achievement would be higher. In School A, most teachers feel confident in their knowledge about reading and believe that if they work hard enough—and are smart enough—students will learn. Test scores at each school reflect teachers' beliefs.

School A's teachers have personal efficacy—the belief that they have the knowledge and skills to teach reading—and outcome efficacy—the conviction that when they use their teaching skills, students achieve. Teachers in School B have low efficacy and, as a result, are more prone to blame others for poor student achievement. They also feel more stress and are less positive about teaching.[6]

Efficacy transcends race, income level, subject matter, and age of students. It is a predictor of group perseverance on special projects. It correlates with higher math achievement, more science learning, improved language skills, and teachers' increased willingness to implement innovation. Efficacy also correlates with positive teacher-administrator relationships, constructive parent-teacher relations, and reductions in teacher stress.

Studies of Cognitive Coaching consistently find significant improvements in teacher efficacy. Efficacy may be the most catalytic of the five states of mind, because a person's sense of efficacy is a prime factor in determining how complex problems are resolved. If a teacher feels little efficacy, then despair, hopelessness, blame, withdrawal, and rigidity are likely to follow. However, research indicates that teachers with robust efficacy are likely to expend more energy in their work, persevere longer, set more challenging goals, and continue in the face of barriers or failure. In sum, efficacy is characterized by the following:

- Efficacy is related to specific areas, such as teaching math or working with middle school kids.

- Efficacy is related to doing certain types of tasks, such as getting things organized.

- Efficacy changes over time with influences from new information and task experiences.

- Personal efficacy stems from self-assessment of teaching skills and influences the effort that teachers expend working with students.

- Personal efficacy also is achieved by professional development: learning about subject matter, pedagogy, students, and self.

- Outcome efficacy stems from self-assessments of teaching results.

- Outcome efficacy influences teachers to modify instruction.

- Outcome efficacy is enhanced through creating learning communities in which teachers collaborate to improve instruction.

- Highly efficacious persons are frequently optimistic, less stressed, able to persevere through difficulties to achieve results, high achievers, self-actualizing, and self-modifying.

Charles Garfield's study of peak performers found that their primary locus of control is internal, not external. One element that stands out clearly among peak performers is their virtually unassailable belief in the likelihood of their own success. Their track records reinforced their beliefs. Conversely, they also recognized when a task was unattainable, and they moved their energies elsewhere.[8]

Efficacy is a prerequisite for improved student learning. Fullan regards teacher efficacy as a vital factor in the successful implementation of change.[9] Rosenholtz found that teachers' efficacy influenced students' basic skills and mastery. The more certain teachers feel about their technical knowledge (personal efficacy), the greater is students' progress in reading. The more teachers are uncertain, the less students learn.[10]

One study on the relation between efficacy and curriculum implementation showed that teachers' efficacy and interdependence significantly predicted the implementation of new curriculum guides.[11] Neither efficacy nor teacher interactions (interdependence) alone produced a significant difference in use of the curriculum, but together they brought about change.

In the Rand Corporation's seminal research on school effectiveness, Berman and McLaughlin[12] found that collective teacher efficacy was the single most consistent variable related to school success. The efficacy identified by the Rand Corporation study is what Fuller, Wood, Rapoport, and Dornbusch[13] label "organizational efficacy," or the link between people's perceptions of valued goals and their expectations that those goals can be achieved by participating in the organization (outcome efficacy).

Laborde and Saunders[14] report that people governed by an internal locus of control show initiative in controlling their environment. They control their own impulsivity, gather information, are cognitively active, eagerly learn information that will increase their probability for success, and show a sense of humor. Compared to individuals with an external locus of control, they are more trustful, less anxious, less hostile, less angry, less suspicious of others, less prone to suicide, less depressed, and less prone to psychosis.

These descriptors provide a vision of the desired state toward which coaches can facilitate growth. One value of efficacy and the resulting self-confidence is that teachers are free to be more flexible. Flexibility is critically important for any creative work in which one wants to see the overall pattern as well as the details.

Flexibility

Destiny is as destiny does. If you believe you have no
control, then you have no control.

—Wess Roberts

Humans can perceive from multiple perspectives and can endeavor to change, adapt, and expand their repertoire of response patterns. In brief, that is a description of flexibility, which is characterized by the following:

- Flexibility is both a disposition and a set of skills.

- The mental skills of flexibility include the ability to shift among egocentric, allocentric, and macrocentric views; between a bird's-eye view (detail) and an eagle-eye focus (gestalt); between the present and the future; between logic and intuition; and between an individual and a group.

- Flexible persons hold multiple goals, consequences, and time frames simultaneously.

- Flexibility in perception and thought requires emotional safety.

- Expertise in an area allows more flexibility, as one can attend to both the mechanics of a situation (the focus of novices) and the underlying causes and effects (the focus of experts).

- Humor is associated with flexibility.

- Flexible thinkers seek novel solutions.

- Flexible thinkers are empathic.

- Flexible thinkers can be comfortable with ambiguity.

- Flexible thinkers change their minds as they receive additional data.

- Flexible thinkers develop and draw from both their "feminine" and "masculine" selves.

Teachers in a certain Minnesota high school were trying to improve the quality and relevance of the school experience for youngsters. They decided to ask the students for ideas. The students organized and produced a series of videotaped interviews with fellow students. They were careful to select high achievers, low achievers, and students in the middle, along with students of ethnic diversity. The data from this production touched the hearts and the minds of school staff members and led to important changes.

An elementary principal in San Francisco offers another example of a flexible perspective that led to creative solutions. Her school was having difficulty with homeless males urinating on the sides of the building at night. Instead of simply calling the police or organizing a committee to look into the situation, she organized a pizza party sleep-in for her entire staff so that throughout the night they could ward off those who were causing the difficulty. Her strategy worked.

Flexibility involves the ability to step beyond and outside oneself and look at a situation from a different perspective. This is what Jean Piaget called overcoming egocentrism. Many psychologists believe that this is the highest state of intelligent behavior. As we shall see later, it is also a prerequisite state of mind for functioning interdependently. The peak performers that Garfield[15] studied had a quality of flexible attention, which he called "micro/macro attention."

Microthinking involves logical, analytical computation and seeing cause and effect in methodical steps. This mode is important in the task analysis portion of planning a lesson or a curriculum. It encompasses attention to detail, precision, and orderly progression.

The macro mode is particularly useful for discerning themes and patterns from assortments of information. It is intuitive, holistic, and conceptual. Macrothinking is good for bridging gaps and enables us to perceive a pattern even when some of the pieces are missing. It is useful in searching for patterns in a lesson or in a week of lessons.

Peak performers also trust their intuition, honoring the mind-body relationship. They tolerate confusion and ambiguity up to a point, and they are willing to let go of a problem, trusting that their creative unconscious will work productively.

Flexibility is also strongly related to creative problem solving. When NASA was developing the Apollo and Mercury space capsules, they needed to deal with the tremendous heat of reentry. A capsule literally glows cherry red as it encounters friction with the earth's atmosphere, and the scientists needed to develop a material that would withstand the heat. Finally, one scientist observed, "You know, we're doing it all wrong. Rather than trying to develop a material that would withstand the heat, we need to conduct the heat away from the space capsule." With this change in perspective, the underside of the spacecraft were lined with tiles that burn up on reentry, conducting heat away from the capsule's surface.

The NASA capsule is an example of reconceptualizing a problem, and it's the kind of thinking that flexible people are able to do. In the classroom, a flexible teacher can deal with a variety of learning styles. He can handle visual, kinesthetic, and auditory learning. She can coordinate a variety of activities simultaneously and is as attuned to the Hmong student as to the Hispanic student.

The flexible teacher is a hypothesis maker who looks upon each experience as a learning opportunity. Flexible people can live with doubt because they have a great capacity to look upon life as a series of problems to be solved. They enjoy problem solving because it's a challenge.

Flexibility, like efficacy, is related to risk taking. David Perkins[16] describes creative people as "living on the edge." They are not satisfied with living in the middle; they are always pushing the frontier. They generate new knowledge, experiment with new ways, and constantly stretch themselves to grow into new abilities. The high jumper Richard Fosbury is a good example. Before Fosbury, high jumpers crossed the bar with a forward leap. However, spectators at the 1968 Olympics in Mexico City saw a far different technique. Fosbury, in midair, turned his back to the bar and cleared it. Fosbury set an Olympic record, and the "Fosbury Flop" became the new standard. Because of Fosbury's novel approach, experimentation, and mental flexibility, this unorthodox manner of getting over the high jump changed the world of high jumping forever.

Craftsmanship

Learn to do uncommon things in an uncommon manner. Learn to do a thing so thoroughly that no one can improve upon what has been done.

—Booker T. Washington

Craftsmanship is the healthy dissatisfaction that humans feel with their own accomplishments. Craftsmanship drives them to hone, refine, and constantly work for improvement.

One fine example of craftsmanship is illustrated in a story told about Tiger Woods after he dominated the 1997 Masters Golf Tournament. Still in his 20s, he was being hailed as the next Jack Nicklaus, considered to be the best golfer of all time. Immediately after the 1997 Masters, Woods studied videotapes of his performance and later told friends his swing was really horrible.

Woods decided to make some serious adjustments to the swing that had brought him to the summit. As he said later, he reasoned that, for now, at this age and with his strength, he had a service-able swing, but could it sustain him as he aged? He decided to reconstruct his total approach to the ball. As golfers know, this is risky. Many fine golfers attempt this and never return to their former prowess.

Woods persevered. He unlearned what had been automatic for him. He concentrated, drilled, and practiced to learn a new tech-nique. He got worse before he got better, but eventually he learned to restrict his hip turn, slow his shoulder rotation, flatten his wrist, and add a split second to his timing, keeping the club face square to the ball longer and producing straighter and more consistent shots. Excellence in performance is the soul of craftsmanship, and Tiger Woods embodies that spirit of excellence.

Craftsmanlike people are characterized by the following:

- They assess their own performance and results.
- They value seeking data about their work in order to study and improve it.
- They envision and set high standards for themselves.
- Their performance may often appear flawless and easy, but underneath that appearance is a great understanding of the complexity of their work.
- They calibrate and monitor progress toward goals.
- They strive for continuous improvement.
- They persevere to close the gap between existing and desired states.
- They monitor and manage refinements in thought and lan-guage.
- They predict, monitor, and manage time.
- They distinguish between perfection and excellence.

To further appreciate craftsmanship, consider studies from the League of Professional Schools. They found that in schools where teachers are the most successful, these same teachers have the high-est dissatisfaction with their work.[17] The drive for elaboration, clarity, refinement, and precision—all attributes of craftsmanship—serve as energy sources from which faculties improve instruction and student learning.

People working toward craftsmanship strive for precision. They seek perfection, elegance, refinement, and specificity. Like Tiger Woods, they generate and hold clear visions and goals. They monitor progress toward those goals.

The holonomous person who is both flexible and craftsmanlike attends to the big picture and to details. In one setting, a holonomous teacher may be excruciatingly detailed. In another setting, that teacher might be artfully vague.

Language plays a critical role in enhancing a person's cognitive maps, and language has a great impact on an individual's ability to think critically, create a knowledge base for action, and feel efficacious. The skillful coach, recognizing that language and thinking are closely entwined, consistently strives to enhance the clarity and specificity of teacher thought and language.

The craftsmanlike teacher is also precise in managing temporal dimensions. Teachers orchestrate across six time dimensions: sequence (in what order), duration (for how long), rhythm (at what tempo, pattern, and speed), simultaneity (along with what else), synchronization (with whom and what), and short- and long-term perspectives. A craftsmanlike teacher strives for excellence in each of these dimensions.

Consciousness

> *The White people think the whole body is controlled by the brain. We have a word, umbelini (the whole intestines): that is what controls the body. My umbelini tells me what is going to happen: have you never experienced it?*
> —Mongezi Tiso, Xhosa tribesman, South Africa[18]

The function of consciousness is to represent information about what is happening outside and inside the body in such a way that it can be evaluated and acted upon by the body. To be conscious is to be aware of one's thoughts, feelings, viewpoints, and behaviors and the effect they have on oneself and others.

Damasio suggests that consciousness begins when

> brains acquire the power . . . of telling a story without words, the story that life is ticking away in an organism, and the states of the living organism, within body bounds, are continuously being altered by encounters with objects or events in its environment, or, for that matter, by thoughts and by internal adjustments of the life process. Consciousness begins when this primordial story—the story of an object causally changing the state of the body—can be told using the universal nonverbal vocabulary of body signals. The apparent self emerges as the feeling of a feeling."[19]

As we have already suggested, consciousness is the medium in which all states of mind are mediated. To make personal change, one must be conscious of one's own inner workings. To mediate consciousness in others, we must be attentive to both verbal and nonverbal communications in order to help others locate the words that represent their experiences.

Recently Bob was on safari in the Ngorongoro Crater in Tanzania. Late one morning, he stepped from his Range Rover to observe some plant life more closely. Suddenly, a glowering hippopotamus—weighing 5,000 to 6,000 pounds and with lower canine teeth 18 inches long—emerged from a waterhole. Grunting and snorting, glistening and frightening, the hippo charged. Terrified, Bob dashed for the car and safety.

What happened in those few seconds? Bob's brain detected threat, and with lightning speed, conjured up a few response options, selected one, and acted. Neural and chemical aspects of the brain's response caused profound bodily changes: surges in metabolic rate and energy. The overall biochemical profile of his body fluctuated rapidly, evoking changes in both brain and body, skeletal muscles contracting. His frightened eyes absorbed the scene connecting the retina and the brain's visual cortices to reactions in his viscera. In time, this memory will become a neural record of many of the changes that occurred, some in the brain itself and some in the body.

Although teaching is rarely this exciting, the same neurochemical processes ignite when a threat or any intense experience is perceived. Cognitive Coaches must realize that "cognitive" always has an "emotional" component. Emotions and the viscera often perform an important role in perception and decision making. This is true in situations of clear and immediate danger, like a charging hippopotamus. It is also true in less obvious dangers, like perceived ego risk in a conversation.

Coaches strive to help colleagues bring to awareness how they feel about a situation. Met in awareness, these feelings sometimes evoke gut reactions that open or close some options to deliberations. Once these feelings are brought to consciousness, colleagues are in a better position to apply their intuitions within the more cognitive processes of decisions making. When feelings are brought to the surface, they can also be examined or challenged to determine if they are interpretations of the real event being worked with or a memory of another event that therefore eliminates viable options from subsequent consideration.[20] Following are some characteristics of consciousness:

- The capacity for consciousness lies in our neurobiology.

- The development of consciousness is influenced by mediational relationships, personal intention, and practice.

- Consciousness is involved when deliberate, rather than automatic, control or intervention is needed.

- We are consciously aware of only a small part of what our minds are taking in at any given time.

- Conscious processes occur one at a time, take effort, and are inefficient.

- Conscious processes are necessary transit zones in which to unlearn old patterns and learn new ones at an unconscious level.

- Unconscious processes produce contradictory interpretations of experience; consciousness provides us with a unique, consistent interruption.

- We can be aware of something without really being aware of it.
- Consciousness can be strengthened through self-observation.

Over centuries of evolution, the human nervous system has become so complex that it is able to affect its own states. We can make ourselves sad or happy, regardless of what is happening outside. Yet the human nervous system is still limited to managing only about seven bits of information at any one time, such as differentiated sounds, visual stimuli, or nuances of emotion or thought. If conscious capacity is limited, however, how do teachers, parents, coaches, or students focus their consciousness to serve them in their goals?

Three stimuli bring data to consciousness: a discrepant event, a flashlight shined by another person, or intention. Imagine you are in traffic, hardly noticing the shapes or occupants of the cars around you, when a car with flashing lights (a discrepant event) suddenly breaks into your consciousness. Or imagine that a friend, serving as a flashlight, asks a question that causes you to examine a feeling or theory or action of yours. Finally, notice that whenever you are clear about your intentions, your attention is riveted that direction.

Consciousness is not unique to Homo sapiens. Cognitive ethnologists claim that animals have intentions, beliefs, and self-awareness and that they consciously think about alternative courses of action and make plans.[21] The great advantage that humans have over animals is that we can strengthen and direct our capacity for consciousness because of the neural anatomy of our brain, which permits development of an autobiographical self. One way of describing human consciousness is that we are aware that certain events are occurring, and we are able to direct their course (metacognition). As humans, we can direct or control whatever we are conscious of within ourselves.

People engaging an enriched state of consciousness often think about their own thinking and feeling. They monitor their values, thoughts, behaviors, and progress toward goals. They articulate well-defined value systems, and they generate and apply internal criteria for decisions. They practice mental rehearsal and edit mental pictures as they seek to improve performance.

Coaches often shine a flashlight on data previously not noticed by the teacher. Christina Linder, a middle school English teacher, reports:

> In learning to more clearly project outcomes for my lessons I found that I was planning more precisely, and that smaller, more tangible goals were appearing in my lesson plans. I had often suspected that at times specific student needs had been sacrificed in attainment of the broader goal.

At the same school, Jan Whitaker wrote the following:

> After a few Cognitive Coaching sessions, I realized it wasn't the material that was important but how it caused thinking in my students. Missing in my very detailed and organized lessons was the opportunity for students to develop creativity, craftsmanship, application, analysis, and higher levels of thinking.

Both teachers commented on how this awareness led to changes in their teaching.[22]

Consciousness is the monitoring arena for each of the other states of mind. If one's personal efficacy becomes depleted, if one is rigidly seeing from only a single perspective, or if one is acting impulsively at the moment of consciousness, one has choice.

Interdependence

We've each been invited to this present moment by design. Our lives are joined together like the tiles of a mosaic; none of us contributes the whole of the picture, but each of us is necessary for its completion.

—Karen Casey and Martha Vanceburg

Humans need reciprocity, belonging, and connectedness. We are inclined to become one with the larger system and community of which we are a part. This is the state of mind called interdependence.

Interdependence was an important state of mind at the Sea View Elementary School (not its real name). At one point, poor performance in student writing began to be seen by the staff as a systems problem. An emerging sense of interdependence and collective responsibility for student learning motivated the formation of vertical teams to address the issue. K–3 staff members were openly supportive of their fourth- and fifth-grade colleagues, and they agreed to work collaboratively on an improvement plan. A skills matrix was developed for teaching both narrative and expository writing. Two-hour rotating planning sessions were structured, with each new team adding to and filling in the gaps of previous teams.

Several by-products emerged. Primary teachers' confidence increased when their efforts in writing instruction were appreciated by upper-grade teachers. Seeing the matrix on the wall helped them to grasp where they became part of the total system. Upper-grade teachers spotted gaps in their writing instruction on the grid. This also inspired changes in other parts of the system, because the district writing rubric did not provide guidance or standards in the area of expository forms.[23]

Interdependent people are characterized by the following traits:

- They have a sense of community.
- They value collective work and are able to be true to their beliefs as they find principled ways to lend their energies to the achievement of group goals.
- They seek resources within the group.
- They know when to integrate and when to assert.
- They contribute themselves to a common good.
- They practice generous interpretations of other people's behavior.

- They pay attention to self and others and unstated systems of communication.

- They regard conflict as a source for learning, as a problem-solving opportunity, and as the other face of community.

- They continue to learn based upon feedback from others and from consciously attending to their own actions and effects on others.

- They seek engagement in holonomous part-whole relationships, knowing that all of us together are more effective than any one of us.

Interdependence is an essential state of mind for Renaissance schools. For example, Rosenholtz,[24] in her study of elementary schools in Tennessee, found that the single most important characteristic of successful schools was goal consensus. Jon Saphier, of Research for Better Teaching, reports that the issue of good schools is so simple that it's embarrassing: in good schools, people have common goals, and they work together toward those goals.

Interdependence modifies working relationships. Sarason finds that "recognizing and trying to change power relationships, especially in complicated traditional institutions, is among the most complex tasks human beings can undertake."[25] The school improvement agenda of the new millennium is moving all educators into more interactive and professional roles. So from the perspective of what's good for schools as well as the perspective of what's good for individuals within the schools, we find that interdependence is a rich and essential resource.

Holonomy describes a characteristic of dynamic or nonlinear systems in which everything influences everything else. Tiny events can cause major disturbances in the system, and you do not need to touch everyone to make a difference. Each autonomous unit in a holonomous system influences the system in addition to being influenced by it. Eleanor Roosevelt's statement that only a small number of people are needed to change the world captures this thought. Interdependence is a two-way street: one gives help and receives help; one influences and is influenced.

MEDIATING RESOURCES FOR HOLONOMY

We either make ourselves miserable, or we make ourselves strong. The amount of work is the same.

—Carlos Castaneda

Of course, the goals of an idealized state of holonomy are never fully achieved. In addition, there is no such thing as perfect attainment of the states of efficacy, flexibility, craftsmanship, consciousness, and interdependence. These are utopian energies toward which we constantly aspire. The journey toward holonomy and the five states of mind is the destination.

Performing intelligently in holonomous systems means living in tensions: whole and part, event and context, individual and group. It is a life work, described by Jung as individuation—an integrated development of the physical, emotional, spiritual, intellectual, and social being. It is a human journey everywhere, across all continents, ages, and cultures. It is most complex in the 21st century in postindustrial societies such as ours, in which Robert Kegan estimates that perhaps as much as 50 percent of America has not achieved the cognitive complexity needed to cope with daily life.[26]

Our dream is that all educators will one day possess the complexity to provide the very best instruction for students. As described earlier, our mission is to foster autonomous, self-directed learners, capable of intelligent, values-based living within holonomous systems. Although there are many important aspects related to mediation, the most critical is to remember one's intention in a mediational transaction.

There is no doubt that school staffs that exercise intelligent membership in holonomous systems also work collaboratively and produce better results with students than do faculties whose members work in isolation from one another. Such workplaces are characterized by clear values and norms, reflective dialogue, deprivatized teaching, and an atmosphere in which the primary focus of energy, attention, and conversation is on student learning.

Mediating holonomy pursues three outcomes: developing capacity among the parts, strengthening the whole, and creating the consciousness and skills with which part and whole inform and support the continuing development of each another. To achieve the first outcome is to support people in becoming autonomous and self-actualizing. Efficacy and craftsmanship especially contribute to this; so does supporting teachers in a continual inquiry into the knowledge base about teaching and developing commitment to setting and working toward high standards.

The second outcome calls for members of the school community to function interdependently, recognizing their capacity to both self-regulate and be regulated by the norms, values, and goals of the larger system. Consciousness, craftsmanship, and interdependence are primary energy sources. To attain this requires clear standards for collaborative work and for teaching, if necessary, the structural, communication, and metacognitive skills required for productive collaboration.

The third outcome is achieved by developing each part and whole to value the other component. This outcome also is achieved by devising and using strategies that draw on the advantages of each while avoiding the shortcomings. We submit that the entire set of states of mind contributes to each of these goals, and that, perhaps more than anywhere else, this is true for this third outcome.

MEDIATING THE FIVE STATES OF MIND

Within you right now is the power to do things you never dreamed possible. This power becomes available to you just as you can change your beliefs.

—Maxwell Malts

Each moment is an intersection between eternity and the present. The choices available to a person will depend on the vigor and accessibility of their states of mind and the richness and complexity of their mental models. In most cases, simply acting like a good friend will help others as they plan, solve problems, and learn from experience. However, there are also times when more complex strategies are necessary. A skillful coach, equipped with these strategies, can mediate in any or all of the five states of mind. The sample coaching cycle in Appendix A illustrates how a coach might invite a colleague to draw forth the states of mind. In chapter 9, we describe special coaching concepts and tools that liberate these five internal resources so they can be applied to the important decisions that educators make about students.

CONCLUSION

The five states of mind can serve as diagnostic constructs through which we can assess the resourcefulness of others and plan interventions. However, assisting others toward refinement and expression starts first with your own states of mind. From there, you can work with others, the system of which you are a part, and even students.

Keep in mind the following three attributes of the states of mind:

- They are transitory; they come and go. A person's state of mind varies depending on a number of factors, including familiarity, experience, knowledge, fatigue, and emotion.

- They are transforming. Dramatic increases in performance accompany heightened states of mind. Just as one's current state of confidence will affect in-the-moment competence, the states of mind access the personal resources required for peak performance.

- They are transformable, either by oneself or by another. A colleague can cheer you up or encourage you, changing in that moment your state of mind and your capacity. Similarly, your own conscious awareness of your states of mind allows you to choose and to change them.

NOTES

1. Paulson, D. (January/February, 1995). Finding the soul of work. *At Work: Stories of Tomorrow's Workplace 4* (1), 18–20.

2. Costa, A. and Garmston, R. (2001). Five human passions: The source of critical and creative thinking. In A. Costa (Ed.), *Developing minds, a resource book for teaching thinking* (pp. 18–22). Alexandria, VA: Association for Supervision and Curriculum Development.

3. Kegan, R. (1994). *In over our heads: The mental demands of modern life.* Cambridge, MA: Harvard University Press.

4. Koestler, A. (1972). *The roots of coincidence.* New York: Vintage Books.

5. Vygotsky, L. (1978). *Society of mind.* Cambridge, MA: Harvard University Press.

6. Soodak, L. C., and Podell, D. M. (April, 1995). *Teacher efficacy toward the understanding of a multi-faceted construct.* Paper delivered at the Annual Conference of the American Educational Research Association, San Francisco.

7. Tschannen-Moran, M., Hoy, A. W., and Hoy, W. K. (Summer 1998). Teacher efficacy: Its meaning and measure. *Review of Educational Research 68* (2), 202–248.

8. Bandura, A. (1997). *Self-efficacy: The exercise of control* (p. 16). New York: Freeman. This is undoubtedly the best single resource on the topic of efficacy.

9. Fullan, M. (1982). *The meaning of educational change.* New York: Teachers College Press.

10. Rosenholtz, S. (1989). *Teachers' workplace: The social organization of schools.* New York: Longman.

11. Poole, M. G., and Okeafor, K. R. (Winter, 1989). The effects of teacher efficacy and interactions among educators on curriculum implementation. *Journal of Curriculum and Supervision,* 146–161.

12. Berman, P, and McLaughlin, M. W. (1977). *Federal program supporting educational change: Factors affecting implementation and continuation.* Santa Monica, CA: Rand Corporation.

13. Fuller, B., Wood, K., Rapoport, T. and Dornbusch, S. (Spring, 1982). The organizational context of individual efficacy. *Review of Educational Press 52,* 7–30.

14. Laborde G., and Saunders, C. (1986). *Communication trainings: Are they cost effective?* Mountain View, CA: International Dialogue Education Associates.

15. Garfield, C. (1986). *Peak performers: The new heroes of American business.* New York: William Morrow.

16. Perkins, D. (1983). *The mind's best work: A new psychology of creative thinking.* Cambridge, MA: Harvard University Press.

17. Garfield, *Peak performers*; Csikszentmihali, M. (1990). *Flow: The psychology of optimal experience* (p. 24). New York: Harper and Row.

18. Buhrmann, D. (1984). *Living in two worlds: Communication between a white healer and her black counterparts.* Cape Town: Human & Rousseau.

19. Damasio, A. (1999). *The feeling of what happens: Body and emotion in the making of consciousness* (pp. 30–31). Orlando, FL: Harcourt.

20. Damasio, A. (1994). *Descartes' error: Emotion, reason and the human brain.* New York: Avon Books.

21. Shettleworth, S. J. (1998). *Cognition, evolution and behavior.* New York: Oxford Press. See also Garmston, R., Linder, C., and Witaker, J. *Cognitive Coaching: two teachers' perspectives.* Alexandria, VA: Association for Supervision and Curriculum Development.

22. Garmston, Linder, and Witaker, *Cognitive Coaching.*

23. Garmston, R., and Wellman, B. (1999). *The adaptive school: A sourcebook for developing collaborative groups.* Norwood, MA: Christopher-Gordon.

24. Rosenholtz, *Teachers' workplace.*

25. Sarason, S. (1991). *The predictable failure of educational reform.* San Francisco: Jossey-Bass.

26. Kegan, R. (1994). *In over our heads: The mental demands of modern life.* Cambridge, MA: Harvard University Press. Also the States of Mind Inventory, developed by Jane Ellison and Carolee Hayes, is intended for use by groups for self-assessment and is available from the Center for Cognitive Coaching at www.cognitivecoaching.cc.

7

Cognition and Instruction

The world is presented in a kaleidoscopic flux of impressions which has to be organized by our minds—and this means largely by the linguistic systems in our minds.
—B. L. Whorf[1]

[The] fact that language shapes perceptions to some extent is widely accepted among psychologists.
—J. M. Anderson[2]

L et's take an imaginary tour of a classroom to observe cognition at work during teaching. As you walk in, you are immediately struck by all the activity around you. A group of students works on a paper mache relief map. Other students work at the computer. A few students are helping each other with their homework. Still others are working at the science table. The teacher sits at a round table working with a small reading group. She listens to Rebecca read; next she listens to and corrects Diane. She diagnoses Tyrell, then Leroy. At that moment, an office monitor enters and delivers a note. The teacher, still listening to Rebecca, reads the note, commends the monitor for coming in so quietly, composes a response, sends him out, and never misses a beat with Rebecca.

Or consider this high school classroom, where George arrives late, noisy, and looking very dejected. Glancing at George, the teacher instantly makes an assessment of his emotional state, what's happening with the class discussion, and George's potential for disruption. She tosses George a humorous greeting: "Hi, George! Good to see you. Make friends with that chair over there and turn to the chart on page 70." She then locates in her mind some appropriate open-ended questions for students to work on. She instructs the students to think-pair-share about these questions for two minutes. In this way, she has achieved two goals simultaneously: providing George a chance to settle in, and offering other students the opportunity to check their understanding of the concept just taught.

One of the great cognitive capacities of teachers is this ability to simultaneously manage a multitude of activities in the classroom. Professionals have an extensive and continually expanding body of knowledge and skills, and they make decisions about when and how to apply which portions of that knowledge in diverse situations. This is what make teaching among the most intellectually demanding professions.

In the past 10 years, great advances have been made in understanding the ways that cognitive systems perform in learning. Teachers who possess cognitive systems with highly developed levels of perception, abstraction, and decision making consistently have students who perform well on both lower and higher cognitive tasks. In this chapter we describe the act of teaching as a highly intellectual process that involves continual decision making before, during, and after instruction.[3] We also examine how linguistic, nonlinguistic, and affective systems affect cognition and teacher thinking, including the implications for Cognitive Coaching.

Many researchers[4] have contributed to an understanding of teacher thought and the stages of cognitive complexity that adults can attain. Cognitive Coaching is a process of engaging, enhancing, and mediating the intellectual functions of teaching, or, as Marzano would describe it, a cognitive system informing teaching.[5] As we shall see, however, the intellectual interrelates with nonlinguistic ways of knowing, including the emotions. Coaches cannot achieve their goals without some understanding of the processes of teacher thinking: how teachers reason as they plan for, execute, and evaluate instruction.

FIVE FINDINGS ABOUT TEACHER COGNITION

Through research on teacher cognition, we have gained valuable insights into what teachers think about as they teach. Research on human information processing, emotional intelligence, effective problem solving, human intelligence, brain capacity, and brain function has revealed five major findings.

1. **All behavior is based on rather simple cognitive maps of reality.** Swedish researchers Dahllof and Lundgren[6] discovered that teachers used a subset of the class, ranging from the 10th to the 25th percentile, as an informal reference group for decisions about pacing a lesson or unit. These mental constructs guided the teacher's behavior toward the entire class. This tendency illustrates how teachers make simple cognitive maps to deal with complex situations.

2. **Talking aloud about their thinking and their decisions about teaching energizes teachers and causes them to refine their cognitive maps.** Teachers refine their instructional choices and behaviors. They have implicit theories about teaching and learning that are "robust, idiosyncratic, sensitive to [their] particular experiences, incomplete, familiar, and sufficiently pragmatic to have gotten [them] to where they are today."[7] Talking aloud about these elements causes examination, refinement, and development of new theories and practices.

3. **Certain invisible cognitive skills drive teaching performance.** These cognitive skills influence teachers' classroom behaviors, students' classroom behaviors, student achieve-

ment, and, reciprocally, teachers' thought processes, theories, and beliefs.[8]

4. **These invisible cognitive skills can be categorized in four domains.** *Preactive* thought occurs as the teacher plans before teaching. *Interactive* thought occurs during teaching. *Reflective* thought occurs when teachers recall and analyze a lesson. *Projective* thought is used to synthesize and apply learnings and plan next steps.

5. **"Thinking" occurs at the intersection of three ways of knowing.** These ways of knowing are linguistic, nonlinguistic, and affective.[9] All information that is perceived by the senses passes through these three processors and is encoded in linguistic representations, sensory images, or affective representations. For example:

-   Teachers' thought processes are influenced by deeply held theories of learning, beliefs about their own efficacy, perceptions of the system in which they work, and beliefs about education or student conduct. In the linguistic mode, these are stored as propositions in the form of abstract concepts (e.g., "A quiet student is a good student."). To describe the concept, the teacher must use token words to express herself.

-   The same concept is also stored in permanent memory in a nonlinguistic mode: in images, sounds, smells, or kinesthetic sensations.

-   Such propositions about students are also stored in an affective mode. *Affect* includes feeling, emotion, and mood. Feelings are purely physiological, the result of chemical reactions in the body. Rational thinking is impossible without the involvement of feelings and emotions. Emotion occurs in relationship to what our thoughts have to say about the feelings. Mood is a dominant emotion, or the most representative emotion that persists over time. (See Figure 7-1.)

Coaching, then, must take into account and utilize these three ways of knowing. Because Cognitive Coaching uses processes that attend to a teacher's language, sensory memories, and feelings, it can raise these deep-structure forms of knowing to a more conscious level so that the teacher can elaborate, clarify, evaluate, and alter them. Ornstein reminds us, "To make a personal change, we have to be able to observe the automatic workings inside ourselves."[10]

An unexpected by-product occurs when teachers talk about their reasons for doing things and respond to questions about their perceptions and teaching decisions. They often experience a sense of professional excitement, and they also speak of renewed joy and energy related to their work.[11]

A BASIC MODEL OF INTELLECTUAL FUNCTIONING

A basic model of human intellectual functioning is useful for the Cognitive Coach who wants to develop strategies, learning activities, and assessment indicators that focus on the intellect rather than on superficial behaviors.[12] Keep in mind that "the body, as represented in the brain, may constitute the indispensable frame of reference for the neural processes that we experience as the mind."[13] Figure 7-1 synthesizes some psychologists' and psychobiologists' current concepts of human intellectual functioning.

Other authors distinguish four basic thought clusters:[14]

- Input of data through the senses and from memory

- Processing those data into meaningful relationships

- Output, or application, of those relationships in new or novel situations

- Metacognition, or self-monitoring of one's own thoughts, actions, beliefs, and emotions

Every event a person experiences causes the brain to call up meaningful, related information from storage, whether the event is commonplace or rare. The more meaningful, relevant, and complex the experience is, the more actively the brain attempts to integrate and assimilate it into its existing storehouse of programs and structures. The most complex thinking occurs when an external stimulus or problem challenges the brain to

- draw on the greatest amount of information, conceptual systems, schema, and structured meanings already in storage.

- expand already existing conceptual systems.

- develop new structures.

A *problem* may be defined as any stimulus or challenge that has no readily apparent resolution. If there is a ready match between what is perceived by the senses and what is already in storage, no problem exists. For example, there is not much need to process information when you are asked your name because the response to the challenge is readily available. Jean Piaget called this *assimilation*.

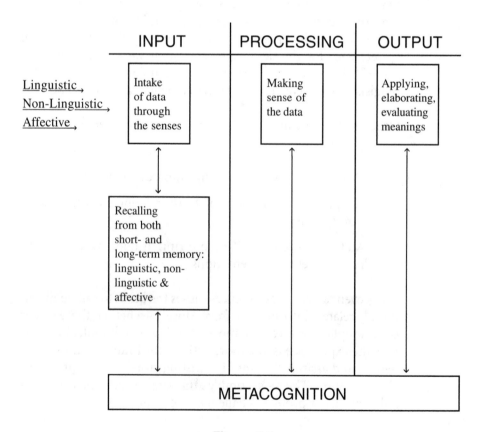

Figure 7-1.

If, however, the challenge or problem cannot be explained or resolved with existing knowledge in short- or long-term memory, the information must be processed. Some action must be taken to gather more information to resolve the discrepancy, and the resolution must be evaluated for its "fit" with reality. Piaget called this *accommodation*, and he saw it as the process by which new knowledge is constructed. Coaching in the area of cognition mediates accommodation.

Consciousness and Cognition

Until recently the quality of consciousness, the awareness of processing information, was not studied. However, new studies reveal several striking phenomena. People apparently process and retain information without awareness. The essence of these studies show "that people may deny seeing or remembering something—that is, be unaware of it—while at the same time showing through their behavior that they do see or remember the thing in question."[15]

As stated earlier, current views of information processing hold that memories are stored within the cognitive system in three forms: linguistic, nonlinguistic, and affective. Information is acquired, stored, retrieved, and acted upon according to the types of memories held in these systems.

TEACHER KNOWLEDGE

Marzano explains that knowledge is composed of information, mental processes, and psychomotor experience. A Cognitive Coach elicits a variety of information in all these areas: subject matter, pedagogy, students, or the teacher herself. The teacher then represents the information linguistically as declarative propositional networks. These facts, time sequences, episodes, vocabulary, generalizations, principles, and concepts will usually also have a strong nonlinguistic representation. Rarely, however, will craft information have strong affective representations. Through mediational conversations, such information can be integrated and refined.

Teachers' Mental Processes

Mental processes are primarily procedural, and they are normally held in linguistic and nonlinguistic modes. Some mental processes of teaching have a wide diversity of uses and products, and they involve the execution of many interrelated subprocesses. For example, teaching a concept attainment lesson to students requires getting students' attention, focusing attention on a conceptual challenge, giving clear directions, classifying student responses as either positive or negative, and performing within acceptable boundaries of teacher responses related to the outcome of the lesson. Other mental processes of teaching are less complex and are made up of a general set of principles that can be applied in several settings. In getting student attention, for example, the teacher can position himself in the room, assume a still and grounded body posture, call for attention in a credible voice, and hold his body and a gesture still until complete attention is achieved.

Experienced teachers will have additional models and mental processes for focusing student attention. Some simple mental processes have narrow uses and are learned to the point of automaticity, such as distributing materials for student work. The more automatic some mental processes become, the more "cognitive space" is available for complex decision making during the lesson. Coaching helps teachers to streamline existing mental models and form new ones.

Teachers' Psychomotor Knowledge

Psychomotor knowledge includes the physical skills and abilities a teacher uses to negotiate daily life in the classroom. Most psychomotor skills are stored in memory in a fashion identical to mental processes, and they are stored in an "if-then" syntax. As such, they have a strong linguistic base: "If students are behaving improperly, *then* a teacher might do the following." For example, *if* the students are misbehaving, *then* the teacher silently moves to a space reserved for group discipline, stands with authority and a serious expression, and directs students in a credible voice about proper behavior. *If* she believes that students have listened and understood, *then* she pauses, walks silently back to the instructional position, changes to a more melodic teaching voice, and resumes teaching.[16]

Because psychomotor skills are usually learned through observation, instruction, and behavioral feedback, they have strong nonlinguistic representations. The affective system is usually not engaged unless a teacher had some strong negative or positive emotional experience connected to the skills. Psychomotor learning is not the domain of Cognitive Coaching; rather, it is the function of a consulting relationship. (See chapter 12 for the distinction between consulting and Cognitive Coaching.)

Our brains constantly strive to satisfy and resolve discrepancies perceived in the environment. Information that the brain has not processed remains in memory for very short periods of time. Merely experiencing something or memorizing without acting on that information commits it only to short-term memory. This fact may explain the unusual power of Cognitive Coaching.

Most data perceived by the brain is either not attended to (and therefore never enters short-term memory) or is not processed and is forgotten within 18 seconds.[17] Much of the daily experience of teaching, therefore, is forgotten and not explained, its potential influence for teacher learning lost. Processing the instructional experience allows the teacher to facilitate construction of new meanings and insights.

The coach's role is to engage and mediate the teacher's cognitive systems. When Cognitive Coaching is used, teachers may process the same teaching event as least six times:

1. Before the planning conference, teachers formulate their objectives and plans.

2. During the planning conference, they engage in deep, preactive mental rehearsal during which the coach questions, paraphrases, and clarifies in ways that help the teacher to be more precise with lesson strategies.

3. Instruction then occurs, with the teacher's conscious awareness about key elements greatly heightened.

4. The teacher recalls the instructional event before the reflecting conferences.

5. The teacher recalls the instructional event during the reflecting conference.

6. Finally, the teacher continues to reflect and refine after the reflecting conference, especially when closure was not reached on a subject or issue.

The long-range goal of Cognitive Coaching is to habituate the intellectual formation of effective thinking. In other words, the goal is acquiring the habits and dispositions of self-directed learning. The teacher must aim to continue growing intellectually by internalizing these intellectual processes and experiencing them when the coach is not present: to be self-modifying, self-referencing, and self-renewing. In this way, the intellectual functions and mental processes of effective teaching become automatic.

As the capacity and skills for self-directed learning develop, another transformation occurs. Teachers who articulate their instructional thinking become more "expert" in three categories: knowledge, efficiency, and insight. Table 7-1 lists ways in which expert teachers differ from novices in these three areas.

TABLE 7-1.

WAYS IN WHICH EXPERT TEACHERS DIFFER COGNITIVELY FROM NOVICES[18]

Knowledge
Expert Teachers

- have more knowledge.
- organize knowledge differently.
- integrate knowledge more thoroughly.
- use more complex and interconnected planning structures.
- generate examples and explanations more easily.
- relate student questions to lesson objectives more effectively.
- have practical knowledge of the social and political context within which teaching occurs.

Efficiency
Expert Teachers

- have more knowledge.
- are able to solve problems more efficiently within their domain of expertise.
- can do more in less time.
- can do more with less effort.
- have automatic, well-learned skills.
- plan, monitor, and revise their approach to problems more effectively.
- use applicable cognitive processes with greater speed and accuracy.
- use richer and more interpretive think-aloud protocols.

TABLE 7-1. *(continued)*

Efficiency
Expert Teachers

- use higher order executive processes more effectively to plan, monitor, and evaluate ongoing efforts at problem solving.
- spend a greater amount of time trying to understand a problem. Novices invest more time in actually trying out different solutions.
- are more likely to monitor their solution attempts.
- are more playful in their approach to classroom discipline problems.
- are more likely to be reflective and continuously learn through experience.
- use new problems as opportunities to expand their knowledge and competence.
- reinvest cognitive resources in the progressive construction of more nearly adequate problem models.

Insight
Expert Teachers

- are more likely to arrive at creative solutions to problems.
- reach ingenious and insightful solutions that do not occur to others.
- do better at distinguishing relevant from nonrelevant data (selective encoding).
- combine information in ways useful for problem solving (selective combining).
- apply information acquired in another context to a problem at hand (selective comparison).

FOUR STAGES OF INSTRUCTIONAL THOUGHT

When we compare the research on human information processing with research on teacher cognition, we are struck by the natural similarities. *Planning* (preactive) consists of all the intellectual functions performed before instruction. *Teaching* (interactive) includes the multiple decisions made during teaching. *Analyzing and evaluating* (reflective) consists of all those mental processes used to reflect, reconstruct, explain, and interpret and judge instruction. Finally, *applying* (projective) abstracts from the experience synthesizes new generalizations, and carries them to future situations.

Planning

Planning may well include the most important decisions teachers make because it is the phase upon which all other decisions rest. Planning basically involves four components:[19]

1. **Anticipating, predicting, and developing precise descriptions of students' learnings that are to result from instruction.** Ironically, this can be a low priority for many teachers.[20]

2. Identifying students' present capabilities or entry knowledge. This information is drawn from previous teaching and learning experience, data from school records, test scores, and clues from previous teachers, parents, and counselors.[21]

3. Envisioning precisely the characteristics of an instructional sequence or strategy that will most likely move students from their present capabilities toward immediate and long-range instructional outcomes. This sequence is derived from whatever theories, beliefs, or models of teaching logic, learning, or motivation that the teacher has adopted. The sequential structure of a lesson is deeply embedded in teachers' plans for allocating their most precious and limited resource—time.

When a person thinks about an action, the brain sends electrical impulses to the nerves and muscles in the corresponding locations of the mind and body associated with the action. This is called the Carpenter Effect,[22] and it is the scientific basis for the practice of mental rehearsal. (See the sidebar "More About Mental Rehearsal.") Mental rehearsal is also beneficial for overcoming the psychological and emotional problems associated with performance.

4. Anticipating a method of assessing outcomes. The outcomes of this assessment provide a basis for evaluating and making decisions about the design of the next cycle of instruction.

There is reasonable agreement among researchers that teachers do not adapt a linear form of planning (e.g., specifying objectives first, then selecting learning activities) Instead, teachers seem to enter the planning process from multiple and various entry points. In fact, several studies find that many teachers think about content first and objectives later.[23]

Even underneath this structure, what is going on in teachers' minds as they plan? Psychologists know that the human intellect has a limited capacity for handling variables. Miller[24] describes this as "M-space," or "memory space." He found that humans have a capacity for handling and coordinating seven different variables, decisions, or disparate pieces of information (plus or minus two) at any one time. This assumes that the person has attained Piaget's stage of formal operations, which not all adults achieve. Other researchers have concluded that most adults can operate on about four disparate variables simultaneously.

When humans approach the outer limits of their capacity, a state of stress begins to set in and they feel a loss of control. Most intellectual energy appears to be invested in techniques and systems to simplify, reduce, and select the number of variables. For teachers, certain planning strategies help to reduce this stress.

During planning, a teacher envisions cues, or definitions of acceptable forms of student performance for learning. This simplifies judgments about appropriate and inappropriate student behaviors. The teacher also selects potential solutions, backup procedures, and alternative strategies for times when the activity has to be redirected, changed, or terminated. This kind of planning causes thought experiments during which a teacher can mentally rehearse activities to anticipate possible events and consequences. This improves the coordination and efficiency of subsequent performance because systematic mental rehearsal prepares the mind and body for the activity. Rehearsal also is the main mechanism for focusing attention on critical factors relevant to the task.

More About Mental Rehearsal

Much of the literature and research on mental rehearsal is drawn from the field of athletics. Olympic pentathlete Marilyn King reports using a combination of three kinds of visualization: visual imagery (being able to project a visual image of herself), kinetic imagery (feeling or physically sensing), and auditory imagery. These three forms of visualization are used in three different areas: long-term goal orientation, envisioning a goal step by step, and centering, or concentrating, to eliminate outside distractions and focus inward.[26] The famous French Alpine skier Jean Claude Killy mentally rehearsed ski slopes with a stopwatch. He concentrated on every turn of the slope, timing himself as he envisioned every inch of his performance from start to finish. Killy claimed that the recorded time for his mental performance closely paralleled the time he actually achieved in the competition that followed.

With mental rehearsal, a preperformance routine often is created.[25] This routine may consist of a smorgasbord of psychological skills that the

continued on next page

athlete feels most comfortable using. The skills are put together in a set order and used routinely before each and every performance.

For example, while on the diving platform, Olympic gold medalist Greg Louganis mentally rehearsed each dive using a self-talk, preperformance routine, which served as an attentional cue or trigger right before his forward three-and-a-half somersault dive. He used the following cue words: "Relax, see the platform, spot the water, spot the water, spot the water, kick out, spot the water again." Note that he is doing this before the dive and not during the dive. The activity prepared his mind for the coming dive and his body for the series of movements. Rehearsal also enabled him to forget everything else in the surroundings.

One common problem as we work is failing to maintain effective concentration. Through mental rehearsal, we learn to direct attention to cues that are most important for performance, and at the same time to close down the perceptions of distracting external stimuli.[27] Much research concerns performance during short physical activities, but we also know that mental rehearsal of complex, interactive activities of longer duration also improves performance. This means that it is helpful to rehearse whole races, entire games, and, of course, entire lesson sequences.[28]

Planning also demands that the teacher exercise perceptual flexibility by engaging multiple perspectives, multiple and simultaneous outcomes, and multiple pathways. However, viewing learning from multiple perspectives requires a certain degree of disassociation from the instruction in order to assume alternative perspectives. Highly flexible teachers have the capacity to view a lesson in both the immediate and long range. They are not only analytical about the details of this lesson (the micro mode), they can also see connections between this lesson and other related learnings. They know where this lesson is leading and how it is connected to broader curriculum goals (the macro mode). Less flexible, episodic teachers may view today's activity as a separate and discrete episode, unrelated to other learning events.

Accomplished teachers teach toward multiple outcomes simultaneously. They have immediate goals for this lesson, but they also know that this lesson leads to a long-term, more pervasive outcome as well. They keep in mind the school's or district's standards of learning. For example, teachers may wish to have students understand the causes of World War II. Simultaneously, they want students to learn interdependence by working in groups, to experience long-range planning for their group project, and to practice the habits of mind of persisting, striving for accuracy, and developing a questioning attitude.[29]

Experienced, effective, flexible teachers draw on multiple strategies to achieve their lesson goals. Based on their knowledge of the content to be taught, the learners in their charge, and the available resources, they can design multiple alternative instructional strategies for achieving their goals. (This becomes even more apparent during teaching—the interactive phase, described below.)

Planning a teaching strategy also requires the cognitive function of analysis, both structural and operational. Structural analysis is the process of breaking down the learning of the content into its component parts. Operational analysis involves putting a series of events into a logical, sequential order.[30] To handle this information overload, teachers often synthesize much of this information into "hypotheses," or best guesses about student readiness for learning. They estimate the probability of successful student behavior as a result of instruction.

Although many studies report on teacher practices regarding planning, Clark and Peterson[31] point out that research is silent on what planning processes are most effective. From our experience, we agree with Shavelson that of the four stages of teachers' thought, planning is the most important because it sets the standard for the remaining three phases. We also place particular emphasis on the value of specifying clear learning objectives. We find that the more clearly the teacher envisions and mentally rehearses the plan, the greater are the chances that the lesson will achieve its purposes. Chances are also greater that the teacher will self-monitor during the lesson and will more critically analyze the lesson during the reflective phase, thus assuming a greater internal locus of control.

Teaching

Teachers are constantly interacting with students in an environment of uncertainty.[32] Teachers are constantly making decisions, that may be subconscious, spontaneous, planned, or some mixture of these. Teachers' in-the-moment decisions are probably modifications of decisions made during the planning phase, but changes made during the fast-paced interaction of the classroom are probably not as well defined or as thoroughly considered as the decisions made during the calmer stage of planning. In-the-moment decisions are spontaneously influenced by teacher information, mental processes, and automated psychomotor processes. Once a lesson begins, teachers have little time to consider alternative teaching strategies and the consequences of each.

Six kinds of temporal dimensions interact constantly with teachers' other thoughts and values to influence their daily decisions. Two of these time dimensions are sequence and simultaneity. *Sequence* refers to ordering instructional events within a lesson. *Simultaneity* refers to the capacity to operate under multiple classification systems at the same time. This means that an instructor can teach toward multiple objectives, coordinate numerous and varied classroom activities at the same time, plan a lesson incorporating several learning modalities, and think about multiple time frames. In addition, teachers plan within a variety of time horizons—daily, weekly, long-range, yearly, and the school term. Effective teachers relate information from all those time frames as they prepare daily lessons.[33]

Keeping the standard of learning and the planned strategy in mind while teaching provides the teacher with a backdrop against which to make new decisions. During the beginning of a lesson, for example, the teacher may emphasize structuring the task and motivating students to become curious, involved, and focused. Later in the sequence, the teacher may use recall types of questions to cue students' review of previously learned information and to gather data to be considered later. Further into the lesson, the teacher may invite students' higher-level thinking and, finally, provide tasks for transference and application.

Clark and Peterson[34] describe teacher thinking related to changing planned content during teaching. They examined influences on those decisions; cues that teachers read in order to make decisions; and the relationships between and among teachers' interactive decisions, teachers' behaviors, and, ultimately, student outcomes. A relatively small portion of teachers' interactive thought deals with instructional objectives. A greater percentage of teachers' interactive thought deals with the content or subject matter. A still greater percentage of interactive thought deals with the instructional process. The largest percentage of teachers' interactive thought concerns learning and the learner.

One of the great mental skills of teaching is simply the teacher's ability to remember the lesson plan during the pressure of interaction. Teachers often suffer cognitive overload—too many things going on all at the same time. Yet skillful teachers respond immediately, intuitively, and spontaneously to how the lesson plan is playing out. Highly conscious teachers are alert to what is going on in the classroom; less conscious teachers continue their lessons regardless of what occurs among students.

For example, alert teachers search for clues that students are prepared. Have the students acted on the information, digested it, and made meaning out of it or used it? Are students staring vacantly, or do body language and facial cues indicate attention? The alert teacher constantly observes, questions, probes, and interprets students' behaviors to make decisions about moving ahead in the sequence or remaining at the present step longer.

Metacognition refers to teachers' critically important capacities to consciously "stand outside themselves" and reflect on themselves as they manage instruction. During a lesson, teachers may ask themselves, "Are my directions clear? Can students see the overhead projector? Am I using precise words to make sure that the students are understanding? Should I speed up?" Such internal dialogue means the teacher is constantly monitoring his own and students' behavior during instruction.

Metacognition is also the ability to know what we know and what we don't know. It is the ability to plan a strategy for producing needed information, to be conscious of steps and strategies, and to reflect on and evaluate the productivity of thinking. David Perkins has elaborated four increasingly complex levels of metacognition:

- The *tacit* level, being unaware of our metacognitive knowledge.

- The *awareness* level, knowing about some of the kinds of thinking we do (generating ideas, finding evidence) but not being strategic).

- The *strategic* level, organizing our thinking by using problem solving, decision making, evidence seeking, and other techniques.

- The *reflective* level, not only being strategic but reflecting on our thinking in progress, pondering strategies, and revising them accordingly.

The metacognitive skills necessary to successful teaching, which a Coach may want to be alert for, include the following:

- Keeping place in a long sequence of operations

- Knowing that a subgoal has been attained

- Detecting errors and recovering from them by making a quick fix or retreating to the last known correct operation

This kind of monitoring involves both looking ahead and looking back. Looking ahead includes the following:

- Learning the structure of a sequence of operations and identifying areas where errors are likely

- Choosing a strategy that will reduce the possibility of error and will provide easy recovery

- Identifying the kinds of feedback that will be available at various points and evaluating the usefulness of that feedback

Looking back includes the following:

- Detecting errors previously made

- Keeping a history of what has been done until the present and thereby determining what should come next

- Assessing the reasonableness of the present and the immediate outcome of task performance

Teachers monitor the classroom for conscious and subconscious cues, and sometimes the cues build up so much they disrupt conscious information processing. Flexible teachers manage their impulsivity by avoiding strong emotional reactions to classroom events. This is an efficient strategy to reserve the limited capacity for conscious processing of immediate classroom decisions.

Flexible teachers have a vast repertoire of instructional strategies and techniques, and they call forth alternative strategies as needed. They are aware that in a math lesson, for example, Samor obviously isn't getting the concept of sequence. Sensing that Samor is a kinesthetic learner, they give Samor a set of blocks and ask him to put them in order.

Many classes are filled with students of a heterogeneous array of languages, cultures, and learning styles. Teachers may have one or more students, or even whole groups, who are Hmong, Vietnamese, Arab, East Indian, and Latino, all in the same classroom. Each must be dealt with employing different strategies, cultural experiences, vocabulary, examples, and techniques. Efficacious and flexible teachers continually cast about in their vast repertoire for, or invent, strategies that may prove effective.

Routines are also helpful in dealing with the information-processing demands of the classroom. Routines reduce the need to attend to the abundance of simultaneous cues from the environment. Efficacious teachers develop a repertoire of routine systems for dealing with classroom management functions (taking roll call, distributing papers and books). They also have systematic lesson designs (e.g., spelling and math drills) and teaching strategies (e.g., questioning sequences and structuring).

Analyzing and Evaluating

Memories are not stored by facts but by the emotions attached to the facts. When accessing the corresponding emotion, the brain reconstructs the memory that is stored as an image from its dispositional representations. Therefore, remembering is first and foremost a matter of accessing the correct emotion.

—Ronald Kotulak[35]

After teaching the lesson, the teacher now has two sources of information: the lesson that was envisioned during planning and the actual lesson as performed. Analyzing involves collecting and using understandings derived from the comparison between actual and intended outcomes. If the teacher finds a great similarity between the two, there is a match. A discrepancy exists when there is a mismatch between what was observed and what was planned. Teachers generate reasons to explain the discrepancy, or cause-and-effect relationships between instructional situations and behavioral outcomes.

Teachers can either assume responsibility for their own actions or they can place the blame on external forces. Teachers with an external locus of control tend to misplace responsibility or situations or persons beyond their control. For example: "How can I teach these kids anything? Look at the home background they come from. Their parents just don't prepare them to learn."

Efficacious teachers have an internal locus of control. They assume responsibility for their own successes or failures: "Of course the students were confused. Did you hear my directions? They were all garbled. I've got to give more precise directions."

Seligman[36] suggests that persons develop "explanatory styles" with which they subconsciously form internal hypotheses or rationalizations to explain to themselves good and bad events in their environment. Hartoonian and Yarger[37] found that some teachers may dismiss or distort information that indicates that students did not learn as a result of their teaching strategy. Less efficacious teachers may give themselves credit for student improvement but misplace blame when performance is inadequate.

Even with this analysis, the cycle of instructional decision making is not yet complete. The learnings must be constructed, synthesized, and applied or transferred to other learning contexts, content areas, or life situations.

Applying

At this stage, the teacher takes new knowledge constructed through analysis and applies that knowledge to future instructional situations or content. Experience can bring change, but experience alone is not enough. Experience is actually constructed: compared, differentiated, categorized, and labeled. This allows the teacher to recognize and interpret classroom events, departures from routines, and novel occurrences. Thus, the teacher can predict the consequences of possible alternatives and activities. Without this conceptual system, the teacher's perception of the classroom remains chaotic.

Self-directed teachers consciously reflect upon, conceptualize, and apply understandings from one classroom experience to the next. As a result of this analysis and reflection, the teachers synthesize new knowledge about teaching and learning. As experiences with teaching and learning accumulate, concepts are derived and constructed. Teachers' practice thus becomes more routinized, particularized, and refined. They are capable of predicting consequences of their decisions, and they experiment more and take more risks. They expand their repertoire of techniques and strategies to be used in different settings with varying content and unique situations. Richard Shavelson[38] states: "Any teaching act is the result of a decision, whether conscious or unconscious, that the teacher makes after the complex cognitive processing of available information. This reasoning leads us to the hypothesis that *the basic teaching skill is decision making.*"

CONCLUSION

In this chapter we have elaborated our beliefs that the craft of teaching is cognitively complex. All the behaviors we see in the classroom are artifacts of these internal mental processes. The myriad decisions are driven by even more deeply embedded conscious or subconscious beliefs, styles, metaphors, perceptions, and habits.

The research on teacher cognition presented here supports our attempt to refocus the definition of teaching away from an archaic, behavioristic model to a more modern and viable cognitive model and thus direct the coach's focus away from overt behaviors of teaching to concentrate on influencing those invisible, inner thought processes of teaching.

These cognitive processes were presented in four clusters of thought: planning, the preactive phase; teaching, the interactive phase; analyzing, the reflective phase; and applying, the projective phase. Based on this conception of teaching, the model of Cognitive Coaching, outlined in chapter 2, directly parallels and is intended to enhance teachers' growth toward even more thoughtful teaching. If teachers do not possess these mental capacities, no amount of experience alone will create it. It is through mediated processing and reflecting upon experience that these capacities will be developed.[39] As Cognitive Coaches, therefore, we are interested in operating on the inner thought processes—in "coaching cognition." Teachers possess wide and expanding bodies of information and skills, and they make decisions about when to use what from the extensive range of their repertoire. Cognitive Coaching assists teachers in becoming more conscious, efficacious, precise, flexible, informed, and skillful decision makers. Together, teachers and coaches create greater student learning.

The ultimate purpose, however, is not only to enhance teaching and the resulting student learning but also to capacitate the teacher for self-directed learning and to cause the teacher to grow toward higher states of mind. In addition, our intent is to support the development of holonomous school cultures that, because they value and have skills in the dual goals of autonomy and interdependence, promote the professional development of teachers, reinvent instruction as appropriate, and increase student learning. Such is the vision of Renaissance schools. Thus the coach continually focuses on these long-range goals in the use of Cognitive Coaching skills.

NOTES

1. Whorf, B. L. (1956). *Language, thought and reality.* Cambridge, MA: MIT Press.

2. Anderson, J. R. (1990). *Cognitive psychology and its implications* (3rd ed.). New York: Freeman.

3. Clark, C., and Peterson, P. (1986). Teachers' thought processes. In M. C. Wittrock (Ed.), *Handbook of research on teaching* (pp. 255–296). New York: MacMillan.

4. Coladarci, A. P. (March, 1959). The teacher as hypothesis maker. *California Journal of Instructional Improvement 2*, 3–6. Jackson, P. W. (1968). *Life in classrooms* (p. 10). New York: Holt, Rinehart, and Winston. Peterson, P. (1988). Teachers' and students' conditional knowledge for classroom teaching and learning. *Educational Researcher 17*, 5–14. Arlin, P. (1990). Wisdom: The art of problem finding. In R. J. Sternberg (Ed.), *Wisdom: Its nature, origins and development* (pp. 230–243). New York: Cambridge University Press. King, P., and Kitchener, K. (1994). *Developing reflective judgement: Understanding and promoting intellectual growth and critical thinking in adolescents and adults.* San Francisco: Jossey-Bass. Kegan, R. (1994). *In over our heads: The mental demands of modern life.* Cambridge, MA: Harvard University Press.

5. Marzano, R. J. (1998). *A theory-based meta-analysis of research on instruction.* Aurora, CO: Mid Continent Regional Educational Laboratory.

6. Dahllof, U., and Lundgren, U. P. (1970). *Macro- and micro-approaches combined for curriculum process analysis: A Swedish educational field project.* Goteborg, Sweden: University of Goteborg Institute of Education.

7. Clark and Peterson, Teachers' thought processes.

8. Ibid.

9. Marzano, *A theory-based meta-analysis.*

10. Ornstein, R. (1991). *The evolution of consciousness: Of Darwin, Freud, and cranial fire—The origins of the way we think* (p. 224). New York: Prentice-Hall.

11. Edwards, J. L., and Newton, R. R. (1995*). The effects of cognitive coaching and empowerment.* Paper presented at the Annual Meeting of the American Educational Research Association, San Francisco. See also Garmston, R. (1989). Cognitive coaching and professors' instructional thought. *Human Intelligence Newsletter 10* (2), 3–4. Garmston, R., and Hyerle, D. (1998). *Professors' peer coaching program: Report on a 1987-1988 pilot program to develop and test a staff development model for improving instruction at California State University.* Sacramento, CA. California State University.

12. Costa, A. (1991). *Developing minds: A resource book for teaching thinking* (p. 25). Alexandria, VA: Association for Supervision and Curriculum Development.

13. Damasio, A. (1994). *Descartes' error: Emotion, reason, and the human brain* (p. xvi). New York: Avon Books.

14. Smith, E. R., and Tyler, R. W. (1945). *Appraising and recording student progress.* New York: Harper & Row. See also Costa, *Developing minds.*

15. Shettleworth, S. (1998). *Cognition, evolution and behavior* (p. 7). New York: Oxford University Press.

16. Grinder, M. (1993). *Envoy: Your personal guide to classroom management.* Battle Ground, WA: Michael Grinder and Associates.

17. Wolfe, P. (1987). *Facilitator's manual: Instructional decisions for long-term learning.* Alexandria, VA: Association for Supervision and Curriculum Development.

18. Sternberg, R., and Horvath, J. (August-September, 1995). A Prototype view of expert teaching. *Educational Researcher 24* (6), 9–17.

19. Shavelson, R. (1976). Teacher decision making. In *The psychology of teaching methods: 1976 yearbook of the National Society for the Study of Education, Part I.* Chicago: University of Chicago Press.

20. Zahorick, J. (1975). Teachers' planning models. *Educational Leadership, 33,* 134–139.

21. Shavelson, R. (1977). Teacher sensitivity to the reliability of information in making pedagogical decisions. *American Educational Research Journal 14,* 144–151. See also, Borko, H., Cone, R., Russo, D., and Shavelson, R. (1979). Teachers' decision making. In D. Peterson and H. Walberg (Eds.), *Research on teaching.* Berkeley, CA: McCutchan.

22. Ulich, E. (1967). Some experiments of the function of mental training in the acquisition of motor skills. *Ergonomics 10,* 411–419.

23. Taylor, P. (1970). *How teachers plan their courses.* Slough, Berkshire, England: National Foundation for Educational Research.

24. Miller, G. A. (1963). The magical number seven, plus or minus two: Some limits on our capacity for processing information. *Psychological Review, 2,* 81–97.

25. Zinsser, N., Bunker, L., and Williams, J. M. (1998). Cognitive techniques for building confidence and enhancing performance. In J. M. Williams (Ed.), *Applied sport psychology* (pp. 270–295). Mountain View, CA: Mayfield.

26. McNeill, B. (1991). *Beyond sports: Imaging in daily life: An interview with Marilyn King* (p. 33). Sausalito, CA: Institute of Noetic Science.

27. Jansson, L. (1983). Mental training: Thinking rehearsal and its use. In W. Maxwell (Ed.), *Thinking: The expanding frontier.* Philadelphia: Franklin Institute.

28. Ibid.; Landers, D., Maxwell, W., Butler, J., and Fagen, L. (2001). Developing thinking skills through physical education. In A. Costa (Ed.), *Developing minds: A resource book for teaching thinking.* Alexandria, VA: Association for Supervision and Curriculum Development. Tolson, J. (July 3, 2000). Into the zone. *U.S. News & World Report,* pp. 39–45.

29. Costa, A., and Garmston, B. (1998). Maturing outcomes. *Encounter: Educating for Meaning and Social Justice 11* (1), 10–18.

30. Clark C., and Yinger, R. (1979). *Teachers' thinking: Research on thinking.* Berkeley, CA: McCutchan.

31. Clark and Peterson, Teachers' thought processes.

32. Harvey, O. J. (1966). System structure, flexibility, and creativity. In *Experience, structure, and adaptability* (pp. 39–65). New York: Springer.

33. Yinger, R. J. (1977). *A study of teacher planning: Description and theory development using ethnographic and information processing methods.* Unpublished doctoral dissertation, Michigan State University, East Lansing.

34. Clark and Peterson, Teachers' thought processes.

35. Kotulak, R. (1997). *Inside the brain.* Kansas City, MO: Andrews McMeel.

36. Seligman, M. (1990). *Learned optimism.* New York: Alfred A. Knopf.

37. Hartoonian, B., and Yarger, G. (1981*). Teachers' conceptions of their own success.* Washington, DC: ERIC Clearinghouse on Teacher Education, No. S017372.

38. Shavelson, R. Teacher decision making.

39. Feuerstein, R., and Feuerstein, S. (1991). Mediated learning experience: A theoretical review. In R. Feuerstein, P. Kelin, & A. Tannenbaum (Eds.), *Mediated learning experience (MLE): Theoretical, psychosocial and learning implications.* London: Freund.

8

Inquiring Into the Knowledge Base of Teaching and Learning

Teaching is one of the most complex human endeavors imaginable.

—Saphier and Gower[1]

The process of teaching is like the flow of busy traffic at an unmarked intersection in Istanbul: only resident drivers know the unstated rules of the road. Similarly, only accomplished teachers know the unspoken knowledge and perceptions that guide their work in the classroom. Cognitive Coaching *accesses* that knowledge and *mediates* to inform teacher practice. Knowing the knowledge base of teaching and learning is important to persons providing support to teachers. In performing the functions of collaborating or consulting (see chapter 12), such knowledge is essential to sound guidance. It is also important in coaching, for through these interactions teachers clarify theories of learning and integrate their knowledge of content, pedagogy, and information about students and themselves into a coherent whole. This depth of learning is available nowhere else—in universities, in books, or from co-workers.

Research supports the conception of teaching as nonlinear inquiry from a rich knowledge base about instruction and learning. Cognitive Coaching mediates, integrates, and extends this knowledge base by focusing on teacher decisions, knowledge, perceptions, beliefs, and values. In this chapter, we specifically consider six domains of continuing inquiry: content knowledge, pedagogy, knowledge of students and how they learn, self-knowledge, knowledge of cognitive processes of instruction, and knowledge of collegial interactions.

WHAT IS TEACHING?

Teaching is knowing about, inquiring into, and experimenting with content and curriculum, learners and learning, fellow teachers and teaching, and educational philosophies and goals. Teaching is also about clear values and working within the contexts of various classrooms, schools, communities, and cultures. Teaching is about applying all of this integrated knowledge in a unit of instruction, a lesson, or an in-the-moment interaction.[2]

Teachers enter the profession as novices, and a small percentage of these develop into experts. Sternberg and Horvath[3] characterize the expert stage as the point at which teachers have greater knowledge, are more efficient, and are more insightful than teachers at any earlier stage of development. Teachers maintain a capacity for learning throughout their careers. However, growth is not automatic. Growth occurs by reflecting on experience and effectively using higher-order thinking processes to plan, monitor, and evaluate educational tasks. Teachers will increase their capacity for learning only when thinking is mediated in the work culture.

Master teachers continue to develop and grow as they construct meaning, reinvest their cognitive resources, and apply new learning. As we discussed in chapter 7, higher-concept teachers produce students who achieve at higher academic levels. Cognitive Coaching mediates this type of career-long development.

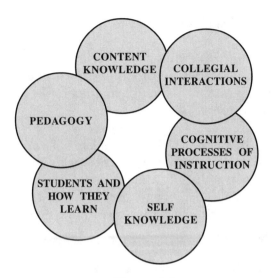

Figure 8-1.
Six Domains of Professional Inquiry.

SIX DOMAINS OF INQUIRY

In this chapter we organize and address the interacting fields of teaching knowledge under six domains of continuing inquiry: content knowledge, pedagogy, knowledge of students and how they learn, self-knowledge, knowledge of cognitive processes of instruction, and knowledge of collegial interactions. The effective coach is familiar with each of these domains and how it influences a teacher's work in and out of the classroom.

Content Knowledge

Expert teachers have a deep reservoir of knowledge about subject matter. They know the structure of their discipline (its organizing principles and concepts). The greater their subject-matter knowledge, the more flexible and student-oriented they are in their teaching.

For example, when a biology teacher presents a lesson about which she has deep personal knowledge, she places fewer boundaries on class discussion and how lab work proceeds. She encourages students to explore more freely. She knows which significant questions to ask, and she knows which problems to pose so that students will inquire into and synthesize the most salient concepts of the discipline. When this same teacher works in less familiar content areas, she limits classroom discourse and restricts learning opportunities. She also resorts to questions at lower, more modest, cognitive levels.

Teachers have always faced the problem of having more content to teach than they have time. Teachers who know the organizing principles of a discipline make better decisions about what to teach. They also make better decisions about how to develop instruction, which effectively serves both short- and long-term learning goals.

For example, some organizing principles of literature are characterization, plot, setting, rising action, and falling action. Many forms of literature can be examined for these dimensions, such as plays, novels, or short stories. An example of an organizing principle in science instruction is the interaction of cycles. Rather than teach about butterflies in one unit, frogs in another, and weather in yet another, a teacher can use her understanding of cycles as an organizing theme to invite learning about comparisons, causal relations, and interactions among the cycles of many living organisms and environmental conditions.

The New Teacher Center at the University of California, Santa Cruz, offers the following expectations for teacher content knowledge.[4] Coaches and other support personnel use these as guidelines to aid teacher reflection about content:

- Organizing and adapting the curriculum to facilitate an in-depth understanding of themes, concepts, and skills in each content area, and demonstrating relationships across the curriculum

- Connecting key concepts and themes within and across the curriculum, and building a wide range of diverse perspectives to extend learning for all students

- Devising and articulating short- and long-term goals with high expectations for learning

- Sequencing instruction to help students synthesize and apply new knowledge and to see relationships and connections across subject matter areas

Pedagogy

The queen on a chessboard is a useful metaphor for the knowledge domain of pedagogy. The queen is the piece with the greatest flexibility and range of movement. So, too, an experienced, effective teacher flexibly draws on a variety of moves during classroom work. This is the knowledge area of pedagogy.

Saphier and Gower, for example, identify 53 ways that a teacher can gain students' attention and keep them on task.[5] Although an individual teacher might not know all 53 of these moves, experienced teachers draw from a large personal repertoire to select the best match for each situation. Teachers also manage momentum, space, time, routines, and discipline. They apply principles of learning, hold high expectations, and design and guide learning experiences that enable students to reach objectives.[6]

Teacher clarity about pedagogy correlates highly with student learning. Clarity is required when teachers present new material, explain concepts, give directions, elaborate on directions, activate prior knowledge, reexplain old material, address confusion, and make instructional connections. Again, expert teachers develop a repertoire in this area and make best-fit matches for individual students and situations. Following are some guidelines in the area of teacher pedagogy from the Santa Cruz project:

- Consistently drawing on an extensive repertoire of appropriate strategies and resources, and adapting and refining strategies while teaching in response to students' needs

- Using questions to revise activities and extend students' abilities to synthesize what they know to achieve learning goals

- Facilitating challenging learning experiences that promote collaboration, independent learning, and choice for all students

- Using a variety of assessments that are embedded in instruction to guide short- and long-term plans and to support learning for all students

---

Expanding Repertoire

Master teachers, like concert artists, consciously expand their performance repertoires. They develop and assemble microroutines that can be
combined and reconstituted to fit a wide variety of settings. These experts
also habitualize many routines to free cognitive space for more complex
perceiving and more sophisticated instructional problem solving. This unconscious competence is the hallmark of the expert in the classroom.[7]

Stanford professor Lee Schulman, president of the Carnegie Foundation for the Advancement of Teaching, defines a special form of
craft knowledge as "pedagogical-content knowledge." This knowledge is formed from the intersection of knowledge about content
and pedagogy.[8] Grimmet and MacKinnon[9] claim that pedagogical-content knowledge is a different kind of knowing. As evidence,
they cite Shulman's assertion that it is derived from a "considered
response to experience in the practice setting, and though it is related to knowledge that can be taught in the lecture hall, it is
formed over time in the minds of teachers through reflection."

Demonstrating pedagogical-content knowledge is a dominant
theme in the performance standards for teacher licensing from the
Interstate New Teacher Assessment and Support Consortium
(INTASC). INTASC believes that assessing specific teaching decisions must occur within various contexts (often the subject matter
being taught), which require various responses.[10]

Knowledge of subject matter and pedagogy also drives certification by the National Board for Professional Teaching Standards.
Certification is specific to subject matter and the age of learners,
Cognitive Coaching has been effectively used in some support programs to support teacher self-reflection and inquiry.

Knowledge of Students and How They Learn

Teachers use knowledge about students as another important tool
of their craft. Like pedagogical-content knowledge, this knowledge
can be taught in workshops. However, knowledge about students
and how they learn comes to life through application of and reflection about teaching experiences. Knowledge in this domain
encompasses several categories of specialized information. This

includes knowing about gender, culture, the developmental stages of cognition, emotional development, physical development, and personalized information about a student.

For example, a teacher may know that only 20 percent of his eighth graders operate at a formal logical level of thinking, but in many cases the curriculum presumes higher levels of abstraction. Informed teachers do not confuse abstraction with intelligence. They know that abstraction in secondary students is content specific, and they adjust their instruction accordingly. Chemistry in the 10th or 11th grade is understandable when taught concretely, but students at this stage find chemistry very difficult when it is taught symbolically.

In Boston recently, teachers discovered how the cultural realities for immigrant students were at cross-purposes with instruction. For many Haitian and Cambodian children, science demonstrations of discrepant events appeared magical, and the students were disturbed. Because the students would not engage in the scientific inquiry, teachers initially interpreted their reaction as laziness. When the teachers learned that these youngsters came from a setting in which the "world of spirit" was very real and therefore dangerous to question, they adjusted their instruction.

Bruce Wellman tells of a middle school in Los Angeles in which a girl had been absent for several days. The science teacher decided to call the girl at home and ask her to do the assignments she had missed. He understood that this daughter of Mexican-American parents believed that her first duty was to her family. He also knew that traditional school responses to absences were not going to motivate her, and might actually push her out of school. Instead, he was prepared to individually negotiate with her how she could get her assignments done and still fulfill her responsibilities at home.

Self-Knowledge

Self-knowledge includes the areas of values, standards, and beliefs. A teacher with self-knowledge is able to overcome egocentric patterns and teach in the ways that students learn best. A teacher with self-knowledge does not teach only in the way that he or she learns.

With knowledge of their own cognitive styles, many teachers discover that the students who distress them the most are the ones with cognitive styles different from their own.

For example, a teacher whose own learning patterns are concrete and sequential may be driven to distraction by students who are abstract and random. This discovery provides another intersection in the domains of knowledge of the discipline being taught, self-knowledge, and pedagogy. Awareness permits the teacher to set aside emotional responses to student style to provide the best learning experiences possible.

Self-knowledge includes information about one's preferred learning styles, preferred representational systems, moral and ethical considerations in teaching, assumptions and theories about learning, and professional mission and values. Deciding what and how to teach is informed by one's beliefs and values. A calculus teacher, very clear about his own values, once said to us, "I do not teach calculus. I teach life through calculus." The following descriptors related to self-knowledge can support teacher reflection:

- Using understanding of self and individual students' development to meet learning goals

- Assessing teaching practice and extending professional development through professional dialogue within the professional community

- Engaging all students in practicing self- and peer-assessment, identifying their own learning goals, and monitoring progress over time

Knowledge of Cognitive Processes of Instruction

Teachers' developmental levels have a direct correlation to their performance in the classroom.[11] Teachers who function at higher conceptual levels are capable of greater degrees of complexity in the classroom and are more effective with students. Teachers with more advanced conceptual levels are more flexible, tolerant of stress, and adaptive in their teaching style. Thus, they are able to assume multiple perspectives, employ a variety of coping strategies, and apply a wide repertoire of teaching models.

Conceptually advanced teachers are responsive to a wider range of learning styles and culturally diverse classes. Teachers at higher levels of conceptual development employ multiple perspectives, including the students' perspectives. They also apply the learners' frames of reference within their own frame of reference for instructional planning, teaching, and evaluation. Furthermore, expert teachers not only seem to perform better than novices do, they also seem to do so with less effort. Sternberg and Horvath[12] outline ways that expert teachers differ from nonexpert teachers in knowledge, efficiency, and insight.

Although teachers' cognitive skills differ from one another on entering the profession, all teachers can develop greater cognitive capacity in the four phases of instructional thought described in chapter 7. One major intention of Cognitive Coaching is to develop these invisible skills of teaching through reflection that utilizes and extends the domains of craft knowledge described so far.

Knowledge of Collegial Interactions

In high-performing schools, faculty collaboration is the norm.[13] Many studies demonstrate the unusual potency of teachers' collaborative action on student learning. Little and McLaughlin report that teacher membership in a learning community is strongly related to students significantly exceeding the learning of control groups. In a study of 24 schools (8 elementary, 8 middle, and 8 high), Louis et al. found that collective responsibility for student learning emerged and schoolwide achievement gains were made when five conditions were present and interacting with one another: a shared sense of purpose, a collective focus on student learning, collaborative activities, "deprivatized practice," and reflective dialogue.[14]

Many school renewal efforts today regard collaboration and democratic governance of instructional issues as an important factor in their success. The League of Professional Schools, founded in 1990 by Carl Glickman, has more than 100 diverse elementary, middle, and high schools in its Georgia league, with affiliated networks in Nevada and Washington. They are committed to democratic governance in determining what students should be able to know and do and how students will demonstrate those competencies, and to continuous action research to test and refine teaching practices. A number of these schools are showing sustained improvements in student learning over a period of years.[15]

Not surprisingly, a teacher's ability to collaborate with his or her peers transfers to classroom practice. There is ample research on learning practices that increase student achievement, learning satisfaction, and success in later life. Glickman[16] reports the following:

> [A] study of 820 high schools and eleven thousand students[17] . . . found that schools that reorganized their academic programs around "active learning" had significantly higher student gains in all achievement domains (mathematics, reading, social studies, and science) measured by the National Assessment of Educational Progress. The same results hold true for recent longitudinal studies of elementary and middle schools.[18]

In these schools, students actively constructed knowledge, used disciplined inquiry, and found applications beyond school for what they had learned.

Teaching is one of the most private professions. For most of its history, teaching has been something that a person does in isolation from other teachers. As long as teachers work in isolation, they do not need a high degree of skill in collective problem solving, consensus seeking, or the technical and interpersonal aspects for collectively analyzing student work. This reality is changing. An important part of teacher work is now being conceived as working with other teachers, support staff, and community members.[19]

TEACHERS AS CONTINUING LEARNERS

The pursuit of perfection in a craft is as old as the human species. Bill Powell, superintendent of the International School in Kuala Lumpur, reminds us that our myths are replete with stories that praise the skill and wisdom of master craftsmen. Whether in art, music, sports, or business, the master craftsman in his or her pursuit of refinement and improvement continues to be featured among our most popular heroes. Powell writes:

> Curiously, craftsmanship is both an attribute and an energy source. The constant striving for improvement is certainly a quality of the master teacher, but it is more than a static characteristic. It is also a dynamic motivating force that compels the teacher towards greater refinement, greater specificity and greater precision.[20]

The master teacher has always constructed clear visions and specific goals. In the mid-1980s, education began an unprecedented journey toward setting standards for students, teachers, and administrators. In schools that already had a norm of self-assessment, this provided new resources with which teachers could examine and set goals for their teaching.

Several characteristics can usually be found in these standards for teaching. First, standards reflect a holistic conception of career development, describing teacher competencies in ways that ensure consistency with emerging visions of teaching development. Second, the core standards describe essential efforts in teaching, regardless of the grade level or students being taught. Third, the standards are performance-based, describing what teachers should know or be able to do. Finally, the standards are linked directly to current views of what students should know and be able to do to learn challenging subject matter.

Because teaching standards most generally describe generic teaching competencies unrelated to subject matter and age of student— and because our knowledge of teaching, learning, and content continues to evolve—such standards are useful mainly as instruments for coaching and self-appraisal. As instruments of evaluation, they fall far short of reflecting the complexity of decision making in which teachers engage as they integrate and apply information from multiple domains of knowledge.

In contrast, the certification process from the National Board of Professional Teaching Standards acknowledges the various instructional contexts within which teachers work. The certificates

are structured around student developmental levels and the subjects taught. In addition, certification requires the application of
sound pedagogical knowledge in each field and a performance-
based assessment that takes at least one year to complete.

Teachers develop a portfolio that includes samples of student
work, a videotape of classroom instruction, and reflective narratives on both of these. They also provide narratives on their contributions to the profession and their work with the school
community. The national achievement rate is approximately 50
percent.[21] Applicants who join a candidates support group or who
work with cognitive coaches or other support programs are generally more successful than applicants who do not.[22]

HOW TEACHERS OWN STANDARDS

Standards are not standards until they are owned. As long as they
remain someone else's expectations, teachers will simply comply
or conform rather than make real, authentic changes. Because systems can mandate compliance but not excellence, schools need
ways in which externally generated standards can be owned by the
faculty and individual teachers. Below are some suggestions for
achieving this goal.[23]

Focus on student learning as central to school conversations. Student learning, is, after all, the end goal of any set of teaching standards. Professional communities focus on student learning as the end
and teaching as the means. As teachers from various grade levels and
disciplines examine external standards for student learning, invite
them to seek agreement on what constitutes good student work in
their school in the subject matter they are addressing. If necessary,
modify the external standards so that a common version for "our students" exists. Next, facilitate processes through which teachers can
agree on developmental schemes and feedback systems that are coherent and consistent across classrooms. As teachers periodically examine actual student work from various classrooms, they construct
practical knowledge about their students related to teaching standards. Three questions drive these collective inquiries: What are our
standards for student work? Does this work meet our expectations? If
not, what do we need to do to see that students are successful?

Relate student standards to teaching standards. Introduce a set of teaching standards based on common agreement about learning and curriculum. As noted above, significant research has been invested in developing standards for teaching, and practicing teachers have offered many refinements. Standards for teaching will always address the six domains of inquiry described in this chapter (though often under different organizational schemes). Table 8-1 offers some sample standards from the California Standards for the Teaching Profession.

Link research-based teaching standards to teachers' daily practice. Several frameworks describe the attributes of effective teaching.[24] They describe a continuum of increasingly more sophisticated competencies, from beginner or novice through intermediate stages to levels of greater experience and mastery. Because these standards are descriptive and nonevaluative, they provide objective, research-based, and theoretically sound descriptors of what constitutes effective teaching.

TABLE 8-1.
CALIFORNIA STANDARDS FOR THE TEACHING PROFESSION

- Creating and maintaining an effective environment for student learning
- Planning instruction and designing learning experiences for all students
- Engaging and supporting all students in learning
- Assessing student learning
- Understanding and organizing subject matter for student learning
- Developing as a professional educator

The six standards are meant to be considered as a whole and not in any particular sequence or order. Each standard contains more specific elements of teaching practice. They are interrelated and work together to provide a complete picture of effective teaching practice.

We mention the California Standards for the Teaching Profession and Descriptions of Practice[25] because these documents suggest processes that are clearly formative in nature and because we have used them in California and in several international schools. Faculties can use such standards to guide inquiry into local definitions of effective teaching. These local elaborations can be used by teachers to prompt reflection about their own teaching and connections to student learning; to develop professional goals; and to guide, monitor, and self-assess progress of professional growth.

Review and adopt standards locally. Discuss, refine, and adapt published teaching standards as a vision for your district. These frameworks provide valuable benchmarks for catalogues of competencies to stimulate discussion and self-reflection.

Discuss the standards in small groups, grade levels, or departments. Talk about what it means to align one's teaching practices with what is known about effective instruction in subject matter for your students. Invite groups to select one standard to work on. Define the standard operationally: What would it look and sound like? For example, what would the standard look and sound like in a third-grade class of mainly bilingual students while teaching reading? How would a standard look and sound in an 11th-grade honors physics class?

Legitimize self-modification through reflective practice. Teaching frameworks are useful resources for helping teachers to reflect on their own practices. After they describe how a standard might sound or look in their classrooms, invite teachers to set goals related to where their teaching fits on the continuum of development. Ask them to consider: What might I do to achieve the next higher level of competency? Master teachers are never complacent about their performance; they always have more to learn.

Talk about real students and real student work. Frequently examine student work together. Compare it to expectations. Is the work good enough? What can be done to "reinvent instruction" so that all students succeed? Relate improvement efforts to teaching standards.

Couch the standards in projects of action research. The most convincing data are not reports of distant and historical research but teachers' own results from using new processes and approaches in their classrooms with their own students and subject matter. Help teachers to establish and employ techniques of data collection to assess the results on student behavior and performance when they use new processes or standards.

Promote in-classroom observation of teaching and learning. Provide release time for all teachers to observe one another as they apply teaching standards in their classrooms. After a conference in which the standards are selected and operationalized, the observing teachers can collect evidence of indicators of the performance of such standards. During a reflecting conference, share the data, allow the teacher to self-assess, and plan for achieving the next higher level of performance on the continuum.

CONCLUSION

Teaching is one of the most cognitively complex professions. Although the knowledge base of teaching and learning is vast and continually expanding, there is still uncertainty as to what works in various schools in diverse communities with each unique group of students. Intersecting with teachers' cognitive and professional development are stages of adult growth and teaching standards. We believe, therefore, that what makes teaching a profession is the continual inquiry, expansion of repertoire, and accumulation of knowledge through practice.

The professional educator continually experiments, inquires, tests, gathers data, revises, and modifies thought and practice. Such accumulated knowledge influences teaching decisions in at least the six domains described here. Continuing inquiry into these areas constitutes career-long agendas for professional growth. Cognitive Coaching helps teachers to integrate, extend, and apply this information in the crucible of classroom work.

NOTES

1. Saphier, J., and Gower, R. (1997). *The skillful teacher: Building your teaching skills.* Carlisle, MA: Research for Better Teaching.

2. Firth, G. (1998). Governance of school supervision. In G. Firth and E. Pajak (Eds.), *Handbook of research on school supervision* (pp. 928–931). New York: MacMillan.

3. Sternberg, R. J., and Horvath, J. A. (1995). A prototype view of expert teaching. *Educational Researcher, 24* (6), 9–17.

4. Santa Cruz New Teacher Project. (1998). *A developmental continuum of teacher abilities: Aligned with the California standards*

for the teaching profession. Santa Cruz, CA: New Teacher Center, University of California.

5. Saphier and Gower, *The skillful teacher,* pp. 13–27.

6. Marzano, R., Pickering, D. and Pollock, J. (2001). *Classroom instruction that works: Research-based strategies for increasing student achievement.* Alexandria, VA: Association for Supervision and Curriculum Development.

7. Garmston, R., and Wellman, B. (1999). *The adaptive school: A sourcebook for developing collaborative groups* (p. 260). Norwood, MA: Christopher-Gordon.

8. Shulman, L. (1987). Knowledge and teaching: Foundations of the new reform. *Harvard Educational Researcher, 57* (1), 1–22.

9. Grimmet, P. P., and MacKinnon, A. M. (1992). Craft knowledge and the education of teachers. *Review of Research in Education, 18,* 387.

10. Darling-Hammond, L., Wise, A. E., and Klein, S. P. (1995). *A license to teach: Building a profession for 21st-century schools.* Boulder, CO: Westview Press.

11. Garmston, R., and Lipton, L. (1998). The psychology of supervision. In G. Firth and E. Pajak (Eds.), *The handbook of research on school supervision* (pp. 242–286). New York: Macmillan.

12. Sternberg and Horvath. A prototype view.

13. Little, J. W. (1993). Professional community in comprehensive high schools: The two worlds of academic and vocational teachers. In J. W. Little and M. McLaughlin (Eds.), *Teachers work: Individuals, colleagues, and contexts* (pp. 137–163). New York: Teachers College Press. See also Newmann, F., et al. (1997). *Authentic achievement.* San Francisco: Jossey-Bass. Louis, K. S., Marks, H. M., and Kruse, S. (1996). Teachers' professional community in restructuring schools. *American Educational Research Journal, 33* (4), 757–798. McLaughlin, M., and Talbert, J. (1993). *Contexts that matter for teaching and learning.* Stanford, CA: Center for Research on the Context of Secondary School Teaching, Stanford University.

14. Louis et al., Teachers' professional community.

15. Glickman, C. (2000). Personal communication.

16. Glickman, C.D. (1998). *Revolutionizing America's schools* (p. 32). San Francisco: Jossey-Bass.

17. Newmann, F. M., Marks, H. M., and Gamoran, A. (1995). *Authentic pedagogy: Standards that boost student performance* (pp. 1–11). Madison, WI: Wisconsin Center for Educational Research.

18. Newmann, F. M., and Wehlage, G. G. (1995). *Successful school restructuring: A report to the public and educators by the Center on Organization and Restructuring of Schools.* Madison, WI: Wisconsin Center for Educational Research.

19. Garmston, R., and Wellman, B. (1999). *The adaptive school: A sourcebook for developing collaborative groups.* Norwood, MA: Christopher-Gordon.

20. Powell, W. (2000). Recruiting educators for an inclusive school. In W. Powell and O. Powell (Eds.) *Count me in: Developing inclusive international schools* (pp. 191–204). Washington D.C. Overseas Advisory Council.

21. Rotberg, I. C., Futrell, M. H., and Holmes, A. E. (2000). Increasing access to national board certification. *Phi Delta Kappan, 81* (5), 379–382.

22. Peterson, J. (2000). Personal communication.

23. Costa, A., and Garmston, R. Peer assistance and review: Potentials and pitfalls. *The Peer Assistance and Review Reader* (Gary Bloom and Jennifer Geldstein Eds.) (2000) Santa Cruz, CA. New Teacher Center, University of California, Santa Cruz (pp. 63–79).

24. Barron, W., and Gless, J. (1997). *Preparing support providers for work with beginning teachers.* Oxford, OH: National Staff Development Center. See also Santa Cruz New Teacher Project.

25. California State Department of Education (1997). *Descriptions of practice.* Sacramento: California Standards for the Teaching Profession.

9

Resolving Problems:
The Third Coaching Map

Our deepest struggles are in effect our greatest spiritual and creative assets and the doors to whatever creativity we might possess. It seems to be a learned wisdom to share them with others only when they have the possibility of meeting them with some maturity. We learn to remain attentive to the mood and outlook of the listener even before we begin to speak about the darker side of our existence.

—David Whyte

In this chapter the most complex of the coaching maps is explored. One dilemma in describing these responsively interactive processes in print is that the context for this map is problem solving, but not in the usual sense. Problem solving is often construed as a linear sequence: tell me a problem and together we can search out possible causes, then envision a desired state with some probable alternative approaches to problem resolution. This lends itself to linear problem solving, in which both parties have the internal resources necessary for problem analysis and solution generation. This process is not effective, however, for the majority of problems that, by definition, are "wicked"; problems that are nonlinear and recursive. These are the types of problems that engage conflicts inherent in holonomous dichotomies and in which the protagonist often approaches the problem situation already feeling defeated, confused, overwhelmed, or simply nonresourceful.

The approach to problems that we present is both simple and sophisticated. On the one hand, it is a search for what the person wants as a desired state. On the other hand, it is the identification and amplification of the internal resources necessary to generate and apply the strategies required to achieve the desired state. In concept it is simple; in execution it is complex. We are describing a pattern known as *pacing and leading*. As illustrated in figure 9-1, it is a coaching conservation that moves one from an existing state of limitations to a desired state of possibilities.

PACING AND LEADING[1]

Imagine that your friend says the following: "I feel awful. I lost my temper during seventh period today. I was exhausted, and when Alex acted up I just lost it. I know I embarrassed him in front of his peers, but I had just had it."

How might you respond? Would you salve the hurt and bolster your friend's spirits? Would you blame the student who was the source of the aggravation? Would you share your similar experiences and feelings about students like Alex? Would you inquire into what Alex did or what your friend said?

This vignette is an example of a tension between our emotional state and our knowledge of appropriate action. Sometimes we are in a position to mediate another person who has temporarily lost access to his or her resourcefulness. Cognitive Coaches, being alert to such situations, use a pattern of pacing and leading. The problem resolving conversation is a map intended to mediate the other person's capacity to liberate and use the efficacy, craftsmanship,

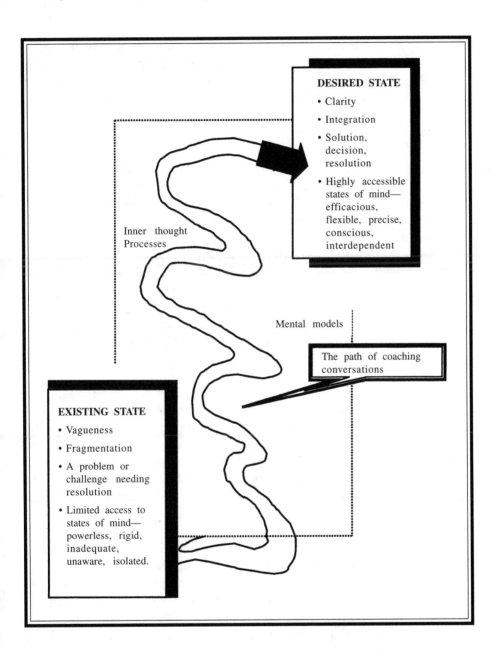

Source: John Dyer. Adapted with permission.

Figure 9-1.
A Paradigm for Problem Resolving

consciousness, flexibility, or interdependence that has been temporarily obscured. The long-range intent of pacing and leading is to help the other person become self-accessing, even when the coach is not present.

When to Use This Map

Accessing internal resources is used to assist a person who, when facing adversity, feels stuck, uncertain of what to do, or so emotionally flooded that it is difficult to make good choices. When people feel trapped in a situation without alternatives, they need two lifelines: states of resourcefulness and strategies to address the specific issue. Yet one without the other is not enough. When people are resourceful, electrochemical interactions occur that make available their inventiveness, their decision-making capacities, and a repertoire of steps they might take. Thus, a coach helps a colleague become more resourceful by accessing internal resources, which, we believe, creates chemical adjustments in the bloodstream.

Most often, pacing and leading is used in conversations specifically focused on resolving a problem about which the person feels stuck. However, if the coach senses the person is stuck and unable to think clearly during a planning or reflective conversation, the coach may transition to this Cognitive Coaching map. Pacing and leading conversations are sometimes brief. More often they are extended, focused conversations in an environment without distractions.

A coach paces to honor the existing state and create awareness of a possible desired state. The coach "leads" a person to locate and amplify his or her own internal resources—states of mind or knowledge—necessary to deal effectively with a problem situation. When nonverbal cues are congruent with verbal descriptions of the desired state and necessary resources, the coach and colleague reflect together about the coaching process. *Matching* or *mirroring* of perceptions might be synonyms for pacing. The goal of pacing is to let the other person know that his or her experience is understood without judgment. Pacing first reflects what is and then makes visible what is possible. In the following example, the response to the speaker might be called a pace and jerk because the speaker's experience was never really acknowledged.

Speaker: "I'm feeling bad."

Friend: "Ohhh. You shouldn't feel that way. Look at the bright side!"

By denying the speaker's feelings, it is more likely that the feelings stay unchanged. To pace, the coach should empathically paraphrase to reflect the emotional state of the speaker and give assurance that the speaker's condition is recognized and acknowledged. After several interchanges with repeated paraphrasing, the coach can then offer a description of what conditions the speaker would like to see instead of the existing state.

Leading begins after the speaker has indicated that the description of a desired state is accurate. Then the coach begins a series of questions intended to help the speaker identify the states of mind or other internal resources necessary to achieve the goal. Leading locates, elicits, and amplifies the internal resources necessary to achieve what is possible. Figure 9-2 illustrates the resolving problems conversation.

Learning the Pattern of Pacing and Leading

The processes of pacing and leading are simultaneously simple and complex. They can be learned from this book, but they must be studied, practiced, tested, and reflected upon to become internalized. For this reason we have organized the information in several ways. First, we have just offered a brief definition of pacing and leading. Second, we offer a more detailed account of the structures and skills of pacing, then leading. Next, we explore theories about the changes in body chemistry during pacing and leading, along with responses of the autonomic nervous system that the coach can observe and use to guide the interaction. We explore more about leading after that, and finally we describe a set of principles of intervention. The coaching conversation in pacing and leading moves from an undesirable existing state toward a desired state, as shown in Figure 9-2 on the next page.

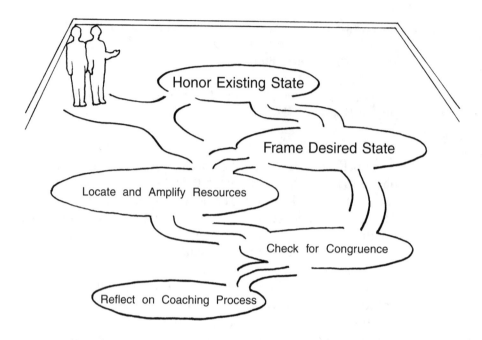

Figure 9-2.
Problem Resolving Conversation

Many relationships exist among territories in a problem resolving conversation and many paths connect them. The pathways of most frequent use by coaches are shown with a center line in pathways between territories. The most critical territories are shown in larger font.

THE STRUCTURE AND SKILLS OF PACING

An effective pace requires complete attention to rapport and to four verbal phases: expressing empathy, reflecting content, inferring and stating a goal, and presupposing a search for a way to get started working toward the goal (i.e., a pathway).

Everything we learned about rapport in chapter 5 becomes extremely important in pacing and leading. Posture, voice qualities, gesture, facial expressions, breathing rates, and other nonverbal manifestations of human experience communicate more authentically than do words. Because the most effective pacing is done by psychologically entering the other person's experience, what the coach's body signals enhances the verbal messages of understanding.

As illustrated in the list that follows, the first two verbal steps are embodied in any well-formed paraphrase. The third is another paraphrase about the coach's inference regarding a goal the colleague desires. The fourth element paraphrases what has been unsaid verbally and presumes a readiness to begin exploring options.

1. Express empathy by matching intonation and accurately naming the person's feeling: "You're frustrated . . ."

2. Accurately reflect the speaker's content: ". . . because you have so many things on your plate you can't keep up . . ."

3. State the goal that you infer the speaker is trying to achieve: "What you want is to be in control of your time and your work . . ."

4. Presuppose readiness to find a pathway to attain the goal: ". . . so you're searching for a way to make that happen."

The above scaffold is simple yet often demanding to learn because it may require unlearning some long-held communication patterns. It is also composed entirely of paraphrases. Any question posed at this stage interrupts the colleague's focus in the story and is experienced as a distraction. Skillful and empathic pacing is essential to effective leading. Repeated and guided practice in pacing is usually necessary for pacing responses to come easily and naturally. Table 9-1 illustrates the neurological effects of the process of pacing.

TABLE 9-1.
THE NEUROBIOLOGICAL EFFECTS OF PACING

Phase	Neurobiological Effects
Empathy "You're worried . . ."	**Distress:** Peptides produced in the limbic brain have stimuated a chemistry of distress. Lung muscles constrict, making breathing shallow and reducing oxygen to the neocortex; heart contractions constrict coronary vessels that supply blood to the heart muscle cells; changes in skeletal muscles and visceral organs produce changes in skin color and muscle tone During the empathy and content phases of pacing, the person often shows signs of distress through muscle tautness and shallow breathing.
Content ". . . because others are perceiving you as negative."	**Distress:** After a few interchanges in which the coach continues to paraphrase, blood chemistry aborts its downward decline and hypothetically reaches a state of balance.
Goal "What you want is to be a good team member . . ."	**Eustress:** This is "good stress." The coach observes shifts in posture, voice qualities, and animation. The coach also notices deeper breathing or other signals that the goal statement, worded as a paraphrase, has shifted the body-mind system into the chemistry of resourcefulness.
Pathway ". . . so you're looking for a way to that happen."	Eustress: The physical manifestations of resourcefulness remain strong. The coach knows the person is ready to enter the lead stage and respond to questions.

Crafting a Goal Statement

Leading without pacing is ineffective. Most people can describe what they don't like. It is only when we are resourceful that we can describe what we want instead. Pacing "listens below the story." During the goal stage, pacing tests the coach's understanding of a desired state. Of the four elements in the pace, formulating an appropriate goal statement is the most complex. A well-formed goal statement does the following:

- It is stated with artful vagueness. ("You want to be in control, be confident, have satisfaction.") If the goal is stated with too much specificity, it narrows the solution possibilities. Vague language here allows the coach to engage the energy of the person being coached to move forward. It does not matter yet if the pictures formed by *confident* mean different things to the coach and the partner.

- It uses verb forms of *be, have,* or *feel,* but never *do.* The latter is used in reference to an action or a plan, not a goal. A useful goal statement is always about a destination (what the person will be or have when satisfied), not a journey (what he or she might do to get there).

- It is stated in positive form (what the person wants, rather than doesn't want).

- It is brief and stated with simple language.

- It acknowledges feelings. (This is sometimes communicated through posture, facial expression, or tone of voice.)

- It assumes nobility of intention on the part of the person being paced.

- It may identify two or more goals that are not always compatible with each other. For example, "You want to be accountable for test results but at the same time be true to your responsibilities to students."

To craft a goal statement, the coach listens for an unexpressed yearning to resolve the tension. What might the person feel, be, or have if the challenging situation were resolved? Search for the tension arising from the drives for self assertion and affliation. Another way to listen is to search for contrasting emotions. If the person is sad, perhaps he wants to be happy. If she is feeling disconnected, then she may want to be connected. If he is feeling powerless, he may want to have control. (See Figure 6-1 on page 125.)

Naming Universal Goals

Another tip for crafting goal statements is to listen for the expression of three universal goals. After the basic survival needs of food, water, shelter, and sex, humans desire three goals: identity, connectedness, and potency. Coaches may use words in the goal statement that relate to these concepts. If, for example, circumstances threaten a colleague's ability to act congruently with his sense of self, the coach may choose goal words that relate to identity. For example, she may use phrases such as "and you want to be true to yourself" or "who you are is a person of integrity and you want to be that with others" or "you want to be who you really are in this situation."

If a situation is challenging one's sense of efficacy, words related to potency may express that desire. For example: "and what you want is to be a catalyst" or "you want to be a person of influence" or "you want to be resourceful in this situation."

If a person feels isolated, words that convey connectedness might be appropriate. For example: "so your desire is be a team player" or "you want a sense of family" or "you want to be a friend."

The above example illustrates holonomous tensions produced by the dichotomy between self-assertion and integration.

Table 9-2 contains a bank of words and phrases that the coach may want to use with this verbal skill.

TABLE 9-2.
A WORD BANK FOR UNIVERSAL GOALS

Identity	Connectedness	Potency
Integrity	Community	Effective
Valued	Bonded	Influence
Creative	Team	Successful
Trusted	Family	Resourceful
Balanced	Unified	Compelling
In Charge	Relationship	Powerful
Self	Unit	Grounded
Unique	Integrated	Strength

Neurological Responses
All behavior is communication.

—P. Watzlawick[2]

Humans have an integrated body-brain system. Transitions from distress to eustress are consistently observed during pacing, as we saw in Table 9-1. *Dis* is a prefix denoting, in general, separation or negation. *Distress* is "bad" stress, separating us from our cognitive resources, leaving our body-mind system primed to protect itself in ancient ways. *Eustress* is "good stress"; *eu* means "good,"as in *eulogy* (good words) or *euphoria* (good feelings).

Often, a colleague begins a pacing conversation with muscle tautness, shallow breathing, and other nonverbal indicators associated with emotional flooding and a shutdown from the neocortex. At the exact moment the coach makes a goal statement congruent with the teacher's desires, an immediate shift into eustress can be observed in breathing, posture, animation, and voice qualities. Given our understanding of the mechanics of information processing, our current hypothesis is that at the moment eustress is achieved, electrochemical energy is released to the body-brain system, stimulating two reactions. One reaction relates to neurotransmitters like seratonin, which move messages from neuron to neuron, make the brain more efficient, and metaphorically allow access to the rational brain.

A second reaction is that peptides,[3] produced in the limbic brain and routed through the bloodstream to the entire body, including the brain, carry chemical signals of hopefulness that are manifested as "gut" reactions and changes throughout the autonomic nervous system. Changes in the visceral, vestibular, and musculoskeletal systems can be observed in pupil dilation, breathing changes, pulse changes, and changes in skin color and muscle tone as skeletal muscles and visceral organs are affected. Even glands respond with discharges of tears, perspiration, or saliva. Hair follicles can become erect. The coach is highly attentive to these signals as feedback about her work.[4]

Peptides are one of three information delivery systems in the body. The other two are neurotransmitters like acetylcholine, norepinephrine, dopamine, histamine, and serotonin; and steroids like testosterone, estrogen, and progesterone. Oxytocin is one example of a peptide. It contracts the uterus in labor and produces maternal behavior. It releases the chemistry of "tend and befriend," which is generally a feminine response to stress. When females are stressed, their oxytocin levels rise.[5] Peptides regulate most of life processes and carry 95 percent of information transmission through the bloodstream to every cell in the body and brain. Less than 2 percent of neuronal communication actually occurs at synapses.

Metaphorically, then, we regard the state of distress as being related to the "chemistry of depression or frustration," and the state of eustress as a shifting to a chemistry of hopefulness or resourcefulness.

We believe the paraphrase to be the heroine of this unfolding neurological drama. Pacing is paraphrasing, and its first function is to interrupt the decline of a chemical-emotional state and restore or refresh the chemistry of hopefulness. Skilled pacing honors and validates the emotions of the existing state *without* increasing the chemistry of defeat or frustration. Questions during pacing counteract this movement and reverse it to plunge the person into deeper negative chemistry. Exploring the speaker's frustration reinforces and often amplifies the body chemistry of negative emotion. Paraphrasing is so consistently associated with the physical signals of these changes because it often clarifies a person's feelings and conflicts, it is accepting of the existing condition (hence lessening physiological "resistance" to it), and it leads the person to feel understood.

Bruce Wellman[6] and Diane Zimmerman offer the following metaphor, illustrated in Figure 9-3. The paraphrase acts as the fulcrum of a lever assisting the increase of chemical resourcefulness. As

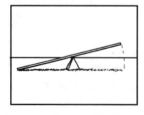
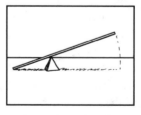
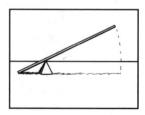

Acknowledge and Clarify   Summarize or Organize   Shift Logical Level

Figure 9-3.
How Paraphrasing "Lightens the Load"

paraphrasing continues, levering action floods the bloodstream (and every cell in the body) with better chemistry. Envison a fulcrum under a lever. Paraphrases that acknowledge and clarify are like a fulcrum placed at about the middle in which some movement will occur. This will balance the chemistry. Paraphrases that summarize and organize move the fulcrum closer to the "load" to be lifted and add more resourceful chemistry. Paraphrases that shift the logical level, which is the form of paraphrase offered in a goal statement, move the fulcrum to its most potent spot, flooding the body-brain system with resources manifested throughout the whole body, including oxygen, which the brain needs for reasoning. A shift from limbic system dominance to npocortical dominance has been completed. Positioning the fulcrum closer to "the load" reduces the amount of "force" required to lift it. Focused inquiry (the lead) is now possible for exploring solutions within the newly identified desired state. (See descriptions of these forms of paraphase in chapter 4.)

During distress, the limbic system is in command, focusing inward, which is its function. The neocortex looks outward and can attend to situations and oneself from a neutral observation point. (See "How Do I Know When I Am Finished?" below for a description of other physical signals stimulated by the autonomic nervous system.)

THE STRUCTURE AND SKILLS OF LEADING

If pacing is paraphrasing, then leading is questioning. When pacing is complete, questioning begins. Your partner has indicated, often through the autonomic nervous system, that the stated goal is indeed congruent with his or her desires. One cue relatively easy to detect is the slowing and deepening of breathing. Now the coach has tacit permission to inquire.[7]

Questions become the coach's primary language tool, supported by paraphrasing and pausing. The map for leading a colleague to internal resources is less clear and less standard than the map for pacing.

In pacing, the coach paraphrases for empathy and content, probably several times, then tested a goal statement, and finally offered the pathway: "So you are looking for a way to do that." Now, however, the coach enters more uncharted water, guided by three overarching questions and the moment-to-moment verbal and nonverbal responses of the person being coached, as shown in Table 9-3. These questions are: Where do I start the lead? Where do I go from there? How do I know I am done?

TABLE 9-3.
A Macro Map for Leading

Since leading another to essential internal resources required for problem resolving is as much art as science, there can be no prescription for how a Cognitive Coach achieves this. There do, however, seem to be at least three stages in the conversation with touch points as follows.

1. Where do I start?	2. Where do I go from there?	3. How do I know when I am finished?
• Initiate a lead question intended to accesses and illuminate a state of mind described in chapter 6	• Emphasize questions that liberate internal resources—feelings, values, subgoals	• Observe major and sudden shifts in voice qualities, posture, breathing, gesture, muscular tone, and/or skin tone.
• If the first question is unproductive, explore other states of mind	• Ask questions to create better goal specificity, if necessary	• Detect congruence between speech content and nonverbal messages
• Continue questioning guided by the colleague's responses	• Paraphrase to shift conceptual levels	• Observe manifestation of cognitive dissonance, as in shifts from certainty to uncertainty or sudden insights
• Maintain empathy and rapport	• Ask questions that shift the focus from a third party to the person being coached	

WHERE DO I START?

One reason we recommend making the pace automatic is that pacing is a complex, multifaceted intellectual task. The coach listens to the feelings and context of what is being expressed, infers an authentic goal, and decides how to begin the lead. The five states of mind serve the coach as a template to initiate a lead statement or question. When verbal and nonverbal messages are congruent related to both goal and pathway, the coach knows she can start the lead.

During pacing, the coach asks himself which of the five states of mind appears to be unawakened in the colleague's experience. If liberated, which of them might convey the necessary resources? The lead to internal resources may begin with a question designed to illuminate that state of mind and its related resources. Although none of the questions listed below would be the first question asked in the lead, they illustrate inquiries that might activate a particular state of mind within the context of an interaction.

For example, if efficacy is unawakened, the coach might ask the following questions:

- **Self-prescribing:** "How do you go about motivating yourself?"
- **Choice making:** "So you can think of several approaches. How will you know which one to choose?"
- **Correcting fate control:** "What was it in *your behavior* that might have caused that?"
- **Shifting toward an internal locus of control:** "What do you need to do?"
- **Identifying resources:** "What knowledge, skills, or attitudes might you need to accomplish that?"
- **Content reframing:** "What might be the positive value of that response?"

If the colleague needs to access flexibility, the coach might ask questions like these:

- **Entering other perspectives:** "Considering their history, what might they be feeling?"
- **Enlarging frames of reference:** "What additional values might there be?"
- **Predicting consequences:** "What might be the result of . . . ?"
- **Considering intentions:** "What do you think they want to achieve?"
- **Testing outcomes:** "What's the worst [or best] possible results of achieving that outcome?"

- **Style checking:** "Given your knowledge of learning styles, what might be going on?"

- **Changing time horizons:** "If you had twice the time [or half the time], what difference might that make?"

- **Context reframing:** "If there were an upside to this misfortune, what might it be?"

A coach who wants to help a colleague access craftsmanship might ask questions like the following:

- **Communicating with specificity:** "How, specifically did . . .?"

- **Managing time:** "How will you know it is time to move on?"

- **Defining criteria for judgment:** "What criteria will you use to . . .?"

- **Striving for refinement:** "How will you know when you are really satisfied?"

- **Exploring standards:** "What are the connections with [curriculum, teaching, district] standards?"

To access consciousness, the coach might ask these kinds of questions:

- **Metacogitating:** "What was your thinking that led to that decision?"

- **Mental rehearsing:** "As you picture this event, what will you be doing?"

- **Mental editing:** "Looking back, what might you change?"

- **Owning intentions:** "What are your intentions?"

- **Considering effects:** "How might your choice influence you and others?"

- **Checking assumptions:** "So you are assuming. . . . How did you arrive at that?"

- **Values searching:** "What is it that makes this so important to you?"

In the area of interdependence, a coach might ask the following:

- **Collaborating:** "Who else is concerned about this?"

- **Talent searching:** "What useful skills do other group members have?"

- **Resource banking:** "How might others assist you?"

- **Group supporting:** "In what ways does this relate to staff concerns?"

- **Envisioning potential:** "As this group continues to develop, what other ways might it handle this?"

- **Coordinating:** "Where else in the system does this value of yours reside?"

Where Do I Go From There?

As Table 9-3 illustrates, the coach begins the lead with questions that illuminate a particular state of mind. If that seems unproductive, the coach may move to another state of mind. Other mediational strategies include paraphrasing to shift the conceptual level and asking questions that illuminate feelings, values, or more details about the goals. The coach might also ask the person to compose self-generated questions or use a series of questions that move from focusing on a third party to themselves. For example:

- What behaviors do you want from the group?

- What knowledge, skills, or attitudes will they need to perform those behaviors?

- What might you do to help them develop these resources?

- What internal resources do you need in order to do that?

Language offers cues to thinking. Language also abides by certain conventions. One thing we want to avoid is detail in which every nuance of thought is expressed. When people talk or write, generalizations, deletions, or distortions are quite common. At times, however, they blur understanding and hide opportunities for choice. Coaches are sensitive to these language forms at all times, but most particularly when leading colleagues to resources. When coaches suspect that one of these forms of language is hiding important information from thinking processes, they may respond in the following ways.

Generalization. Generalization eliminates the necessity to relearn a concept or behavior every time we are confronted with a variation of the original. However, generalizations can carry imprecision and inaccuracies that limit thought and choices. Examples of three forms of generalization follow, along with examples and sample responses.

A *complex equivalent* is a statement that ties two separate ideas together as if they were inseparable: "He is failing; he doesn't study enough." In that case, the coach might ask, "Have you ever known someone to study hard and still fail?" or "Can one not study at all and still pass?"

A *lost performative* is a statement in which the performance criteria for a value judgment are missing: "That was a good paper." The coach might then ask, "Good in what way?" or "What criteria are you considering when you rate it as good?"

A *modal operator* (derived from mode of operation or modus operandi) is a rule word like *can't* or *impossible:* "I can't do this." Then the coach might ask, "What is stopping you?" or "What would happen if you did?"

In all of these situations, the coach's intention is to illuminate possible inaccuracies represented by the generalizations. Fritz Perls, the originator of Gestalt therapy, used to say, "Don't say can't. Say won't!"

Distortion. Distortion is the process by which we alter our perceptions; it is the source of creativity, play, humor, and multiple versions of remembering or interpreting an event. Three linguistic cues may signal distortions that are limiting to the speaker.

Cause-and-effect statements inaccurately name the source of an event. This type of distortion may be a cue to low efficacy, placing the power outside oneself for responses: "They make me mad." In that case, a coach might respond, "They have that much control over you?" or

"When do you first notice that you are becoming angry?"

Mind reading is the expression of interpreting another person's intentions, thinking, or feelings. It differs from the paraphrases in a pace in that it is expressed as an explanation of another person's behavior rather than an attempt to understand when someone says something such as: "He is doing that to annoy me." In that situation, the coach might respond, "What other possible reasons might he have?" or "Can you think of a time when you have done something similar for a different purpose?" or "If he had a positive intention, what might it be?"

A *nominalization* names a process as if it is a thing. It describes a verb as if it were a noun. The words *relate, love, learn, communicate,* and *trust* are all nominalizations. In the sentence, "They don't respect each other," the word *respect* is used as an abstraction, or nominalization. Respect can mean a number of things. The question "What might they be doing when they are respecting each other?" returns action and specificity to the abstraction.

Coaches seek to return active status to nominalizations because we are doomed to frustration and failure whenever we try to solve an abstraction. For example, nothing can be done about "resistance," because the language form characterizes it as a nominalization, a thing, an immovable object. "Resisting," however, has form: a beginning, a middle, and an end with which a person can observe, interact, and intervene. Denominalized words allow participation. Nominalized forms suggest choicelessness. Many nominalizations in a person's speech are sometimes a cue about low efficacy. When someone says, "Their resistance is the problem," the coach might respond, "What are they doing when they resist?" or, "How does the resisting begin?" or, "What would they be doing if they were not resisting?"

Deletions. Deletions are information left out of statements. Deleted information occurs more frequently in speech than either distortions or generalizations because if we were to speak inclusively of all details, our conversations would take a century: "The man—that is, the tall, moustached man with the gray suit, green shoes, and white tie (and holding a cane), standing three feet from and to the north side of . . ."

The sensitive coach is selective about the frequency of challenges to deletions. We cannot emphasize strongly enough, however, that paraphrasing gives permission to ask any type of probing questions. For example, when a person says, "They say it will get better," the coach can respond, "So, they believe it will improve. Who is they?" If the colleague says, "We want them to think," the coach can respond, "Think how, specifically?"

How Do I Know When I Am Finished?

> *Conversation does not have to reach conclusions in order to be of value.*
>
> —Parker Palmer

Pacing and leading releases a person from the trap of impotency about how to approach a problem. Pacing and leading does this by accessing and amplifying the internal resources necessary for clarity, courage, and right action. Most often these require amplifying states of mind, as depicted in Figure 9-4. In other consulting conversations, where the goal is to solve problems, you know you are finished when the person has articulated a plan of action. When the goal, however, is to liberate sufficient internal resources to restore states of mind, different indicators of completion are needed.

Observations of physiological changes will often provide cues.

Mind and body are inseparable. An observant coach sees and hears physiological changes that may be interpreted as movement from distress to eustress during pacing. Similar indicators also guide the coach's choice of interactions during leading and are signals that conversational goals have been met. Emotions play a commanding role in being stuck or becoming resourceful and are registered in the body. Behavioral manifestations of internal resource states (BMIRS) will appear involuntarily as they are informed by chemical shifts affecting the autonomic (self-regulating) system. Look for verbal and nonverbal congruence.

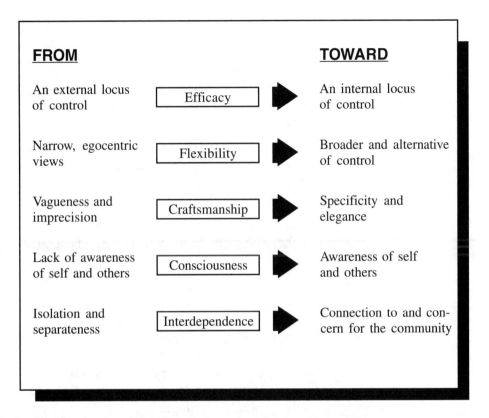

Figure 9-4.
Dimensions of Holonomy: Five States of Mind

In a typical emotion, regions of the brain send commands to other regions of the brain and to almost every area of the body. The commands are sent by two routes. One route is the bloodstream, where chemical molecules act on cell receptors. The other route consists of neural pathways, and the commands along this route take the form of electrochemical signals that act on other neurons, on muscular fibers, or on organs. Organs (such as the adrenal gland) in turn can release chemicals of their own into the bloodstream. Each emotion shares a common biological core described by neurologist Antonio Damasio:[8]

  • Emotion travels via the bloodstream and neural pathways. Chemical molecules act on electrochemical signals, which act on cell receptors, neurons or muscular fibers, or organs. Organs release chemicals into bloodstream.

- Emotions are collections of chemical and neural responses. All emotions contribute in some way to the advantage of the organism. The role of emotions is to assist the organism in maintaining life.

- Emotions are biologically determined processes, depending on innately set brain devices, established by a long evolutionary history. Learning and culture may alter the expression of emotions.

- Emotions both regulate and represent body states. They are produced in the brain stem and move up to the higher brain.

- All the triggering devices for emotions can be engaged automatically, without conscious deliberation. While individual variation and culture play a role in bringing on emotion, there is still a "fundamental stereotypic, automaticity and regulatory purpose of the emotions."

All emotions use the body as their theatre, but emotions also affect numerous brain circuits. The coach is attentive to bodily changes that signify involuntary changes in the autonomic nervous system. While the coach can never know the exact meaning of each behavioral change, the coach combines observations of BMIRS with their knowledge of the person, the conversation taking place, and their intuition to presume that a pacing and leading goal has been met. Voice, posture, breathing, gesture, muscular tone, and skin-tone color shifts are major sources of data. Specifically, the coach will look for the following:

1. Major and sudden shifts in any of the above systems, as well as congruence in content of speech, voice, posture, and gesture.

2. Manifestations of cognitive dissonance, as in shifts from certainty to uncertainty or in sudden insights. Bilateral body movements—gestures with both hands—allow the coach to infer that right and left hemisphere integration is present regarding a topic.

THE COACH'S INVISIBLE SKILLS

In chapter 3 we discussed three listening techniques useful to coaches: autobiographical listening, inquisitive listening, and solution listening. While pacing and leading, three additional metacognitive skills are useful; coaches should set aside their own need for closure, comfort, and comprehension.

Closure. Humans have a natural need for closure: to understand the end of a story, to be satisfied that we know how it turns out, to put an end to a dilemma. Two internal questions regarding closure inform the coach's decisions during problem-solving conversations: What are my intentions? How will I know when my work is finished?

In pacing and leading, the coach's intention is to help a colleague illuminate and accept tensions, clarify goals, and to locate the internal resources needed to meet the challenge. This is different from helping the colleague to identify a solution and devise a plan. The latter is a legitimate consulting goal, but most often it is attainable only when the teacher already has the confidence and emotional resources for that level of thinking. Thus, in pacing and leading, the coach sets aside his or her own natural interest in knowing "the end of the story" or what specific action the teacher will take. Instead, the coach looks for the involuntary nonverbal cues that signify the colleague has accessed the necessary resources to proceed. Internal resources may include knowledge, skills, and states of mind.

Comfort. Because pacing and leading is the most complex of the maps and depends on moment-to-moment sensory acuity, the coach may not always know what to say next. Being comfortable with this dimension of ambiguity is a critical resource to both parties. For the coach, living with this ambiguity helps to prevent premature and inappropriate comments. For the colleague, it is reassuring to have someone fully present and not discomforted as he works through his uncertainties.

If the coach becomes uncomfortable by being lost in her own emotional reactions to the issues being discussed, two strategies can be employed. First, she can remind herself to set aside autobiographical listening. Second, she can use a paraphrase. Paraphrasing helps to focus the coach's emotional attention on the colleague, not on the coach's discomfort. If the coach becomes lost in the process and a way out is not apparent, living with the discomfort at these times is often the best action. In doing so, the coach communicates his trust in the colleague and in the process.

Comprehension. Since the coach's intentions are to support the other person in clarifying goals and to locate the internal resources to meet those goals, the coach doesn't need to know the history, background, context, and sources of the problem. Process knowledge is paramount for the coach; specific information about the situation is secondary. The only time one needs to know extensive details about a problem is when one intends to be the problem solver.

NINE PRINCIPLES OF INTERVENTION

To support colleagues in getting "unstuck" and back to resourceful states, a coach uses the strategies of pacing and leading. This strategy has been described in two stages: pacing, with four major verbal phases, then leading, with a more generalized map to guide choices. In addition, larger ideas than these are useful guides in promoting thinking and development. These ideas are principles of intervention we have adapted from the work of Stephen Lankton and Carol Lankton.[9]

While theories of personality or human behavior are useful, they have shortcomings because resolutions are sought within the frame offered by the theoretical model. Since all models illuminate only selected views of human behaviors and place others in shadow, interventions based on theories of personality will always be doomed to partial success. In contrast, coaches working with the principles of intervention listed below will find themselves limited by only their own flexibility.

1. People act on their internal maps of reality and not on sensory experience. Each person perceives the world from his own unique vantage point, seeing it through frames of personal history, belief systems, representation systems, and cognitive styles.

This principle reminds the coach to learn how the world appears to the other person and to sensitively gather data to understand the other person's maps and how they are constructed.

2.   People make the best choice for themselves at any given moment. This principle does not suggest that people make the best choice possible, only the best choice available to themselves at the moment. High emotionality will limit choices, as will strongly held positions or points of view.

3.   Respect all messages from the other person. Empathy and respect are critical resources the coach brings to the coaching relationship. Skilled coaches nonjudgmentally attend to and respect both verbal and nonverbal messages. This requires being attuned to the more subtle elements of communication—voice, tone, gestures, facial expressions, eye shifts, and speech metaphors.

4.   Provide choice; never take choice away. In several cases, Milton Erickson worked with suicidal persons. His approach was, in effect, "Yes, that's one choice. What are others?" When we attempt to limit a person's choices, she is often drawn even more stubbornly to the choice we've removed. Effective coaches exercise options.

5.   The resource each person needs lies within their own personal history. Erickson would frequently tell students or clients that their "unconscious contains a vast storehouse of learning, memories, and resources." Coaches need to be mindful that they are there to facilitate the teacher's access to these inner resources, not to offer a solution.

6.   Meet the other person in her own model of the world. The skills of rapport are especially helpful in connecting with another person psychologically. However, this does not imply that the coach must stay in the other person's model.

7.   The person with the most flexibility or choices will be the controlling element in the system. The greater a repertoire that teachers have, the greater flexibility and choice they have in terms of instructional strategies and classroom management. The same is true for the coach or any person in a helping relationship. When interventions fail, it is frequently due to the coach's inability to exercise the necessary flexibility.

8. A person cannot not communicate. Even if a person is not communicating verbally, he is still sending nonverbal messages. Some behaviors are very subtle, such as breathing shifts or a slight nod of the head. These behaviors are very important for the coach to attend to when using the language of empowerment.

9. Outcomes are achieved at the psychological level. This principle is based on the reality that several levels of communication operate simultaneously. One of these is the social level message carried in words. Another is the psychological message usually reflected in the voice tone, gesture, or emphasis. When these two levels of communication are incongruent, the psychological message will determine the outcome of communication.[10] This principle reminds coaches to be conscious of and clearly intentional about their own levels of communication.

CONCLUSION

The danger in writing about a subject like accessing internal resources is that the examples can too easily be seen as mechanical formulas for given problems. Nothing could be further from the truth. For example, on these last pages, we have displayed only what Lankton and Lankton[11] call the "social message" carried in words. Missing on these pages are the postural shifts, inflections, breathing changes, and all the many ideomotor responses that send the psychological message.

The skillful coach attends to these states not by mechanically observing and interpreting nonverbal signals but by caringly, intuitively, with her entire presence being committed interdependently, one human being to another, to entering the other's model of the world, accessing resources, and illuminating choice. Skillful coaching does not mean applying formulas. Rather, it means continually designing, testing, and refining an ever expanding repertoire of new and more efficient ways to be catalytic in a colleague's growth.

As coaches become increasingly skillful in working with the map of problem resolving, there is a reciprocal effect on themselves. In recognizing the five states of mind in others, the coach recognizes these states in himself. The *external* attention and skill of coaching others becomes *internal* in the coach, who thus mediates herself to higher states of holonomy. The model of Cognitive Coaching, then, becomes self-mediating, self-transforming, and self-modifying for coaches themselves. As Erich Fromm[12] wrote:

> In thus giving of his life, the mentor enriches the other's sense of aliveness. He does not give in order to receive; giving is in itself exquisite joy. But in giving he cannot help bringing something to life in the other person, and this which is brought to life reflects back to him; in truly giving, he cannot help receiving that which is given back to him.

NOTES

1. Costa, A., and Garmston, R. (1985). Pacing and Leading: A Coaching Strategy. In *Leadership training for Cognitive Coaching: A training syllabus.* Hayward, CA: Office of the Alameda County Superintendent of Schools.

2. Watzlawick, P., Beavin, J., and Jackson, D. (1967). *Pragmatics of human communication.* New York: Norton.

3. Pert, C. (1997). *Molecules of emotions: Why you feel the way you feel.* New York: Scribner.

4. Ledoux, J. (1996). *The emotional brain: The mysterious underpinnings of life.* New York: Simon and Schuster. Sylwester, R. (2000). *A biological Brian in a cultural classroom.* Thousand Oaks, CA: Corwin.

5. Pert, C. (1997). *Molecules of emotions: Why you feel the way you feel.* New York: Scribner.

6. Wellman, B. (2001). Personal communication.

7. Grinder, M. (1997). *The science of nonverbal communication.* Battle Ground, WA: Michael Grinder & Associates.

8. Damasio, A. (1999). *The feeling of what happens: Body and emotion in the making of consciousness* (pp. 51–52). New York: Harcourt Brace.

9. Lankton, S., and Lankton, C. (1983). *The answer within: A clinical framework for Ericksonian hypnotherapy.* New York: Brunner/Mazel.

10. Garfield, C. (1986). *Peak performers: The new heroes of American business.* New York: William Morrow.

11. Lankton and Lankton, *The answer within.*

12. Fromm, E. (1956). *The art of loving.* New York: Harper & Row.

Part III

Engaging in Coaching

This section provides information about how to flexibly navigate the three mental maps of planning, reflecting, and increasing resourcefulness in problem resolving. Human variability in meaning-making and its implications for coaching is presented. Issues related to consulting and coaching—when to do which and how to do both and still maintain the integrity of mediational goals—are also explored.

10

Navigating Coaching Maps

A map displays the territory so a traveler can choose a path to a destination. In a similar vein, mediators use a variety of Cognitive Coaching "maps" to guide mediational interactions. In this chapter, we describe how coaches make conscious decisions to navigate within and among the maps, using them in various settings and for different purposes. We also describe how coaches use the maps in relation to the teachers' states of mind (see chapter 6), the cognitive processes of instruction (see chapter 7), and the knowledge base of teaching (see chapter 8).

NAVIGATING AMONG THREE MAPS

In chapter 2, we elaborated on the basic structures of the Cognitive Coaching process, and we described two of the three mental maps that guide the coach's interactions. The third was described in chapter 9. These three maps are:

1. *The planning conversation,* conducted before participating in an event, solving a problem, or attempting some task.

The coach may not be present during the event or available for a follow-up conversation.

2. *The reflecting conversation,* conducted after an event or after a task is completed. The coach may not have participated in or witnessed the event or task. (As a variation, these two maps may be combined into a "coaching cycle." A coaching cycle occurs before and after an event during which the coach will be present. This cycle is explained more fully below.)

3. *The problem resolving conversation,* employed when a colleague feels stuck, helpless, unclear, or lacking in resourcefulness; experiences a crisis; or requests assistance from a mediator.

These mental maps serve as guidelines for coaches to use as they navigate in a variety of coaching situations.

MANEUVERING WITHIN AND AMONG THE MAPS

Skillful Cognitive Coaches know these maps intimately so they can use them spontaneously yet still be aware of exactly where they are in the process. By being alert to cues from the other person and the context, coaches may decide to shift from one map to another, depending on the needs of the person they are coaching, the amount of time available, and context of the situation. Figure 10-1 illustrates this entwining of maps.

For example, toward the end of a reflecting conversation, a colleague may express some frustration and confusion, so the coach may decide to shift to the map for problem resolving. While coaches visit the various regions of the maps and shift from one map to another, the maps provide the basic structure of the coaching process.

As a coach interacts with a colleague, he or she may detect an opportunity to switch from a reflecting to a planning conversation. For example, in a reflecting conversation with Raul, the coach might seize the opportunity to begin planning: "So, Raul, upon reflection on the year so far, you'd like to implement project-based learning with your primary students. What might you do to get started?"

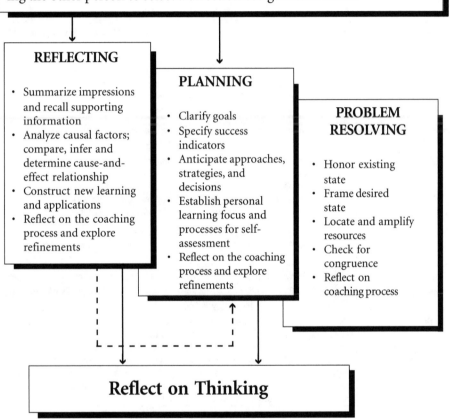

The coach mediates by (1) attending to trust and rapport and (2) inviting the other person to select a direction & significant focus.

REFLECTING

- Summarize impressions and recall supporting information
- Analyze causal factors; compare, infer and determine cause-and-effect relationship
- Construct new learning and applications
- Reflect on the coaching process and explore refinements

PLANNING

- Clarify goals
- Specify success indicators
- Anticipate approaches, strategies, and decisions
- Establish personal learning focus and processes for self-assessment
- Reflect on the coaching process and explore refinements

PROBLEM RESOLVING

- Honor existing state
- Frame desired state
- Locate and amplify resources
- Check for congruence
- Reflect on coaching process

Reflect on Thinking

Figure 10-1.
Cognitive Coaching Conversations

Or, during a planning conversation, a coach might take a cue from a colleague's comments to switch to a reflecting conversation: "What was it about some of those projects you saw that you might use in your planning for your students?"

Sometimes problems arise in a conversation, or tensions and conflicts surface. In this case, the coach might decide to mediate the moment with the map that liberates internal resources, as the following dialogue illustrates.

Knowing the various mental maps deeply, skillful coaches can flexibly maneuver within each and draw forth components as the situation demands.

Teacher:	I have a meeting with one of my parents after school today to talk about Timothy's progress.
Coach:	What do you hope to accomplish by this conference?
Teacher:	Well, I'm hoping to enlist her support in dealing consistently with Timothy's behavior at home. It seems she doesn't want to discipline him, and I'm having trouble because when he acts out in class, he claims his mom will "bail him out."
Coach:	So what's your strategy for the conference?
Teacher:	I'm planning to have his portfolio available, his test scores, and some other examples of his work so that she can see that he's just getting by. He seems so distracted by every little interruption. It's hard for him to stay focused. I want to find out from her about his study habits and behavior at home so that we can get to the bottom of his behavior problems.
Coach:	So you want to gather data from her that may help you and her to work together.
Teacher:	Yes, but Tim's mom is really flighty, and I'm nervous about it. Last time she came to see me she screamed at me. If she does that again, I don't know what I'll do. I might lose my cool.
Coach:	[Switching from a planning conversation map to the map for problem resolving and using the technique of pacing.] You're feeling anxious about your meeting with Mrs. Hammond because you anticipate she might raise her voice to you. You want the conversation to be focused and rational because you need her help in solving Timothy's behavior problems. You're searching for a strategy to guide you in case she becomes defensive and emotional.

SPECIAL APPLICATIONS OF THE MAPS

Skillful coaches also have the capability of navigating within and among these mental maps to meet the needs of special circumstances and purposes. Such coaches are always alert to the "mediational moment," when an opportunity for learning presents itself. There are many such occasions every single day; below are just a few variations of how the mental maps can be used. We include sample dialogues to illustrate each variation. Locations on the mental maps are provided in the column to the right.

Corridor Conversations

Corridor conversations are casual encounters among colleagues conducted while walking to work, in informal settings, in the lounge or lunchroom, or in other conditions in which time is limited. Consider the conversation in Table 10-1 on the way to class after lunch.

TABLE 10-1.

SAMPLE CORRIDOR CONVERSATION

	Conversation	Regions of the Reflecting Map
Sarah	Hey, Tyler, did you finish that book you were reading last week?	
Tyler	Yeah, it was pretty good.	
Sarah	What was it about?	
Tyler	Well, it's about different ways of assessing student thinking.	
Sarah	So, what did you think of it?	Summarize impressions
Tyler	It was pretty helpful.	
Sarah	What was it about the book that made it helpful?	Recall supporting information
Tyler	Well, the directions were clear and the strategies for assessment were practical. I can use a lot of the ideas with my students.	
Sarah	Why are alternative strategies for assessing students' thinking so important to you?	Analyze
Tyler	I suppose it's because we're being pressed for accountability, but standardized tests don't measure creativity and reasoning and problem solving. We have to find some better ways.	
Sarah	So, from what the book suggests, what are you going to use with your class?	Commit
Tyler	I've been thinking about that. I'm intrigued with having students make their own electronic portfolios They can scan their work, videotape their demonstrations, and burn their own CD-ROMs.	
Sarah	I'd like to see some examples when you get them.	
Tyler	Sure. And thanks for asking about the book. Gotta get to class now. Ciao!	

Professional Standards Conference

A professional standards conference usually centers on a teacher who is new to the profession. The coach and the teacher seek to bring out one domain or competency area on which to focus. Teacher efficacy is enhanced, and motivation to improve increases, when the teacher identifies which standard to concentrate on rather than having the standard imposed from outside.[1] (This was elaborated in a discussion of current research on best teaching practices[2] in chapter 7.) Table 10-2 gives an example.

TABLE 10-2.
Sample Professional Standards Conference

	Conversation	Regions of the Planning and Reflecting Maps
Coach	Come on in, Maria! Let's talk. You've had a chance now to review the district's professional standards. Which ones interest you?	
Teacher	Well, something I'd like to learn more about is this one on "involving all students in assessing their own learning."	
Coach	Under that standard, which elements are of particular interest to you?	Clarify goals
Teacher	I picked out two: "Making assessment integral to the learning process" and "Developing and using tools and guidelines that help all students assess their own work."	
Coach	So, you're interested in integrating assessment as part of students' learning?	
Teacher	Yes. You know, at the university we learned about test construction in my tests and measurements course. I think I can write pretty good test items that challenge my students. I also go over the tests with them so that they learn from their mistakes, but that doesn't really make assessment integral to the learning process.	
Coach	So you'd like to find better ways to integrate learning and assessment and to have your students learn from the process?	Establish goals
Teacher	Exactly.	
Coach	Maria, besides learning to become the best teacher you can be, what other interests do you have outside school?	
Teacher	Well, my hobby is cooking and baking. I'm taking a course on weekends now, and I'd like to become an expert pastry chef.	
Coach	In that course, how does assessment and feedback help you in your learning?	Summarize impressions

TABLE 10-2. *(continued)*

	Conversation	Regions of the Planning and Reflecting Maps
Teacher	I suppose one way is that the instructor gives us the criteria by which we judge our products: taste, appearance, flakiness, texture. Things like that. She also gives us feedback while we are preparing the dough and the filling. We share with others in the class so we can taste each other's work, and then, of course, I take some home and try it out on my husband. If he asks for seconds or wants me to make it at home, I know I did something right!	Recall supporting information
Coach	So, feedback from the expert, critiquing each other, and responses from an "outsider" (in this case your husband) all contribute to your learning. How does having those criteria ahead of time help you?	
Teacher	Well, if I know what it should look like and taste like, I can judge for myself. When I took the course in cake decoration, I had to take pictures of my cakes and put them into a scrapbook. We also had to analyze each picture and tell why we chose it, what made it a good example, and what we would do different next time. The instructor gave us feedback as well.	Analyze, infer, and draw cause-and-effect relationships
Coach	So, from what you have said about how assessment and feedback was helpful to your learning, how might you use some of these same strategies with your students?	Construct new learnings and applications
Teacher	Hmm. Well, one thing that comes to mind is for our creative story writing. I could get the students to generate a set of criteria for what makes a good story. I could put students in pairs to critique each other's work according to the criteria. They could put their best stories into a folder and reflect on why they chose each one. I'd like to see what they chose, and I could give my thoughts as well.	
Coach	So, you're suggesting some ways to help students incorporate assessment and feedback into their own learning processes?	
Teacher	Yes. You know, having them evaluate themselves can be combined with my evaluation and each other's so they can get feedback from several sources.	
Coach	Maria, as you reflect on this conversation, how has it been of help to you?	Reflect on the coaching process and explore refinements
Teacher	Having me look at my own assessment and learning really helped me think about how I could apply those same processes to my students. Assessment is a lot more than giving and taking tests, isn't it?	

Action Research

Teaching occurs under ambiguous, uncertain, complex, and often conflicting situations. Teaching is embedded with actions that require invention, testing, and reflecting. To guide their classroom routines and instruction, teachers often use tacit knowledge developed from construction and reconstruction of their own professional experiences. Gleaning professional expertise from these experiences requires reflection in which teachers learn to consciously "watch their own actions and decisions."

The action research conversation presents an opportunity for the coach to serve as mediator of a research task in which experimental data will be collected to be used as feedback to guide and inform reflective practice. In an action research conversation, the coach causes the teacher to explore his own "personal action theories." Sagor[3] describes a seven-step action research process, which becomes a repeating cycle for the inquiring teachers: selecting a focus, clarifying theories, identifying research questions, collecting data, analyzing data, reporting results, and taking informed action. (This cycle is similar to the planning and reflecting maps.) Table 10-3 shows how the teacher can increasingly assume this role of conscious monitor, data gatherer, and researcher.

TABLE 10-3.

SAMPLE ACTION RESEARCH CONVERSATION

	During a Planning Conference	**Action Research Themes Within the Coaching Cycle**
Coach	So, what will you be looking for in students' behavior to let you know your strategy is working?	Select a focus; determine success; indicators
Teacher	I'll be observing their participation. By that I mean their excitement, their involvement: the questions they ask and the responses they give.	
Coach	How would you want that data recorded?	Collect data
Teacher	I'll give you a seating chart, and I'd like you to keep track of not only who responds but also record the key ideas of what they say.	
Coach	How will you use these data when we analyze them in the postconference:	Analyze data

continued on next page

TABLE 10-3. *(continued)*

	During a Planning Conference	Action Research Themes Within the Coaching Cycle
Teacher	I'll be able to tell if my strategy was successful. I'm hoping that all of the students are involved and that their responses to my questions cause them to hypothesize, speculate, and theorize.	
	During a Reflecting Conversation	
Coach	How do you think the lesson went?	Summarize impressions
Teacher	Well, there were parts that went well, and there are other parts that didn't go so well	
Coach	Say more.	Probe
Teacher	I thought that some students really didn't listen to each other's ideas. They almost always repeated what the previous students said. Mark's response was almost the same as Eric's. Danielle just repeated Elena's comments.	
Coach	What hunches do you have to explain this behavior?	Clarify theories
Teacher	I suppose there could be lots of reasons: These kids come to me with years of trying to get right answers. They've been rewarded for giving the answer the teacher is looking for. They've never been encouraged to take risks and to venture forth with a new, divergent idea. I also think that the tests we give signal them to be satisfied with and to only want the "right answer." I often have students who say, "Just tell us the right answer!" or "Aren't you going to tell us when we're right?" They seem to feel safe in knowing their answer is "the correct one."	
Coach	[Notice that the coach enters the planning map at this point.] What did you want from them?	Clarify goals
Teacher	Well, I had hoped for more creative, divergent responses, not just repeating what the previous speaker said or what's in the book or what I've said.	
Coach	So, what might you do to cause more students to give original ideas rather than merely repeating or giving similar strategies, decisions, and ideas as the previous speaker?	Establish action plan; anticipate approaches and how to monitor
Teacher	Hmm. I guess I could put them into groups of three or four and have them generate as many hypotheses as possible. Then, I could have each group share their answers, and they couldn't repeat. They'd have to state a hypothesis that had not been given before. I could also make sure that they realize that what I want is a creative answer, not necessarily a "safe" answer.	

continued on next page

TABLE 10-3. *(continued)*

	During a Reflecting Conversation	Action Research Themes Within the Coaching Cycle
Coach	So your hypothesis is that if you structured the groups and told them they had to generate and share many hypotheses without repetition, you'd get more variety and less "parroting" of each other's ideas?	Paraphrase the teacher's hypothesis; identify research questions
Teacher	Exactly!	
Coach	You place great value on students thinking for themselves rather than depending on others for ideas.	Paraphrase; infer values
Teacher	Yes. I want students to be creative, to think for themselves, to take risks, and to support their hypotheses with a rationale or data.	Select a focus
Coach	How would you know that students are getting better at thinking for themselves and taking risks as a result of your teaching? Over time, what would you look for as indicators that students were growing in their risk-taking abilities?	Collect data
Teacher	Well, I'd see it in their writing. They'd ask less about "What do you want me to write about?" They'd volunteer what they want to write about. During classroom discussions, they'd state their own ideas, give their opinions rather than ask me if that was the right answer.	
Coach	How would you collect such data?	Collect data
Teacher	Well, I could—no, students could collect examples. I'd need to tell them that risk taking is a goal for our class and school. I could tell stories about athletes and scientists so they would see how taking risks causes great achievement. We could talk about when they take risks, when they shouldn't take risks, and what risk taking does for us. They could describe their risk taking in their journals. Then, over the year, we could add entries. Through sharing the entries, we could determine if students not only value taking risks but also become more inclined to do so.	
Coach	And what will you do to make all this happen?	Design action plans

This conversation continued as the teacher suggested an action plan for testing her own hypothesis. She also developed a technique to collect data (in this case for the students to self-evaluate) and to interpret the data.

Cognitive Coaching helps to cast teachers in the role of researchers: gathering evidence, formulating experiments, interpreting data, and then using the data to modify or reinforce practice.

More important, however, are the powerful signals that (1) teachers are empowered to gather and use data about their own curriculum and instructional decisions, and (2) traditional ways of assessing and evaluating students need to give way to Renaissance forms of assessment, including teachers' assessment of their own growth.

Journal Conversations

Many schools encourage staff members (and students) to keep journals as a powerful form of reflection and growth.[4] Journal conversations provide additional opportunities to apply the Cognitive Coaching mental maps. A coach and teacher might meet early in the school year for a planning conversation to decide the goals and purposes of the journal, how it should be organized, and the focus of the entries. Journals may be of several types:[5]

- *Action research journals* assess the effect of informal research on student learning.

- *Professional growth journals* focus on personal learnings and self-assessment.

- *Staff development journals* provide a record of learnings gained by participating in course work, inservice, and other staff development activities.

- *School improvement journals* describe and reflect on various school programs, initiatives, and restructuring efforts.

- *Study group journals* may be kept by members of a department or grade level as they attempt to improve practice by applying, testing, and refining their understanding of a particular theory or practice.

- *Child study journals* track work with one child who needs special attention.

Occasionally throughout the year, conferences are scheduled to share progress. These conversations, centered around the rich information in the journal, allow the coach to mediate learning from the everyday events in the life of the teacher. A final reflective conversation might be conducted toward the end of the year.

Portfolio Conversations

Teacher portfolios have become increasingly popular tools for reflection and growth.[6] These portfolios contain collections of artifacts and writings related to the teacher's goals. A portfolio can also serve as a stimulus to a mediated learning experience with coaches.

There are five components of the map of the portfolio conversation (Figure 10-2), and they share elements of the planning and reflecting conversations described above:

- Outcomes: A planning conference might clarify goals for the portfolio activity.

- Collection: What student-made and teacher-produced artifacts should be collected throughout the year as evidence that goals were achieved?

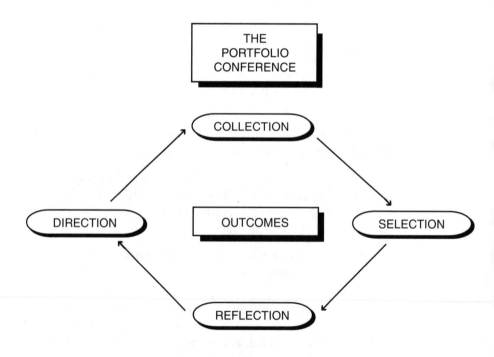

Figure 10-2.
Portfolio Map

- Selection: The teacher shares his or her rationale for including particular artifacts in the portfolio.

- Reflection: The coach and the teacher reflect on the significant learnings and meanings derived from the portfolio activity.

- Direction: The teacher applies learnings to future practice.

THE COACHING CYCLE

As described in Chapter 2, another variation in a coach's repertoire is the coaching cycle. If time permits, coaches may find the opportunity to engage in the full coaching cycle, which is a combination of the planning and the reflecting maps. Whereas in Chapter 2 we presented the coaching cycle around a teacher conducting a lesson, other examples might include a food service manager conducting a conference with a worker, a guidance counselor conducting an interview, or a school administrator facilitating a meeting. The coaching cycle bears revisiting here.

The coaching cycle is engaged before, during, and after a goal-directed event. The coach is present at each of these phases. In the following discussion, we will use the facilitation of a meeting as the setting for a coaching cycle. We will use the terms *conference* and not *conversation* because a conference implies a more formal or planned event, whereas a conversation may be more casual and spontaneous.

The diagram of the coaching cycle in Figure 2.3 depicted a continuous process of learning in which goals are set; actions are taken; data is monitored, collected, and interpreted; changes are made; and new goals are set. Coaching is a continuous process. Although the process is mediated by a coach, the intent is for the colleague to internalize this cycle of continuous learning to achieve self-directedness and holonomy.

A planning conference for an event such as a facilitated meeting where the coach will be present differs slightly from the planning conversation, described in Chapter 2, where the coach would not attend the meeting. During a planning *conversation*, the coach, in addition to helping the administrator clarify goals, success indicators and the plan, will have the administrator identify a personal learning focus and processes for self-assessment. The coach may mediate by helping the administrator establish mental mechanisms for self-observation or self-monitoring. The coach may ask such questions as:

- What success indicators will *you* be alert to during the meeting?

- In addition to paying attention to evidence of the meeting's success, how might you use this experience for your own growth?

- What might you focus on and gather data about, to support your own continuing growth?

In a coaching cycle however, because the coach will be present during the event, the coach may share with the administrator the task of monitoring performance of either the participants in the meeting or the administrator himself. The coach may collect data as well as mediate the planner by establishing mental mechanisms for self-observation or self-monitoring.

For example, in addition to the mediative questions described in the planning conversation above, the coach may also ask:

- You mentioned earlier that there was something you'd like *me* to look for. What is it that you'd like *me* to observe while you are conducting the meeting?

- What behavior of the participants do you want *me* to observe?

- Which of your behaviors do you want *me* to collect and record?

- In what form should *I* collect the data that will be most helpful to you?

- When, during the meeting, will be the most appropriate time for *me* to collect the data?

The Planning Conference

The planning conference is powerful for several reasons. Not surprisingly, many professionals are reluctant to have an "outsider" observing their performance. Having an "outsider" in attendance produces stress, and coaches know that learning will more likely occur in an atmosphere of eustress. Establishing and maintaining this is paramount.

When the coach meets with, in this example, an administrator before the event, she is seeking several kinds of information. First are the goals and objectives the administrator wants to accomplish in the meeting. We have discovered that as the coach probes and clarifies in an attempt to better understand the plan, the planner also becomes clearer about the outcomes and design. The coach is engaging the planner in a process of mental rehearsal similar to what athletes do before their performances.

To continue our example of the facilitated meeting, the coach also invites the administrator to describe which strategies will be used to accomplish the goals. The coach invites the administrator to anticipate what the participants will be doing if they are, indeed, successfully performing the goals and objectives desired during the meeting. The coach helps the planner specify what will be seen or heard within or by the end of the event to indicate goal achievement. Throughout the discussion, the coach clarifies her role in the process, the kind of data she is to collect, and the format of data collection.

We have found that in addition to the cornerstone information displayed in Table 2-3, the two additional areas of planning conference talk most frequently useful to coach and colleague are: (1) information regarding the relationship of this event to the long range outcomes, mission statements, vision, and relationships to district initiatives and (2) information about the administrator's concerns. The coach may ask the administrator, "Any concerns?" This artfully vague question allows the planner to say no or to discuss anything that might be troubling them.

When we've asked administrators what information they would like observers to have prior to an observation, we get an extensive list of requests. These are situational, of course, and depend on many environmental and personal factors:

- Where this event fits into the school's overall, long-range plan, and what's happened previously on this topic.
- Information about the social dynamics of the group.
- Behavioral information about specific individuals.
- Aspects of the meeting about which the planner is unclear.
- Concerns about participant behavior.
- Concerns related to trying a new meeting technique.
- Why this meeting is important to staff and students.
- Events beyond the school or district affecting the deliberations of this group.

A planning conference is not unique to Cognitive Coaching. Indeed, the planning conference is a mainstay of most all Clinical Supervision models[7]. What makes Cognitive Coaching unique, however, is the focus on colleague's perceptions, thought processes, and decisions. While the description of the planning conference described above appears to be focused on the event, the Cognitive Coach maintains her focus on the long-range outcomes: developing and automating the intellectual patterns of efficacy, flexibility, consciousness, craftsmanship and interdependence.

Observing the Event

Coaches do not specify data-gathering instruments, nor do they offer judgments about them. Instead, they assist their colleague in designing the instrument in the planning conference. Then they assist with evaluating the instrument in the reflecting conference. The intent is to cast the colleague in the role of experimenter and researcher and the coach in the role of data collector.

The coach must help their colleague to specifically define what should be recorded. This is not the place for subjective judgments. Clearly defining observable indicators of what a behavior will look like is key to gathering the data. For example, a coach might say, "You want me to determine if participants are engaged in the task. What will you hear them saying and see them doing when they are engaged?" Or the coach might say, "So your goal is to have the staff grasp the significance of the school's mission statement as a guide for decision-making. What are some examples of comments staff members might make if they grasp the significance?

It is also important that the coach invite the colleague to construct the system for collecting the data. The data must make sense to the colleague during the reflecting conference, or the colleague may be unable to draw any meaning from them. For example, a coach might say, "So my job is to collect evidence of staff member's statements of advocacy. When during the meeting should I record it? How often should I collect the data? Do you want me to record it as verbatim comments on a checklist? Are there specific staff members you want me to observe?" Or the coach might say, "In what form might I collect evidence of the staff's reaction and discussion of the mission statement? Should I record all their comments? At what point in the staff meeting should I start recording? Do you want me to specify which staff member made which comments?"

Having clarified the goals and purposes of the event and how the administrator and coach will be collecting evidence of their achievement—and having determined with the administrator exactly what data should be collected and how it should be recorded—the coach is now prepared for the observation. During the event, the coach simply monitors for and collects data regarding the behaviors and performance as discussed in the planning conference. The coach may use a variety of data-collection strategies including room/table maps, audio and video recordings, verbal interaction patterns, participation, on-task counts, or frequency counts of certain behaviors. Of more importance, however, is the colleague's perception of the data and the format in which it is collected. Both must be meaningful and relevant to the colleague's self-improvement efforts.

The Reflecting Conference. Whereas the planning conference is best done just before the event, when planners are clearest about their objectives and strategies, we have found that the reflecting conference is most beneficial when a period of time has elapsed after the event. This intervening time allows for reflection on the event, and it encourages deeper processing and self-analysis.

The coach can use this time to organize the data and plan the reflective coaching strategy. The coach may wish to review the data collected and organize rough notes in a more presentable form to give to the administrator. She may wish to reflect on the quality of trust with that administrator to decide which goals are paramount at this stage of their relationship and which coaching tools should be selected to achieve those goals. The coach also may wish to plan and construct questions at an appropriate depth and level of complexity for the colleague at his present stage of career development.

As the reflecting conference begins, the coach encourages the administrator to share his impressions of the event and to recall specific instances that support those impressions. We have found that it is important for the colleagues to summarize their own impressions at the outset of a conference. This way, the colleague is the only participant who is judging performance or effectiveness.

At this point, the coach would also invite the administrator to make comparisons between what he remembers from the meeting and what was desired (as determined in the planning phase). The coach facilitates the administrator's analysis of the goals by sharing data and using reflective questioning. The aim is to support the administrator's ability to draw causal relationships between his actions and outcomes. Drawing forth specific data and employing a variety of linguistic tools are important coaching skills in supporting the colleague as he makes inferences regarding in-the-moment decisions, behaviors, and the achievement of outcomes.

As the reflecting conference continues, the coach will encourage the colleague to project how future events might be modified based on new learnings, discoveries, and insights. The coach also invites the administrator to reflect on what has been learned from the coaching experience itself. The coach invites their colleague to give feedback about the coaching process and to suggest any refinements or changes that will make the relationship more productive. (A sample dialogue of the Coaching Cycle of a coach and teacher appears in Appendix A.)

CONCLUSION

One of the basic and critical capabilities of the effective coach is navigating within and among the three Cognitive Coaching mental maps. Skillful coaches have internalized these maps so thoroughly that they are able to draw upon them as the situation and circumstances demand. The maps become habituated so that little conscious energy is expended in using them, which frees the coach to focus on the relationship and coaching interactions.

In this chapter we have revisited the mental maps basic to Cognitive Coaching: planning, reflectiving, and problem resolving. These might take place in conversations in informal settings or in more formal meetings or conferences. The maps are applied in a variety of settings, which demonstrates how the coach is constantly on the lookout for ways to provide a mediated learning experience. Although this chapter has described several types of experiences, you will undoubtedly spend the rest of your career exploring the many different settings and situations in which these maps can enrich your own and others' learning.

NOTES

1. The videotape series *Another Set of Eyes* provides observation strategies and data-gathering tools. For additional information, contact the Association for Supervision and Curriculum Development, 1702 N. Beauregard St., Alexandria, VA 22311-1714 (703-933-ASCD; www.ascd.org).

2. For additional information, see California Commission on Teacher Credentialing. (1997). *California standards for the teaching profession.* Sacramento: California Department of Education. Danielson, C. (1996). *Enhancing professional practice: A framework for teaching.* Alexandria, VA: Association for Supervision and Curriculum Development. Osterman, K. F., and Kottkamp, R. B.(1993). *Reflective practice*

for educators: Improving schooling through staff development. Newbury Park, CA: Corwin Press.

3. Sagor, R. (2000). *Guiding school improvement with action research* (p. 3). Alexandria, VA: Association for Supervision and Curriculum Development.

4. Vicksburg Community Schools. (2000). *A reflection on teaching: A journey through the seasons.* Vicksburg, MI: Author.

5. Dietz, M. (1998). *Journals as frameworks for change.* Arlington Heights, IL: IRI Skylights.

6. Martin-Kniep, G. O. (1999). *Capturing the wisdom of practice: Professional portfolios for educators.* Alexandria, VA: Association for Supervision and Curriculum Development.

7. Danielson, C. and McGreal, T. (2000). *Teacher evaluation to enhance professional practice* (p. 84). Alexandria, VA: Association for Supervision and Curriculum Development.

11

Human Variability in Meaning-Making

When you pass strangers on the street, the unfamiliar faces blur. When you let your lives touch and make the effort of asking questions and listening to the stories they tell, you discover the intricate patterns of their differences and, at the same time, the underlying themes that all members of our species have in common.

—Mary Catherine Bateson[1]

Humans differ in temperament, tempo, signature, and thumbprint. We like different books, people, music, work, and leisure. Some of us are sloppy; some of us are fastidious. Many of us are serene; many others among us are stressed. We are light-skinned, dark-skinned, slim, and stout. Genetic, family, and environmental histories combine to make each of us truly unique.

In this chapter we present information about eight of the many human variables that influence the human quest for meaning: (1) representational systems, (2) cognitive styles, (3) response filters, (4) educational belief systems, (5) gender, (6) race, ethnicity, nationality, and culture, (7) adult stages of development, and (8) career stages of development. Skilled coaches are sensitive to differences in each of these areas, and they adapt the coaching process for each person with whom they work.

In addition, this chapter considers a coach's need for flexibility. We examine how skillful coaches draw upon flexibility to enhance coaching effectiveness by attending and adapting to differences in the ways that humans process and make meaning. Effective coaches constantly sense, search for, and detect cues about another person's thinking processes, beliefs, modality preferences, and styles. Coaches also deliberately expand their repertoire so they can match their style to a variety of situations and individuals.

UNDERSTANDING   PERCEPTION

None of us experiences the world in exactly the same way as another. In fact, all the information we receive through our eyes, ears, nose, mouth, and skin has been selected and distorted before it even reaches our brain.

Perception, in large part, is the result of genetics and neurology. Seventy percent of a human's sense receptors cluster in the eyes, and we appraise and understand the world mainly through seeing it.[2] Women see differently than men. Women have a higher percentage of cones in their eyes, which allows for a greater awareness of space and relationship and less of the "targeting" focus that early humans found essential for hunting.

A surprising number of animals see in color, but the colors they see are often different from the ones we see. Prairie dogs are color-blind to red and green; ants can't see red, either. Deer and rabbits see humans in shades of gray.

Similar selections, distortions, and constructions occur within each of a human's five senses: seeing, hearing, touching, tasting, and smelling. This is why human processing is often discussed in terms of "representational systems." That is, what we hear is a representation in our mind of the original sound, and what we see is a representation of a picture. The reality is created deep inside our brain.[3]

Neuroscientist Antonio Damasio explains, "Representations are constructed based on the momentary selection of neurons and circuits engaged by the interaction. In other words the building blocks exist in the brain, available to be picked up and assembled."[4] The part that remains in memory is built according to the same principles. So, when we think, we reexperience (reconstruct) the information in the sensory form in which we first experienced it: pictures, sounds, feelings, tastes, or smells.

For Cognitive Coaches, understanding how each person creates different perceptions allows them to accept others' points of view as simply different, not wrong. They come to understand that they should be curious, not judgmental, about other peoples' impressions and understandings. The more we all understand how someone else processes information, the better we can communicate with him or her.

REPRESENTATIONAL SYSTEMS

In Western culture, the primary nonlinguistic systems in which we think are the visual, auditory, and kinesthetic. All persons think using these three primary representational systems, and we each favor one or two, even though we are often unaware of our thoughts in more than one system. In addition to having a "highly preferred" representational system, each person has a lead system. Reviews of a number of studies and conversations with observers in this field lead us to believe that roughly 40 percent of the U.S. population uses the visual system as the preferred mode. Another 40 percent is primarily kinesthetic, and 20 percent is auditory. Figure 11-1 shows these systems.

Eric Jenson estimates that 20 percent of classroom learners function auditorily.[5] He feels that "state," or the current processing preference, matters most in learning. However, different cultures

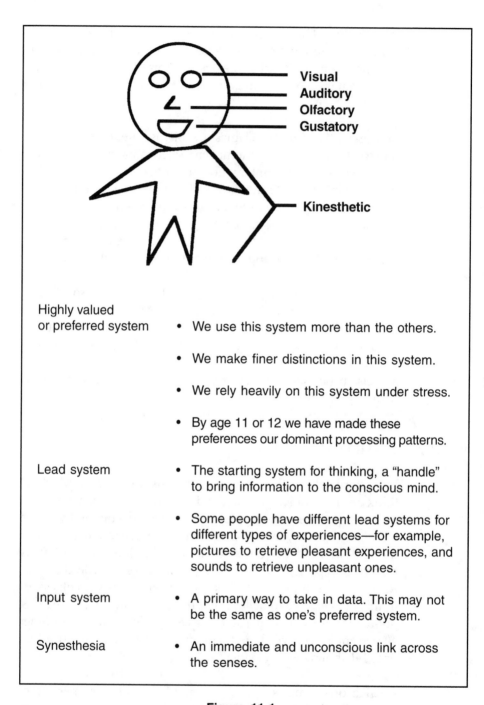

Highly valued
or preferred system

- We use this system more than the others.

- We make finer distinctions in this system.

- We rely heavily on this system under stress.

- By age 11 or 12 we have made these preferences our dominant processing patterns.

Lead system

- The starting system for thinking, a "handle" to bring information to the conscious mind.

- Some people have different lead systems for different types of experiences—for example, pictures to retrieve pleasant experiences, and sounds to retrieve unpleasant ones.

Input system

- A primary way to take in data. This may not be the same as one's preferred system.

Synesthesia

- An immediate and unconscious link across the senses.

Figure 11-1.
Representational Systems

mediate for different representational systems. Ultimately, the coach needs (1) consciousness of her own preferences, (2) awareness of her current state, and (3) sensory acuity to detect the state of the colleague with whom she is working.[6]

Stop right now and think back to your last great meal. Did you first see pictures, hear sounds, or experience feelings? This is your lead system, the jump-start to your thinking process. Perhaps you saw a picture of a friend's face, followed by feelings of relaxation. In that case, your lead system would be visual and your preferred system kinesthetic.

The person with the most flexibility has the greatest influence in any interaction. The most effective coaches are conscious of their own and others' personal styles, patterns, and predispositions. They flexibly work in different ways with each individual according to the ways that person is unique. This trait is important for the development of trust because we all tend to be more comfortable with, and therefore trust more easily, people with similar styles.

In most cases, flexible coaches personalize each moment of communication to the individual, responding to the representational systems the other person is using. (Exceptions do exist. For example, sometimes a coach wants to stretch a person's thinking into a system not being used.) When a coach uses the other person's representational system, trust is enhanced, rapport in the moment is strengthened, and the communications require no translation. Two types of cues indicate which representation system a person is using in the moment: language and eye movement.

Language Cues

Vocally, affiliated pairs and groups may converge their speech patterns. By matching a partner's speech style a person may emphasize similarities and enhance attraction.[7] Specific behaviors on which people match speech include accent, rate, volume, pause length, vocalization length, and language choice. When a parent says, "I see what you are saying," we might infer that the parent is actually making some kind of image based upon the words. When a student says, "I don't see what you are saying," we could interpret the child's communication to mean "I can't make a picture out of your words, and, until I can make a picture, I won't be able to understand it."[8] In this sense, we take people literally and adjust our communication styles to theirs.

Words are often clues to thinking processes. We've heard several stories about how this was first discovered. In one version, Bandler and Grinder[9] noticed certain speech patterns as they watched therapist Virginia Satir at work. One client said to Satir, "Virginia, I just can't *see* things *clearly*. I've lost my sense of *perspective*. My prospects are *dim*." Satir responded, "Let me see if I get the *picture*. Your horizons are *dark*. Your prospects are *cloudy*. You'd like to develop a *brighter focus*." Both the client and Satir spoke in rich, visual terms.

Another client told Satir, "I am feeling *low*. I'm just *down* a lot of the time. I've lost my *grip*. I can't seem to get *moving*." These words are primarily kinesthetic, referencing emotions, tactile sensations, and sensorimotor or positional aspects of experience. Satir responded, "What I get is enormous depression. It's like you're living *under* a rock and you have this great *weight* on your shoulders. You're feeling *pressure*. You'd like to *push* these *feelings* away and be *relaxed, at ease*."

Representational Language in the Real World

We once observed Ann, an administrator, who was biased against Mariko, a teacher, for some unknown reason.

Mariko was working on gaining skill in detecting representational system language. By writing down words participants used in staff meetings, Mariko discovered that Ann primarily used auditory phrases. (Other cues were there but were unnoticed until then: dimmed lights in Ann's office, classical music in the background.)

Mariko was highly visual, but she knew the research on representational system matching and trust. She also wanted a better working relationship with Ann. So Mariko began to use auditory terms when she was around Ann. In a remarkably short amount of time, Ann's attitude toward Mariko became positive. After that, Mariko no longer had to match language systems with Ann all the time; the connection had been made.

As coaches listen to a person talk, they may discover that most of the words are from one of the sensory-based representational systems listed in Figure 11-2. These words are an indicator of how the person is representing an experience. The words are also cues, so that you can best communicate by using metaphoric language from the same representational system.[10] We refer to this as language congruence. For example, when someone says, "They play hardball around here," you can respond by saying, "Yeah, it's really tough. Bases are loaded, you go up to bat, and the team is counting on you."

Following is an example of a discussion between two teachers in which the coach (Maria) matches her colleague Andra's language, which is primarily visual:

Andra:	Thanks for agreeing to *observe* my third-period economics class.
Maria:	I'm *looking* forward to *watching*. What will I *see* students doing?
Andra:	What you will *see* is students taking notes from a *videotape* about the influence of political philosophy on economic policies before, during, and after President Reagan's two terms of office.
Maria:	So I'll *see* students taking notes. What specifically do you want them to learn?
Andra:	The *focus* of today's lesson is on two world leaders: Ronald Reagan and Margaret Thatcher. We're *looking* at how their political philosophies influenced their nations' economies. Today the students will *watch* a video program about the Reagan era. I want them to understand the concept of conservatism and to *see* its relationship to world trade, domestic policy, and inflation.
Maria:	Can you *illustrate* for me what you mean by "*seeing* the relationship"? What will you *observe* students doing as evidence that they are *getting that picture*?

Many methodological errors can be found in the research on language congruence, unfortunately, but several solid studies—and our own experience—have affirmed the relationship between language and representational systems.[11]

How We See

Damasio observes, "[The] images you and I see in our minds are not facsimiles of the particular object, but rather images of the interactions between each of us and an object which engaged our organisms, constructed in neural pattern form according to the organism's design." The object is real, and the images are as real as anything can be. Yet the structure and properties in the image we end up seeing are brain constructions prompted by an object.[12]

As you listen to a person talk, you may discover there are times when a majority of his or her predicates (descriptive words and phrases—primarily verbs, adverbs and adjectives) are from one of the modality or representational systems listed below. This person is choosing, usually at an unconscious level, to isolate one system from his or her ongoing stream of representational system experiences. This is an indicator for you of how this person is best understanding his or her experiences and how you can best communicate.

Visual	Auditory	Kinesthetic
see	hear	feel
look	listen	grasp
observe	speak	handle
watch	tell myself	energetic
clear	verbalize	in touch
viewpoint	told	gut feeling
perspective	talk	firm
point of view	say	foundation
visualize	clear as a bell	on the level
eyeball	tune in	relaxed
hazy	resonate	tense
fuzzy	tone	weighty
murky	harmonious	heavy
vivid	volume	come to grips
light	loud	lightweight
transparent	dissonant	raise an issue
lighten up	pitch	grasp the situation
look something up	high-pitched	let go
picture	low-key	sleep on it
reflect	squeaky	hurt
acuity	singsong	touchy
see the light	ring my chimes	irrational
focus	unheard of	pushy
image	well said	pain in the neck
mirror	answer	itchy
insight	so to speak	foot the bill
foreshadow	drum it in	shoulder the blame
red	mellifluous	soft touch
purple		

Olfactory	Gustatory	Nonspecific
smell	taste	think
odor	tasteless	experience
scent	tasteful	know
aroma	salivate	intellectualize
fragrant	mouthwatering	understand
rotten	tip of my tongue	perceive
fresh	delicious	respond
	lip smacker	accurate
	sweet	solution
	spicy	resolve
	bitter pill to swallow	strategy
	bit off more than she or	logical
	he could chew	

Figure 11-2.
Representational Systems:
Language Indicators of Modality Preferences

Eye Movement

With the advent of research in brain specialization, scientists have investigated the relationship between particular types of eye-movement patterns and variations in brain functioning.[13] Although controlled laboratory testing has yielded inconsistent results,[14] the relationship between eye movements and cognitive functioning has been well documented.[15]

Cognitive activity in one hemisphere triggers eye movements in the opposite hemisphere. The following eye-movement patterns provide an external graph of internal sensory activity[16] for 90 percent of right-handed persons (Figure 11-3). This information is reversed for many (but not all) left-handed persons.

- Looking up and to the left allows us to access stored pictures (visual recall). This is seen often in reflecting conversations (Figure 11-4).

- Looking up and to the right indicates the creation of new images (visual construct). This is seen often in planning conversations.

- Eyes go horizontally to the left when we are accessing stored sounds (auditory recall), as when we are recalling in a reflecting conversation.

- Eyes go horizontally to the right when we are creating new sounds, as in mentally rehearsing before we speak (auditory construct).

- Eyes down and to the left is common when we are talking to ourselves (internal dialogue). This position and the next must be differentiated from another cause of looking down: a learned behavior that indicates respect, in some cultures.

- Looking down and to the right is common when we are experiencing feelings (kinesthetic).

- Looking straight ahead when answering a question may mean accessing memorized information, such as "What is your name?"

Our experience is rich with examples of coaches who understand and communicate with others based on their attentive reading of

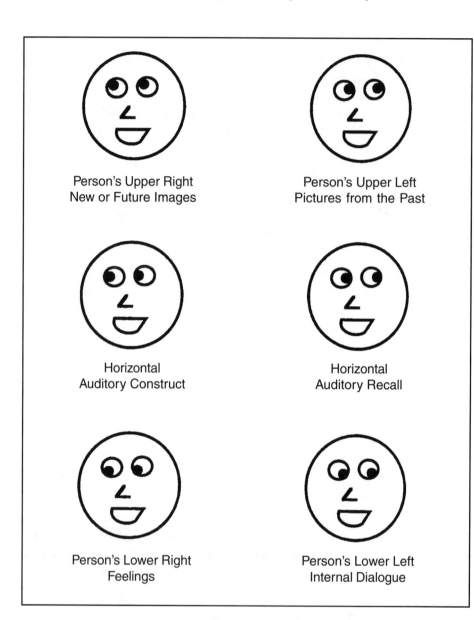

Figure 11-3.
Eye Movements and Representational Systems

(Depicted as you are looking at a normally organized
right-handed person)

Photo by Bruce Wellman, Mira Via, Guilford, CT.

Figure 11-4.
Accessing Her Visual Memory

eye patterns. Coaches use eye-movement information to select language congruent with the representational system the teacher is using. More important, because eye movements reveal the duration of cognitive processing, the coach knows when to use wait time and how long to wait. Eye movements signal that someone is focusing attention internally, when additional comments or questions can't be processed. To witness eye accessing cues and their relationship to thought and language production, see the videotape displaying a live planning conversation produced by the Center for Cognitive Coaching.[17]

Auditory processing is quick. Persons who process information visually take slightly longer, and processing kinesthetically takes the longest. Science educator Mary Budd Rowe found that teachers who extended their wait time after asking students questions (from the normal one-half second to three to five seconds) produced impressive gains in students' higher order thinking.[18] Later neurological research finds that it takes that long to receive information, process it, and formulate a response.

COGNITIVE STYLES

Two persons looking at the same invitation to a dinner party may literally see something different. Angela will notice the time, date, and location of the affair as well as the recommended dress. John will register with pleasure that he has been invited to a party by a friend. He notices that the event is planned for Thursday, an evening he's usually free. It wouldn't be unheard of for him to arrive at the party on the wrong Thursday or get lost on the way because he didn't pay attention to details. Angela's and John's readings of the party invitation illustrate differences in cognitive styles.

Numerous models and theories explain stylistic differences,[19] but we have found that Herman Witkin et al.'s field dependence-independence theory of cognitive style is a simple yet effective construct for learning how teachers' perceptions, intellectual processing, and instructional behaviors differ.[20] Witkin's work is solidly grounded. The results of more than 35 years of research on field dependence-independence are compiled in a bibliography listing more than 2,000 studies.[21] We define styles as behaviors, characteristics, and mannerisms that indicate underlying psychological frames of reference. These are usually developed as preferences between the ages of two and five.[22] Most of us lean toward one of two poles: exacting attention to detail where perception is not influenced by the background, or *field independence*; or strong influence by the context of information, or *field dependence.*

Over time, Witkin and his associates became convinced that field dependence-independence influences not only perceptual and intellectual functioning but personality traits such as social behavior, career choice, body concept, and defense.[23]

Field Independence

The field-independent person is task oriented and competitive. The term field independence is used because such a person doesn't need to view the whole system to make sense of things. She can isolate and work effectively with the details. This person often likes to work alone and emphasizes getting the job done. She works part to whole, perceiving analytically. The field independent teacher is logical, rational, and likes to figure things out for herself. She learns through books, computers, and audiotapes. She is good at sequence and details, and she likes theoretical and abstract ideas.

The field-independent person who's placed on a committee might say, "Just give me a job, and I'll go off and do it. Why are we talking so much? We don't need to get to know each other. We need to complete the task."

The field-independent person wants the coach to focus on tasks. She wants independence and flexibility to make decisions based on data and analysis. She looks to the coach to be knowledgeable about curriculum and instruction, to maintain a professional distance, and to give messages directly and articulately.

Jan, a middle school field-independent teacher, looked back on four months of Cognitive Coaching and reflected that previously she had been extremely curriculum-focused in her teaching, devoting her time and attention to the details of each activity. She had been "administering knowledge" and successfully keeping students busy, but at the expense of some aspects of the students' cognitive development and personal growth. Through coaching sessions, Jan developed more balance in her teaching. The coach matched her interest in details and her language of specificity, which gave the coach and the teacher the safety to explore bigger questions: How does this lesson relate to long-term goals? What personal meaning do you want students to construct from this? Why is this important to you?

Field Dependence

The field-dependent person needs to perceive the whole context (the "field") to make meaning. This person enjoys working with others in collaborative relationships. He takes in the overall scheme of something and may have difficulty with individual parts. He works from intuition and gut reactions but likes and needs concrete experience. Metaphors, analogies, patterns, and relationships appeal to him because he likes to see things holistically.

Field-dependent persons are often oriented toward relationships, even seeking mentors in their lives. They have a sense of the large picture, and they know where they are going for the semester or the year. They often understand what is occurring in their class through intuition, reading subtleties of body language and voice.

The field-dependent teacher in a faculty meeting appreciates the conversation and interaction about ideas. He finds it important and valuable to share feelings on a topic. He is more tolerant of ambiguity than his field-independent peers and more skillful in processing.

Field-dependent teachers want a coach to be warm and show personal interest and support. They want guidance and modeling, but they also want the coach to seek their opinion in decisions. They want the coach to have an open door, practice what she preaches, and use voice tones and body language that support her words.

Christina was a field-dependent teacher in the same school as Jan. Her style of teaching focused heavily on the affective domain. She writes that when she encouraged a focus that was often subjective, students learned through exploration, but specific learnings were often sacrificed in attainment of the broader goal. Jan and Christina both believed that Cognitive Coaching helped them access the "lesser used" sides of their brains. Through self-analysis and "self-remediation" (their words), they searched every corner of their minds, bringing to the surface feelings and ideas that might have otherwise gone untapped. In becoming more bicognitive, they became better thinkers and better teachers.[24]

Although it is always possible to err by stereotyping with certain characteristics, the traits of field independence and dependence are useful cues for communication in the coaching relationship.

RESPONSE FILTERS

A response filter is a prevalent pattern that describes how people respond in contrast to how they take in information or process it. These may be somewhat related to cognitive style, but other psychological factors help to shape them. Flexible Cognitive Coaches must learn to be compassionate toward both, because humans are prone to annoyance or judgment when another person's styles in these areas are different from our own.

Although no one performs solely in one style characteristic, you can probably locate which of these descriptors in Table 11-1 best characterizes your responses. Is there someone in your work or home environment with whom you frequently find yourself frustrated or annoyed? Check their response patterns and cognitive style. The chances are great that they process and respond in different ways than you do.

TABLE 11-1.
PATTERNS OF RESPONSE

Internally referenced: This person responds using herself as the judge of appropriate behaviors. She maintains independence in thought and action.	**Externally Referenced:** This person responds primarily based on what others think. She uses the group's norms or values as sources for her behavior.
Analytical reflective: This person responds internally. He takes information and processes it reflectively. He tends to be a pragmatist and is more likely to be past-or future-oriented.[25]	**Impulsive experimental:** This person responds with immediate action on thoughts. His pattern is to "do it," then engage in trial and error. He is likely to be present oriented.
Matcher: This person responds by noting similarities. She agrees easily, likes consistency, and tends to approve of something that has been done before.	**Mismatcher:** This person responds by noticing differences. She finds flaws in propositions, prefers variety, and likes change. She is not negative, merely contrary. A mismatcher is more likely to sort incoming data by differences.

EDUCATIONAL BELIEF SYSTEMS

To be truly flexible, coaches must be discerning about and work congruently with educational philosophies different from their own. Different educators have different aims in education. Whether they verbalize them or not, educators hold deep convictions about their professional mission, their work, their students, the role of schools in society, the curriculum, and teaching. Furthermore, these beliefs are grounded in and congruent with deep personal philosophies and are powerful predictors of behaviors. They drive the perceptions, decisions, and actions of all players on the education scene.

Beliefs are formed early and tend to self-perpetuate.[26] Changing beliefs during adulthood is a relatively rare phenomenon, and beliefs about teaching are well established by the time a student gets to college. Because beliefs strongly influence perception, they can be an unreliable guide to the nature of reality. The filtering effects of belief structures ultimately screen, distort, or reshape thinking and information processing.

EDUCATIONAL IDEOLOGIES

People's ideologies significantly influence their educational decisions. The flexible Cognitive Coach recognizes colleagues' prevailing educational ideologies through their use of metaphors, educational goals, instructional methods, approaches to assessing outcomes, and teaching. The coach respects these beliefs (with the obvious exception of destructive orientations like racism) and works with them to help fellow educators articulate and be increasingly effective in achieving their educational goals.

The coach's goal is to maintain trust and communication rather than to change beliefs. When the coach works within a colleague's educational belief system, trust is deepened, rapport is enhanced, coaching services are valued, and the coach becomes more influential. Ultimately, the colleague may become more conditional regarding his or her own educational philosophies and more understanding and appreciative of the educational beliefs of others. This movement, as a step toward greater cognitive complexity, is a developmental goal for all human beings.[27] In their seminal work on educational belief systems, Eisner and Valance[28] describe at least six predominant ideologies that influence educators' decision making and fuel the ongoing debate among policy makers, politicians, parents, and the public in the 21st century. We do not intend to describe those ideologies fully here, but we present a brief summary of our interpretation of each to illuminate their differences and manifestations in classrooms and schools.

Religious Orthodoxy

Coming from a Christian tradition and with a firm belief in God, the early Pilgrims in the United States provided an educational policy in which schools were legally mandated to teach biblical literacy. Today, numerous religious schools in the United States such—as Roman Catholic, Church of Christ, Evangelical Christian, Seventh Day Adventist, Muslim, Jewish, Lutheran—have a common goal: to teach the habits and values that will lead students to live in accordance with their faith.

Proponents of religious orthodoxy in the Christian sects include such groups as the Christian Coalition as well as such orders as the Jesuits, the Christian Brothers, and the Sisters of Mercy. Their metaphors lie in the Bible. Others may draw inspiration from the Qur'an, the Torah, Tao-te-ching, or the Veda. They may model their ways after David, Moses, Jesus, Mohammed, Budda, or Confucius. They wish to transmit the beliefs, laws, commandments, and truths of their interpretation of their scriptures.

Educators with the orientation of religious orthodoxy enable students to learn appropriate norms of morality. They encourage students to conduct their lives in accordance with those norms. Students are assessed, in part, to the degree that they profess the teachings of that religion.

In some of these schools dialogue, debate, and critical thinking are encouraged. In others, questioning, doubt, and the exploration of competing views are often discouraged. Faith in Allah or in God's word may be held to transcend human thought. Fundamentalist Christian parents, for example, may criticize a public school's efforts to teach "critical thinking," questioning, evolution, or other attitudes that might weaken religious commitment. Likewise, such issues as vouchers, school prayer, and dialogues about the separation of church and state often illuminate differing beliefs.

Cognitive Process

With an orientation to cognitive psychology, cognitive processors believe that the central role of schools is to develop rational thought processes, problem-solving abilities, and decision-making capacities. They are drawn to educational theorists and authors such as Jerome Bruner, Hilda Taba, Robert Sternberg, Jean Piaget, Reuven Feuerstein, Maria Montessori, Howard Gardner, David Perkins, and Edward deBono. They believe that the information explosion is occurring at such a rapid rate that it is no longer possible for experts in any field to keep up with new knowledge. Thus, we no longer know what to teach but instead must help students learn how to continuously learn throughout their lifetimes.

Cognitive processors select instructional strategies that involve problem solving and inquiry. They use concepts like Bloom's taxonomy, intellectual development, habits of mind, metacognition, and thinking skills. They organize teaching around the resolution of problems and the Socratic method, and they bring in discrepant events for students to explore and analyze. They assess student growth by how well they perform in problem-solving situations. Their metaphorical model of education is that of information processing: human beings are meaning makers, and schools and teachers mediate those capacities.

Self-Actualization

Those who believe in self-actualization regard the ideal school as child-centered. They believe the teacher's role is to liberate each human's inherent capacities for learning. They believe that the purpose of teaching is to bring out the unique qualities, potentials, and creativity in each child. They support multisensory instruction, with many opportunities for auditory, visual, and kinesthetic learning. They value student choice, whether for classroom topics, the nature of assignments, or classroom activities. They value self-directed learning and individualized instruction and support schools of choice and magnet schools so as to better meet the unique interests of each learner.

To provide for students' unique and multiple needs, interests, and developmental tasks, those who believe in self-actualization use learning centers focused around themes. They value student autonomy and look for increases in self-directedness as a central measure of teacher effectiveness. They are drawn to such humanists as John Dewey, Abraham Maslow, Arthur Combs, Carl Rogers, and Sidney Simon along with George Leonard, Gerald Jampolsky, and Depak Chopra.

The self-actualizer's vocabulary includes words referring to the affective domain and concepts such as the whole child, nurturing, peak experiences, choice, democracy, holism, self-esteem, continuous progress, creativity, and caring. Their metaphoric model of education is grounded in a vision of each child's potentials.

Technologism

Influenced by the behavioral psychology of B. F. Skinner, Ivan Pavlov, and Edward Thorndike, technologists may be attracted to such education authors as Robert Mager, Madeline Hunter, and Seymour Papert. They place strong emphasis on accountability, test scores, learning specific subskills, and measurable learning. Their metaphor for education is as an "input, through-put, output system" in which data and opportunities to learn skills are provided.

Technologists are skilled at task analysis and are interested in technology-based learning systems and instruction. They value opportunities to diagnose entry levels and prescribe according to what is known and what is yet to be learned. They are probably more field independent and skilled in detail, with great ability to analyze, project, and plan. They talk about accountability, evaluation, reinforcement, task analysis, time on task, mastery, templates, diagnosis and prescription, and percentiles. When policy-making bodies adopt this orientation, external assessments and high-stakes testing abound.

Academic Rationalism

Keeping company with such philosophic leaders as Robert Maynard Hutchins, Mortimer Adler, Diane Ravitch, E. D. Hirsch, Arthur Bestor, William Bennett, and Chester Finn, academic rationalists are drawn to teacher-centered instruction. They believe that knowledgeable adults have the wisdom and the experience to know what is best for students. Their metaphors for education are the transmission of the major concepts, values, and truths of society, and they consider students as clay to be molded or vessels to be filled. They value and are highly oriented toward increasing the amount and rigor of student learning. They are drawn to the Classics (preferably original sources), Great Books, and traditional values. They appreciate basic texts and the teaching strategies of lecture, memorization, demonstration, and drill. They evaluate students through summative examinations, achievement testing, and content mastery. They speak about authority, humanities, basics, the disciplines, scholarship, standardized tests, standards of learning, and other aspects that value higher academic standards.

Social Reconstructionism

Social reconstructionists are concerned with problems of society such as the future of the planet, the destruction of the food chain, the hole in the ozone, global warming, endangered species, the deforestation of timberland, the protection of wildlife, and the threat of overpopulation. Social reconstructionists view the learner as a social being: a member of a group, a responsible citizen, one who identifies with and is proactive regarding the environmental ills and social injustices of the day.

They believe that we have gone beyond the age of representative democracies and have moved to a stage of participative democracies. They believe that this is a world in which we must care for our neighbors and take action at the grassroots level. The social reconstructionist teacher engages students in recycling centers, contributing to social issues, community service, cooperative learning, environmental education, and global education. Their metaphor of education is as an instrument of change, and they believe that schools are the only institution in our society charged with the responsibility of bringing about a better future and a better world. They are drawn to such activists as Marilyn Ferguson, Alvin Toffler, Jane Goodall, Margaret Wheatley, John Naisbitt, Ralph Nader, Fritjof Capra, and Jean Houston. They employ concepts such as environmentalism, democracy, consumer education, student rights, the 21st century, multiculturalism, futurism, global intellect, pluralism, change, save-the-Earth, ecology, peace, and love.

All of these belief systems are necessary and valuable aims of education. As Carl Glickman[29] observes: "When one concept of education wins out over all others and we are left with a single definition determined by others for all of us, then we all lose." We want students to find spirituality and to become effective problem solvers, to be self-actualized, knowledgeable, efficient, and concerned. So the task for coaches is to become at ease with a variety of educational beliefs and refine their ability to work with people whose beliefs may be different from their own.

Belief systems don't change easily. The older we become, the less likely we are to change. However, change usually occurs in two instances. If the prevailing culture begins to shift its values persistently and pervasively, we may begin to move our thinking. For example, the 1960s saw the pervasive influence of individualized instruction, and many of us began to behave more like self-actualizers. In the 1970s, social reconstructionism came to the forefront as we became aware of globalization and confronted environmental problems. With the onset of the information age in the 1980s, we realized that information overload demanded the exercise of intellectual prowess, and cognitive processing became paramount. The technological paradigm of the 1990s influenced our educational thought with high-stakes accountability and international comparison of various countries' science and mathematics test scores.

Teachers also adapt their belief systems to accommodate new realities. For example, a 12th-grade history teacher may take a position as a kindergarten teacher, or an instructor may move from an affluent school to one of pervasive poverty. In these cases, the teachers' paradigm changes and so do the beliefs they use to explain their role in their new environment.

GENDER

A man and a woman are standing outside enjoying the sunset. The woman says, "What a beautiful sunset." The man answers, "Yes. Do you know what it is caused by? There have been several volcanic eruptions to the west of us, and what we are looking at is the volcanic ash in the air." If the second speaker were a woman, her response might be, "Yes, that's a lovely sunset. It makes you feel good, doesn't it?"

Recent neurological and psychological studies reveal very real biological differences between men and women that influence their perceptions of the world in subtly different ways. A number of gender differences are found in the hypothalamus, the portion of the brain associated with sexual behavior. Although some researchers caution that most gender differences are, statistically, quite small,[30] recent brain scans from healthy people have confirmed that parts of the corpus callosum are 23 percent wider in women than in men. Some researchers speculate that the greater communication between the two sides of the brain caused by a thicker corpus callosum could enhance a woman's performance in certain communication tasks.

At birth, more boys than girls are left-handed. Females are better at reading the emotions of people in photographs; males excel at rotating three-dimensional objects in their heads. Women excel in their ability to simultaneously process emotion and cognition. However, these same abilities may impair a woman's performance in certain specialized visual-spatial tasks. For example, the spatial ability to tell directions on a map without physically rotating it appears strong in those individuals whose brains restrict processing to the right hemisphere. Brain research indicates that men listen with different parts of the brain than women, who listen with their "whole brain." By contrast, more women listen equally with both ears, while men favor the right one.

Sociolinguist Deborah Tannen[31] finds that men and women converse for different purposes. Men talk, she says, to establish independence and status and to report information. Women, on the other hand, tend to use talk to establish intimacy and relationship. In a sense, women's talk is about establishing the fact that we are "close and the same," and men's talk is to establish the fact that we are "separate and different."

Men tend to operate in conversations as individuals in a social world in which they are either one-up or one-down. Women tend to operate as individuals in a network of connections. This is not to say that women are not interested in status and avoiding failure, but these are not consistent goals. Tannen summarizes these differences as "men talk to report, women talk to rapport."

At work, men are inclined to jockey for status and challenge the authority of others, wheras many females lack experience in defending themselves against such challenges. Women may misinterpret challenges as personal attacks on their credibility. It is as if men ask, "Have I won?" whereas women ask, "Have I been helpful?"

In faculty meetings, men tend to talk more often and for longer periods of time. Because women seek to establish rapport, they are inclined to play down their expertise in meetings rather than display it. Because men place more value on being center stage and feeling knowledgeable, they seek opportunities to gather and disseminate factual information.

Women are more likely to be auditory than men are. Women tend to ask more questions and give more listening responses than men do. In one startling study, Sadker and Sadker[32] reported that teachers who were shown a film of classroom discussion overwhelmingly thought the girls were talking more. In actuality, the boys were talking three times more than the girls.

Because sex differences have been misused in the past to assert male "superiority" and female "inferiority," many people are suspicious of the notion that physiological differences between the sexes can lead to different abilities or predispositions. Now we know that differences do exist but that they are also culturally reinforced. This does not guarantee that all men or all women will have the same characteristics, but it does speak to the bulk of the bell-shaped curve. The majority will have that learning style.

One of the most important coaching findings from Tannen's work relates to the misunderstandings that sometimes develop out of the different purposes of conversation. For example, many women feel that is natural to consult with a partner before making a decision. Men, however, may view consulting with a partner as tantamount to asking for permission. Because men strive for independence, they may find it more difficult to consult. This drive for independence may also explain their difficulty in asking a stranger for directions.[33] Women, on the other hand, are more comfortable in asking a stranger for directions when they are lost because it literally affords another person an opportunity to be helpful to them.

Although research conclusions sometimes seem to conflict, the bottom line for the coach is to be aware of gender differences that may or may not exist. The most successful coaches tend to be androgynous in their communications, drawing on both the masculine and feminine characteristics reported by Deborah Tannen and others.

RACE, ETHNICITY, NATIONALITY, AND CULTURE

The shoe that fits one person pinches another; there is no recipe for living that fits all cases.

—Carl C. Jung

A female vice-principal of a math-science magnet high school had on her staff an Iranian male teacher. She confessed to us that she couldn't understand why it was so difficult to coach this man until she realized that some Middle Eastern cultures do not view the role of women in the same manner as other cultures. She may have been at least partially right.

Data gathered during the 2000 census discloses an increasingly complex picture of diversity in the United States. Non-Hispanic Whites remain the majority, but their share of the population dropped from 76 percent to 69 percent in 2000. Hispanics of any race now make up 12.5 percent of the population. The racial breakdown of other groups is: Blacks, 12.1 percent; Asians, 3.6 percent; American Indians, 0.7 percent; Native Hawaiians, 0.1 percent; and "some other race," 0.2 percent. Furthermore, 2.4 percent of the total population is multiracial. By 2000, 20 percent of children in the United States were living with a foreign-born parent. Increasingly, Cognitive Coaches will have to draw upon their flexibility as they interact with colleagues whose racial, ethnic, national, and cultural orientation is different from their own.

Culture is a set of rules for living[34] and is based on who people think they are, where they think they are, and the resources they perceive are available. There are cultures of age, gender, geography, religion, and race. All learning styles are culturally reinforced.[35] Southern Europeans are more likely to be auditory. Northern Asians are more likely to be "matchers" (see Table 11-1), as are Midwesterners. Research suggests Native Americans are strongly right-hemisphere dominant, as are a high percentage of African Americans. A higher percentage of Hispanics are kinesthetic. Rural learners tend to be more field dependent. Israelis and Australians have a higher than usual percentage of "mismatchers." Northern Europeans and Asians are more likely to prefer visual learning.[36]

STAGES OF ADULT DEVELOPMENT

Another important area of human variability relates to the stages of adult development. There is developmental growth beyond the childhood ages of Piaget's studies, and many grandparents today will attest that their own children did not seem "fully adult" until about age 30.

Developmental psychologists Robert Kegan and Lisa Lahey[37] outline three stages of adult development. Not all individuals successfully move through all three stages. Some maintain stability at a given stage for most of their adult life. Each new stage carries traces of the former, so in new situations thinking and behavior may temporarily revert to a previous stage. These stages represent principles for how one constructs experience and organizes thinking, feeling, and social relating. These stages are of special interest to the Cognitive Coach because they may operate as containers for all the other ways of making meaning.

Progression through these stages represents a curriculum of sorts for adult development. They are the products of environments of mediation, not of age. Kegan and Lahey call the first stage interpersonal, the next institutional, and the last post-institutional. Progression through these stages requires increasingly complex mental operations.

Interpersonal. At this stage, validation comes from external criteria. It is usually arrived at somewhere in late adolescence, and the person identifies with models external to the self. Both people and ideas can serve as models, and the person, without critical examination, strives to emulate these models. "I am my relationships," might be a metaphor for this stage. Adults at this stage may be prone to have dependency relationships, to seek approval, and to uncritically accept the values of others. "How am I doing?" this person frequently wants to know from students, colleagues, administrators, or coaches. Efficacy may be an important state of mind to help a person's development into the next stage.

Institutional. Self-authorship, self-ownership, and self-initiative define this stage. Validation comes from internal criteria. Personal standards and self-evaluation shape the values and beliefs that form the institution of the self. This "institution" holds assumptions about how the world works and one's place in it. A limitation of this stage is self-sealing logic. Metaphorically, this person's identity might be stated as "I have relationships." Flexibility may be a means to the final stage.

Post-Institutional. Most people who achieve this stage do not do so before age 40. Here is found the richest expression of interdependence. Identity continues to develop through reflection and self-modification. Validation comes through openness to questions, possibilities, conflict, and reconstruction of meaning. Continual inquiry and data from outside oneself shape values and beliefs. Adults at this stage are consciously interdependent with others. "There are relationships and I am part of them" neatly summarizes this stage. Figure 11-5 on page 267 elaborates on these stages.

CAREER STAGES

Adults learn, retain, and use what they perceive as relevant to their professional needs. As teachers mature in their professional roles, their needs change as well. Early-career teachers and expert teachers view their practice differently. Expert teachers draw largely from their tacit knowledge acquired from years of experience to create classroom conditions that facilitate access to and successful

Interpersonal	Institutional	Post-Institutional
• Personal identity depends on relationships • Wants to be supported, accepted and praised • Hard to set limits, especially if creates risk of losing popularity • Relationships take priority over performance • Longs for interpersonal needs to be met and requires others to fulfill needs • Flexibility—allocentric to please others to keep self well-liked  **Tips** • Keep person in relationship • Objective evaluations felt to be dehumanizing • Non-contingent reinforcement • Mediate toward autonomy and 5 states of mind	• Self-authoring, self-owning, self-initiating, self-dependent • Can create relations of caring and collegiality but is not dependent on them • Can separate work from person  • Sets own standards, self-evaluation • Personal well-being linked to smooth running of own system • Craftsmanship—moderately developed, goal-oriented, but self-sealing logic **Tips** • Respects those who hold own opinions • Satisfied by supervisor who trusts their judgment • Values opportunities for learning and advancement • External standards or laissez-faire distressing • Coach for interdependence	 • Reflects on and modifies own organization of self • Open to questions, possibilities, conflict, and reconstruction • Views problems as possibilities • Questions system's norms, goals, and policies • Practices double-loop learning • Supervisors at first two systems of logic are disconcerting **Tips** • Values communication of feelings • Supervisor observation and analysis of teaching behaviors repugnant • Flourishes in collaborative cultures respecting individuation

Adapted from Robert Kegan and Lisa Laskow Lahey

Figure 11-5.
Three Systems of Adult Meaning

learning for diverse groups of students across content areas.[38] Experts possess a special kind of knowledge about learners that is different from novices, knowledge that influences classroom management and is the basis for the transference and application of subject matter. Richly developed appreciation of and strategies for accommodating student differences and learning variables result in experts designing more effective learning environments and solving problems at a much higher conceptual level. Expert, experienced teachers tend to perceive problems from a much broader context and are able to draw upon their tacit knowledge to determine effective interventions. These conceptual strategies do not automatically appear in a teacher's mind; they are constructed through years of experience.[39]

Teachers' developmental levels have a direct correlation to their performance in the classroom.[40] These levels also correlate to their interactions with other adults in the school environment. Teachers who function at higher conceptual levels are capable of greater degrees of complexity in the classroom and are more effective with students. Teachers with more advanced conceptual levels are more flexible, stress tolerant, and adaptive in their teaching style. Thus, they are able to assume multiple perspectives, employ a variety of coping strategies, and apply a wide repertoire of teaching models. In addition, they are responsive to a wider range of learning styles and culturally diverse classes. Teachers at higher levels of conceptual development can take an allocentric perspective, employing the learner's frame of reference in instructional planning, teaching, and evaluation. Understanding and being sensitive to these dimensions of expert teacher thinking can inform coaching practices with accomplished teachers.

In addition, expert teachers seem not only to perform better than novices do, they also seem to do so with less effort. "Cognitive resources are limited in human beings but experts seem at times to stretch these limits; they seem to do more at a given level of expenditure of resources."[41] (Refer to Table 7-1.)

Early-career teachers, on the other hand, tend to focus their attention on the immediate situation, on practical teaching techniques, on classroom management, and on relationships with students.[42] (As with all factors of human variability, there are always exceptions. Some early-career teachers focus on the broader level and some highly experienced teachers focus on the more technical level, probably as an influence of cognitive style.)

Beginning teachers move through several stages of emotional relationships to their job that influence what they need from a coach. When they have completed a teacher training program, *anticipation* characterizes their emotional state. They are eager to engage and have big plans. *Survival* is the next stage, as reality hits. They are overwhelmed with aspects of the job they could not anticipate. *Disillusionment* often follows. They feel they are working hard but not getting anywhere. Perhaps this is not the right profession for them, they think. *Rejuvenation* often follows the winter break. They have completed half a year, they have rested, the end is in sight, and they have gained some coping strategies to manage the problems they encounter. Toward the end of the year, *reflection* begins as they think about changes that they want to make for the next year. Finally, a second stage of anticipation begins as they look forward to the next year. Beginning teachers in year-round environments may not experience the extremes of the lows reported by teachers in traditional programs.[43]

Any educator working with new teachers knows how profound these differences are between the novice and the expert teacher. Career stage is one factor that calls for another form of coaching flexibility, adjusting the functions within a supporting relationship to match teachers' developmental needs without compromising Cognitive Coaching.

CONCLUSION

Each person constitutes a distinct system of mental, emotional, cultural, and physical interplay, characterized by the unique ways in which all humans hold and process information, communicate, relate to others, learn, problem-solve, and become stressed. All of these ways of being are of equal value. Any combination may be more or less intelligent, compassionate, or capable.

Cognitive Coaches continually inquire into and learn about these differences in groups of people and their ways of representing and communicating meaning. Although this topic is far beyond the scope of this book, we offer several general assumptions that are useful guidelines for achieving communication free of racial or ethnic bias. These guidelines also apply to gender sensitivity.[44]

1. If you are a different race or gender than I, you carry experiences, perceptions, and meanings that I cannot know directly.

2. The origins of your perceptions, processing, and communication styles emerge from personal experience. Because they are ecologically sound, they become persevering patterns.

3. To the degree that our personal histories are different, my communication may be misinterpreted by you and yours by me.

4. When we have misunderstandings about communication style differences, it doesn't make them go away, but understanding the source of the differences can diminish mutual mystification and blame. This makes the world a more familiar and comfortable territory.

5. Our communication and the mutual interests that bring us together provide valuable opportunities to grow and learn from each other. Our differences enrich us both.

6. We all have unexamined prejudices and biases. We can work respectfully together and accomplish tasks important to us to the degree that we can become conscious of and set aside these thoughts and feelings.

7. My most useful personal attributes in communicating with you are integrity, consciousness, flexibility, and interdependence, manifested through respect, openness, curiosity, and inquiry. From these sources, you and I can continue to learn more about each other.

8. As a result of these assumptions, I strive to be free of ethnic, racial, and gender bias in my communication.

Cognitive Coaches use the following guidelines in their private and public communication:[45]

- They guard against making generalizations that suggest all members of a racial, ethnic, or gender group are the same. Generalizations and stereotypes may lead to insupportable or offensive assumptions while ignoring the fact that all attributes may be found in all groups.

- They avoid qualifiers that categorize others and call attention to racial, ethnic, and gender stereotypes. A qualifier is additional information that suggests an exception to a rule (e.g., a "sensitive" man, a "mathematically gifted" girl).

- They identify others by race or ethnic origin only when relevant—and few situations require such identification.

- They consciously avoid language that to some people has questionable racial, ethnic, or sexual connotations. While a word or phrase may not be personally offensive to you, it may be to others.

- They are aware of the possible negative implications of color-symbolic words. They choose language and usage that does not offend people or reinforce bias.

Because the making of meaning is an individual process, Cognitive Coaches are conscious of human variability. They not only promote diversity but also are effective in working with others who possess a wide range of human variables. They recognize, respect, and understand them so they can make better connections, work together more effectively, learn and teach successfully, leverage their own and others' diverse gifts and affinities, and consciously foster individual and collective development. This is critically important to developing trust, to accelerating the learning of the coach and the person being coached, and to enhancing interdependence.

The opportunities for coaches to assist others in the process of meaning-making demand continual learning about human differences and developing their capacities of consciousness and flexibility. The person with the greatest flexibility has the greatest influence.

Human diversity is valued in Renaissance schools. Like the workers on the sugar plantation described in the sidebar, we learn to

> **I ka noho pu ana—a'ike i ke aloha.**
> It is living together that teaches the meaning of love.
>
> In Hawaii, the sugar planters mixed ethnic groups on purpose, their idea being that different folks would not naturally mix, and dissension among the workers would make them easier to manage and less likely to band together against their bosses, the Lunas. What actually happened, however, is a tribute to the adaptability and resiliency of the human spirit. The workers not only got along, but of necessity they shared the very elements that made them different, even as they maintained their ethnic integrity.
>
> First they had to adapt to their new situation. There were things they were used to in their home cultures that they simply couldn't get in Hawaii. Second, they adopted the good things from other cultures they were exposed to, but they retained some of the important cultural elements of their own ethnic groups. Finally, they made special contributions to their new multicultural society on the plantation, a working-class culture made up of many minorities.

recognize the different capacities inherit in each person and to develop skills to work together. This is more than an organizational need. It is a human need: to enhance the quality of life that people individually and collectively express.

NOTES

1. Hateley, B., and Schnidt, W. (1995). *A peacock in the land of penguins.* San Francisco: Berrett-Koehler.

2. Acherman, D. (1990). *A natural history of the senses* (p. 230). New York: Vintage Books.

3. O'Connor, J., and Seymour, J. (1990). *Introducing neuro-linguistic programming: The new psychology of personal excellence.* Hammersmith, London: HarperCollins.

4. Damasio, A. (1999). *The feeling of what happens: Body and emotion in the making of consciousness.* Orlando, FL: Harcourt.

5. Jensen, E. (2001). Personal communication with Bruce Wellman.

6. Swanson, L. J. (1995). *Learning styles: A review of the literature.* ERIC Document No. ED 387 067.

7. Burgoon, J., Buller, D., and Woodall, W. (1996). *Nonverbal communication: The unspoken dialogue* (2nd ed., p. 322). New York: McGraw-Hill.

8. Dilts, R., and Epstein, T. (1995). *Dynamic learning.* Capitola, CA: Meta.

9. Grinder, J. (1994). Personal communication.

10. Garmston, R. (1988). *A guide to neuro-linguistic programming and counseling in education.* Course syllabus. School of Education, California State University, Sacramento.

11. Einspruch, E., and Forman, B. (1985). Observations concerning research literature on neuro-linguistic programming. *Journal of Counseling Psychology 32* (4), 589–569.

12. Damasio, *The feeling of what happens,* p. 321.

13. Lipton, L., and Garmston, R. (1998). *Pathways to mastery: A cognitive coaching exercise* (videotape and manual). Highlands Ranch, CO: Center for Cognitive Coaching. This videotape of a planning conference with a staff developer in Texas shows her congruent eye-accessing cues as she recalls information about the group she is about to teach and later as she constructs ideas for the group. This tape also displays the connection between eye accessing and the words she is saying.

14. Trevarthen, C. (1990). *Growth and education of the hemispheres.* In L. Trevarthen, and C. Colwyn (Eds.), *Brain circuits and functions of the mind: Essays in honor of Robert W. Sperry.* New York: Cambridge University Press.

15. Jensen, E. (1996). *Brain-based learning.* Del Mar, CA: Turning Points. Galin, D., and Ornstein, R. (1973). Individual differences in cognitive style: Reflective eye movements. *Neuropsychologia 12,* 367–376. Kinsbourne, M. (1972). Eye and head turning indicates cerebral lateralization. *Science, 58,* 539–541. Kocel, K., Galin, D., Ornstein, R., and Merrin, E. (1972). Lateral eye movement and cognitive mode. *Psychonomic Science, 27* (4), 223–224.

16. Bandler, R., and Grinder, J. (1975). *The patterns of the hypnotic techniques of Milton H. Erickson, M.D.*, Palo Alto, CA: Behavior and Science Books. Beck, C., and Beck, E. (1984). Test of the eye-movement hypothesis of neuro-linguistic programming: A rebuttal of conclusions. *Perceptual and Motor Skills 58*, 175–176. Dilts, R. (1983). *Roots of neuro-linguistic programming.* Cupertino, CA: Meta.

17. Garmston, R., and Lipton, L. (1997) *Pathways to mastery.* (videotape and manual). Highlands Ranch, CO: Center for Cognitive Coaching.

18. Rowe, M. (1996). *Science, silence and sanctions: Science and children* (pp. 35–37). Washington, DC: National Science Teachers Association.

19. Lozano, A.(2001). A survey of styles of thinking: From learning styles to thinking styles. In A. Costa (Ed.), *Developing minds: A resource book for teaching thinking.* Alexandria, VA: Association for Supervision and Curriculum Development.

20. Guild, P., and Garger, S. (1985). *Marching to different drummers.* Alexandria, VA: Association for Supervision and Curriculum Development.

21. Witkin, H. A., Oldman, P. K., Cox, W., Erlichman, E., Hamm, R.M., and Ringler, R. (1973). *Field dependence-independence and psychological differentiation: A bibliography.* Princeton, NJ: Educational Testing Service.

22. Jenson, *Brain-based learning,* p. 139.

23. Witkin, H. M., Goodenough, D., and Cox, P. (1975). *Field dependent and field independent cognitive styles and their implications.* Princeton, NJ: Educational Testing Service.

24. Garmston, R., Linder, C., and Whitaker, J. (October, 1993). Reflections on Cognitive Coaching. *Educational Leadership 51* (2), 57–61.

25. For more information on time orientations, see Jensen, E. (1996). *Brain-based learning.* Del Mar, CA.: Turning Point.

26. Pajares, M. F. (1992). Teachers' beliefs and educational research: Cleaning up a messy construct. *Review of Educational Research 62* (3).

27. Kegan, R. (1994). *In over our heads: The mental demands of modern life.* Cambridge, MA: Harvard University Press.

28. Eisner, E., and Valance, E. (1974). Conflicting conceptions of the curriculum. Berkeley, CA: McCutchan. See also Eisner, E. (1994). *The educational imagination: On the design and evaluation of school programs.* Upper Saddle River, NJ: Prentice-Hall.

29. Glickman, C. (2000–2001). Holding sacred ground: The impact of standardization. *Educational Leadership 58* (4), 46–51.

30. Gorman, C. (January 20, 1992). Sizing up the sexes. *Time,* pp. 42–48.

31. Tannen, D. (1990). *You just don't understand: Men and women in conversation* (p. 17). New York: Ballantine Books.

32. Sadker, M., and Sadker, D. (1985). Sexism in the schoolroom of the '80s. *Psychology Today,* pp. 54-57.

33. Goldberg, H. (1991). *What men really want.* New York: Penguin Books.

34. Brown, J. (1999). Personal communication.

35. Brenner, D., and Parks, S. (2001). Cultural influences on critical thinking and problem solving. In A. Costa (Ed.), *Developing minds: A resource book for teaching thinking* (pp. 216–221). Alexandria, VA: Association for Supervision and Curriculum Development. Payne, R. (2001). *Thinking in a culture of poverty.* Costa, *Developing minds,* pp. 229–233.

36. Jensen, E., *Brain-based learning,* p. 139.

37. Kegan, *In over our heads.* See also, Kegan, R., and Lahey, L. (1984). Adult leadership and adult development: A constructivist view. In B. Kellerman (Ed.), *Handbook on socialization theory and research* (pp. 199–229). Chicago: Rand McNally.

38. Berliner, D. (1988). *The development of expertise in pedagogy.* Paper presented at the meeting of the American Association of Colleges for Teacher Education, New Orleans.

39. Sparks-Langer, G. M., and Colton, A. (1991). Synthesis of research on teachers' reflective thinking. *Educational Leadership, 49* (6), 37–44.

40. Garmston, R., and Lipton, L., with K. Kaiser. (1998). The psychology of supervision: From behaviorism to constructivism. In G. Firth & E. Pajak (Eds.), *Handbook of research on school supervision* (pp. 242–246) New York: Macmillan.

41. Sternberg, R. J., and Horvath, J. A. (1995). A prototype view of expert teaching. *Educational Researcher, 24* (6), 9–17.

42. Leat, D. (1995). The costs of reflection in initial teacher education. *Cambridge Journal of Education 25* (2), 161–174.

43. Foundations in Mentoring New Teachers. (2000). New Teacher Center at University of California, Santa Cruz.

44. Kochman, T. (1983). *Black and white styles in conflict.* Chicago: University of Chicago Press. Harris P., and Moran R., (2000). *Managing Cultural Differences.* Houston, TX: Gulf.

45. Bettman, Ellen. (1984). *Without bias: A guidebook for nondiscriminatory communication* (2nd ed.). New York: Anti-Defamation League.

12

Repertoire of Support Functions

Whatever we can do to facilitate learning on the one hand and loving on the other is important, because those are the most healing forces available to us.

—Na'im Akbar[1]

No single form of support serves all purposes. The power of Cognitive Coaching has been applied in many different forms of support models. Some models are technical, some are humanistic, and some are developmental or reflective. Ed Pajak[2] has created a summary of current models that distinguishes the unique features of many programs, but all of these approaches have certain tenets in common. Among them is the belief that teaching is "untidy" and uncertain. Structured collegial conversations to help make meaning from complex instructional situations, and reflective conversations help to generate knowledge, expand teaching repertoire, and promote teacher development.

This chapter considers a support provider's need for situational flexibility to achieve the ultimate goal of developing high performing, self-directed individuals. Specifically, we answer a variety of questions about the many different kinds of support provided to teachers. For example, when does one coach, and when does one consult? Can these functions ever be blended? Isn't everything evaluation? Can one person provide support *and* evaluation? If so, how can that be achieved?

SITUATIONAL FLEXIBILITY

One of our collaborators in the development of Cognitive Coaching, Bill Baker, once heard a teacher say, "Bill, you don't always coach me." Taken aback, Bill asked what she meant. "Sometimes," she said, "you co-ponder with me."

Bill now thinks about what he does in four dimensions. First, he always maintains trust and rapport. Second, he mediates thinking by promoting inquiry, probing for clarity, and encouraging self-directed reflection. Third (but not necessarily in this sequence), he supports data acquisition. This might include sharing personal experience or supplying access to resources such as other teachers, materials, and research. Fourth, he co-ponders, entering a phase of thinking together with the teacher in which they consider problems, choices, and concerns.

Support providers frequently have other responsibilities. There may be a few situations in which a person's full-time job is to coach others. However, most often the coaching function is just one of the job duties of a principal, teacher advisor, mentor, peer coach, staff developer, director, or superintendent. Persons in these roles sometimes coach, sometimes consult, sometimes collaborate, and sometimes evaluate. As described in chapter 1, we have come to think of these various roles in two categories: (1) support providers, in which assisting teachers is the primary function of the role, or (2) supervisors, in which assisting teachers is but one of many responsibilities.

Programs to support teachers have proliferated in a number of states and provinces. They go by many names: peer coaching, mentoring, performance assessment, performance review, and coaching. Because more people, untrained in any form of performance support, are providing direct assistance to teachers than ever before, answers about when and how to cognitively coach—and when not to cognitively coach—are even more urgent.[3]

In chapter 1, we described four types of support provided to teachers as they mature in the profession: Cognitive Coaching, collaboration, consulting, and evaluating. Table 12-1 summarizes the central purposes of three of these.

TABLE 12-1.
PURPOSES OF COACHING, COLLABORATING, AND CONSULTING

Cognitive Coaching—a relationship with a mediator of thinking	Collaborating—a relationship with a colleague	Consulting—a relationship with an expert
• Enhance and habituate self-directed learning: self-managing, self-monitoring and self-modifying.	• Solve instructional problems, apply and test shared ideas, learn together.	• Increase pedagogical and content knowledge and skills. Institutionalize accepted practices and policies.
• Transform effectiveness of instructional decision making to maximize effectiveness of actions toward reaching goals.	• Form ideas, approaches, solutions, and focus for inquiry.	• Inform regarding pedagogy, curriculum, policies, and practices.
• Habituate reflective practice and build capacity for professional effectiveness.	• Gather and interpret data to inform collaborative practice.	• Provide technical assistance and improve teaching.

As can be seen in Tables 12-1 and 1-1, these forms of interaction are guided by consciously chosen intentions. These support functions share a set of skills (described in chapter 4) and, for our purposes, exist within a framework of beliefs and concepts that we call Cognitive Coaching. Therefore, each is used as a stance within a support provider's repertoire for its contribution to the development of professional expertise and self-directedness.

Skillful coaches may depart from Cognitive Coaching periodically to conduct these other forms of interaction. Because they continually strive to consummate their identity as mediators, however, they consciously return to the beliefs, values, principles, maps and tools of Cognitive Coaching as their "default position."[4]

AN EXEMPLARY SUPPORT SYSTEM

Sometimes we are asked, "When coaching, is it all right to give a suggestion? What if you sense the teacher's plan will not work? Should you tell him?"

Coaching, collaborating, and consulting each serve a valued purpose to the teacher, the institution, or both. Ideally, each takes place in transactions devoted to only one of these functions at a time. There are situations, however, that call for an *occasional*, skillful transition to another function. There are no simple rules to guide the coach, but there are some prerequisite conditions.

Of paramount importance is interpersonal trust and trust in the process. Next is a collegial relationship between the coach and the person being coached. Finally, the coach needs exquisite coaching skills and a rich knowledge base of the topics being coached.

We've had the good fortune to visit an exemplary program for new teachers at the University of California, Santa Cruz.[5] There, teacher advisors demonstrate elegant, seamless, and effective situational flexibility across the functions of coaching, consulting, and collaboration. What makes this possible are a number of conditions.

The teacher advisors are maestro coaches. The associate director has 14 years' experience and is a graduate of both the cognitive coaching foundations and leadership programs. Other advisors have been coaching and teaching coaching skills to others for as many as eight years.

The teacher advisors' only responsibilities are to support beginning teachers. For years, these advisors have spent every single school calendar day in classrooms working with beginning teachers or conferencing with them about their work. The advisors have no responsibilities for teacher evaluation.

Teacher advisors practice continuous inquiry into their own practices. New and veteran advisors are paired in coaching relationships. Center staff members meet weekly to share experiences and seek ideas from each other. They continue to build a collective body of knowledge and skills about supporting beginning teachers.

Each teacher advisor receives intensive training in classroom observation on (1) how to recognize, along a developmental continuum, classroom manifestations of each of the California Teaching Standards, and (2) how to use a variety of data-gathering instruments.

The teacher advisors are clear that their mission is to develop independence, not dependence, in these relationships. They regard collaboration as a vehicle for developing the beginning teacher's professional independence, and they move to establish this early in their relationships.

For beginning teachers, these advisors are their lifelines to survival. Advisors communicate a reaffirming certainty that each beginning teacher is okay, has the capacity to survive and learn, and contributes value to students' education. Such consistently positive presuppositions are especially important during the early months, when beginning teachers encounter feelings of overwhelming self-doubt and inadequacy.

Part of the sense of a seamless fabric in the work of the New Teacher Center may be explained, we think, by noting that many coaching practices are applied in either consulting or collaborating. For example, trust and rapport are fundamental to any helping relationship. Paraphrasing, with its profound influences on the chemistry of resourcefulness, is prominent in both collaborative consulting and coaching. In consulting, as in coaching, there is a need for data. Good practices in either function require clarity about what data to gather, how to collect it, and how it will be useful. Data may sometimes be reported within the consulting role without interpretation from the consultant. During consulting, clarity is needed about the teacher's goals. A consultant, like a coach, will use open-ended questions and pause, paraphrase, and probe for specificity. Given these common features, the question "How do you know when to segue from coaching to consulting, and how do you do it?" is often met with puzzlement.

WHEN TO CONSULT

How does a support provider know when to switch from coaching to consulting? One teacher advisor described her thinking process as follows. First, she knows the teacher well enough to detect when the teacher is stuck. Second, based on her knowledge of what has worked for this teacher in the past (including the teacher's information processing style and the degree of risk to the teacher in acting on possibilities in this situation), she knows the teacher has the capacity to implement ideas the advisor might offer.

Wendy Barron, associate director of the New Teacher Center and senior teacher advisor, describes how coaching and consulting are woven together over a three-week period with a beginning teacher.

1. **Coach:** The teacher expresses interest in literacy circles. Wendy invites reflection about her intention, values, goals, and planning.

2. **Consult:** The teacher realizes there are gaps in her knowledge about how to conduct literacy circles. Wendy shares ideas, locates information, and gives the teacher an article about literacy circles.

3. **Collaborate:** Wendy discusses the article and engages the teacher in co-planning. She and the teacher share ideas about how to get started.

4. **Consult:** At the teacher's request, Wendy models a lesson teaching students to generate processing questions. When asked for strategies, she offers some for consideration.

5. **Coach:** The teacher asks Wendy to observe. Wendy gathers requested data and conducts a reflecting conversation after the lesson.

6. **Collaborate:** Wendy and the beginning teacher examine student papers together and determine an area for future instruction. Together they plan the next lesson.

Teacher advisors see their work as a dance in which they are constantly deciding when to turn, dip, or bop while maintaining a partnership with the teacher.

When coaching, support providers may be especially generous with silence. They also might ask teachers to elaborate on values and beliefs they hold about learning. Sometimes they allow teachers to "fail forward" in order to develop rich learning from lessons that did not go as the teacher wanted. They also ask "take-away" questions for the teacher to ponder after the coaching conversation. Take-away questions do not require an answer in the moment. Rather, they are inended for later reflection. Occasionally, coaches model their own reflective thought.

Practices unique to collaboration might include physically helping a new teacher to arrange a classroom or supplies, procuring materials, demonstrating, advising, suggesting, co-planning, or co-teaching.

Although support providers might do more consulting than coaching at the beginning of the year with new teachers and incrementally modify the ratio to a greater use of coaching, we do not regard these functions as points on a continuum. Rather, we see them being chosen in the moment, based on perceived appropriateness to meet various intentions and teacher permission.

In fact, support providers may want to start interactions with coaching and collaborating and move to consulting only when they see a need. Teachers report far more satisfaction with coaching than with consulting, and even young and inexperienced teachers bring the cognitive capacity for coaching.

ISN'T EVERYTHING EVALUATION?

We're often asked, "Isn't everything just evaluation?" This is a complex question to answer. First, it's useful to consider the various meanings of *evaluate. Webster's Unabridged Dictionary* provides this definition: to determine the worth of; to find the amount or value of; to appraise.

The word *evaluate*, used as a verb, is a nominalization. Nominalizations name ideas as events when they are actually processes. Nominalizations are abstractions, separate from the actual doing of the thing. Because abstractions trigger different representations in people's minds, it is useful to ask, "What specifically does one do when one is evaluating?"

When we claim Cognitive Coaching should be separated from evaluation, two issues often arise in people's minds. First, to evaluate is to make a judgment, but aren't humans judgment machines? Our very survival depends on rapid assessment of situations and determining the relative safety of our environment. Don't all actions and questions arise from the foundation of judgments we have made, either consciously or unconsciously?

We agree that judgment and action are inextricably intertwined. Yet one can choose to act without communicating judgment about events, behaviors, or choices that another has made if one is free of judgment about the individual. To be nonjudgmental of others is both a perspective and a discipline, developed as one gains in personal maturity. Harvard Professor Robert Kegan[6] describes this stage of adult meaning-making as "post-institutional thought," when one's thinking is freed from the certainties of right and wrong, compassion is a state of being, and one can compare (judge) actions with standards without either blame or praise.

Of course judgment is associated with coaching (and consulting and collaborating). However, the judgment required in these settings is about comparing behaviors against standards, results against goals, not about the worth or motivation of the individual.

Webster's says that a judge is one who has skills or experience sufficient to decide on the merit, value, or quality of something. Judgments will always be a necessary part of our work. We can make judgments, however, without being judgmental. We can judge without criticizing, censuring, or praising.

CAN ONE PERSON EVALUATE AND SUPPORT?

Research by Carl Glickman at the University of Georgia sought an answer to the question "Is it possible for one person to serve as both a supporting supervisor (coach, consultant) and an evaluator of performance?"[7]

Glickman's findings were a cautious "yes," if three conditions are present:

1. Trust exists in the relationship and the process.

2. The teacher is clear about which role the principal is performing in the moment.

3. The principal's behaviors are pure. That is, when evaluating, only evaluating behaviors are used. When consulting, only consulting behaviors are used (providing data, making judgments, interpreting possible relationships, making suggestions, offering advice, advocating). When coaching, only coaching behaviors are used (giving data, asking questions, inviting self-assessment, eliciting analysis, inviting synthesis of learning, requesting commitment). Mingling these three classes of behavior sends a mixed message, and the learning potential of the brain shuts down, which is one more indicator of the power of emotions to disrupt thinking. Anxiety signals from the limbic brain can create neural static, sabotaging the ability of the prefrontal lobe to maintain working memory.[8]

Glickman's findings become especially important as many school districts encourage teachers to serve in support roles with their colleagues. Among the forms this support takes are beginning teacher induction programs, peer coaching, mentoring, peer assistance, and peer review. Being an outstanding teacher, however, does not automatically translate into being an effective mentor for other teachers. Just one or two teachers unskilled with the functions of mentoring, consulting, coaching, or peer-assisted review can disastrously affect morale and teachers' willingness to be open to collegial support.[9]

On the other hand, many programs have developed thoughtful curricula for preparing teachers to work in support relationships with their peers. Throughout California, for example, local Beginning Teacher Support and Assessment programs have developed training modules for supporting new teachers. Two reliable sources of curricula and seminars for supporting teachers are the New Teacher Center at the University of California, Santa Cruz, and the Center for Cognitive Coaching in Highlands Ranch, Colorado.[12]

MAKING IN-THE-MOMENT DECISIONS

During our university days, we were jolted as we realized how valuable it could be to shift supervision styles. We were working with a graduate student administrative intern. Both of us, by nature, tend toward a mediative, inquiry-based style of supporting others. Examination of progress with "Paul," however, revealed little follow-though on his part and insufficient understanding of the administrative position in which he was interning. Recalling Glickman's description of levels of abstraction and levels of commitment, we decided that Paul was relatively low on both continuums and therefore might benefit from a more direct information approach. Paul's performance and understanding immediately improved as he was provided with descriptions of what he should do next. Even though we had switched to a more direct informational style with Paul, we had not lost sight of our mission: extending his capacity for self-directed learning.

Paul's story represents the coach's dilemma of not knowing what kind of support to offer. More often, the issue is not if to offer information or questions, but *when*. This is a delicate situation, and it is possible that only the most experienced coaches can make sound judgments most of the time. Many factors come into play. Is this a new teacher, a new assignment, or a new relationship? What is the person's general state of efficacy and craftsmanship? What is he asking for? How do you know if what she asks for is what she needs? What degree of stress is present?

Our colleagues Laura Lipton and Bruce Wellman address similar issues related to mentoring. They believe that a mentor's major responsibility is to increase the novice teacher's capacity to generate knowledge. Lipton and Wellman envision three stances that a mentor might take along a learning-focused continuum of interactions:

> The mentor might consult; that is, inform a teacher regarding processes and protocols, advise based on the mentor's expertise, or advocate for particular choices and actions. Another stance is to collaborate; that is, to participate as equals in planning, reflecting, and problem solving. At other times, the mentor might decide that coaching, that is, the nonjudgmental

mediation of thinking and decision making, is the most effective option.[10]

Whether to deviate from coaching is the most critical question for a support provider. Lipton and Wellman suggest that mentors give thought to three related questions: if, when, and how. If their answer to "if I should deviate" is yes, then consideration must be given to when and how.

Decisions about when and how to deviate from coaching are largely driven by the coach's attention to the verbal and nonverbal cues that signal what someone is thinking and feeling. The coach must read the colleague's communication: Is it confidence, confusion, or discomfort? This may move the coach to offer a summarizing paraphrase, leave an area of inquiry for another time, or ask a penetrating question. Inexperienced coaches sometimes move to consulting because of their own discomfort, not the teacher's.

Whether to move to another type of support behavior seems to be the most complex question. In general, one moves along a sliding scale of support behaviors as a teacher gains experiences and matures in reflection. For a beginning teacher, for example, it is most likely that one enters the relationship primarily as a consultant but exits it as a coach.

Several factors influence the choice of services to provide. As in the case of Paul, Glickman's concepts about the level of abstraction and commitment may apply. Abstraction refers to the teacher's ability to examine situations from a variety of perspectives, to generate and examine alternative solutions, to test and modify instructional practices, and generally to reflect about their work. In brief, the support provider determines how much initiative, thought, and action the teacher expends in his teaching. Glickman[11] regards these two factors as developmental. He would have support providers increase the ratio of collaborative, or nondirective, work (coaching) as teachers become more highly abstract or committed.

Another variable is culture. Glickman cautions that a support provider might incorrectly interpret limited language production from a teacher as a lower level of abstraction when, in fact, it might stem from a cultural cause. The percentage of foreign-born persons in the United States is increasing. Coaches must be aware of how a foreign-born speaker's language might color a coaching interaction differently.

SIGNALING A CHANGE

When the teacher knows which function is driving an interaction, he can respond congruently. The greatest risk of confusion comes when a support provider decides to shift from one function to another. Laura Lipton does this elegantly. Here are some of her moves.

First, she seeks permission to change functions: "I've been coaching. I'd like to shift roles and offer some ideas to consider. Then you decide for yourself which might be useful. Okay?"

Then she physically moves, in essence creating a visual paragraph for a new beginning of the conversation.

She pauses and uses a frozen gesture, which initiates a neutral zone in which the teacher mentally separates from the coaching function.

When Laura sees that the teacher's breathing is regular and unlabored, she knows that she has permission to transition into consulting. [13]

MENTAL PREREQUISITES FOR FLEXIBILITY

Skillful coaches shuttle among a variety of perceptual orientations. Each provides unique information unavailable in the other two perceptions. These three orientations are as follows:

- Egocentric, the coach's point of view.

- Allocentric, the other person's perspective.

- Macrocentric, a wide-angle view of the interaction between the coach and other person.

The Coach's Perspective

This perceptual frame operates whenever we are intensely aware of our own thoughts, feelings, intentions, place on a coaching map, and physical sensations. To be aware of our own boundaries requires egocentricity. Being egocentrically conscious allows us to monitor of our own processes. With consciousness, we can recognize that we are doing autobiographical or solution listening and decide to set it aside to better understand the other person. Without consciousness of our own thinking and feeling processes, we have no other choice but to stay stuck in whatever internal reality is happening at the moment. Listening egocentrically may generate sympathy for the person we are coaching.

The Other Person's View

Shifting focus from myself to the other person characterizes this perspective. It is the mental resource for rapport. With this point of view, we become aware of how a situation looks, sounds, and feels from the other person's experience. To work within this point of view, the coach must be exactingly attentive to the other person. Listen with your eyes to the physicality of communication, with your ears to the delivery and tone of the words, and with your feelings to what you sense about the other person's state. Allocentricity is the catalyst for empathy.

Listening "From the Balcony"

Compassion, or observation without value judgment, is often a by-product of the macrocentric perspective. In the macrocentric mode, one listens from a view outside the perspective of either party—"listening from the balcony." To a degree, you are detached from the feelings of identification you might have been experienced with either the egocentric or the allocentric view.

Coaches gather the most information about an interaction from this position. The deeper that coaching maps, tools, and values are internalized, the greater the ease of going to the "balcony." Coaches have some understanding of their own feelings, some understanding of the other person's perspective, and an awareness of the systemic nature of the conversation. To be macrocentric is to observe the interaction from a distance without identifying with either person.

Knowing one's intentions and choosing behaviors from a range of possible options that are congruent with those intentions requires the ability to move in and out of these three positions. This may be the most essential requirement for exercising situational flexibility. It is also the most valuable resource in modifying coaching interactions to match the other person's ways of processing information and making meaning.

CONCLUSION

The mission of Cognitive Coaching is to develop the cognitive capacities for self-directed learning. Ultimately, the support person with the greatest flexibility in choices and repertoire has the greatest influence. It is for this reason that Cognitive Coaches, devoted to mediating thinking, will occasionally draw from the other support services of collaborating and consulting to achieve these ends.

The constructivist coach knows that through her services in collaboration and consulting she can provide data, ideas, and structured experiences which can be mediated to enhance the teacher's skills and dispositions of meaning making.

The coach also knows that through collaboration and/or consulting, opportunities will arise that can enhance the teachers development of resourcefulness related to the five states of mind: efficacy, flexibility, consciousness, craftsmanship, and interdependence.

Thus, even though a coach may enter other support functions, their "default position" is always from their stance that is grounded in the values, principles and purposes of Cognitive Coaching.

NOTES

1. Riley, D. W. (Ed.). (1991). *My soul looks back, 'less it forget: A collection of quotations by people of color* (p. 181). New York: Harper-Collins.

2. Pajak, E. (2000). *Approaches to clinical supervision: Alternatives to improving instruction* (2nd ed.). Norwood, MA: Christopher-Gordon.

3. Baker, B. (2001). Personal communication.

4. We are grateful to Michael Dolchemascolo, Jane Ellison, Judy Gottschalk, Lynn Sawyer, Sue Pressler, and Sharon Storrier, associates at the Center for Cognitive Coaching, for helping us to make these distinctions.

5. Moir, E., Barron, W., and Stobbe, C. (2001). Personal communication. Starting with a foundation of Cognitive Coaching principles, protocols, and skills, the Santa Cruz New Teacher Center has become a leader in training support providers in California and other states. Center advisors in Santa Cruz support beginning teachers using a blend of practices that we had earlier thought not to be possible. What has emerged from their work is a support system in which Cognitive Coaching, consulting, and collaboration work together almost seamlessly. The advisors blend Cognitive Coaching with what we will term *collaboration or consulting*. We do not necessarily recommend their practices in settings in which a number of factors we describe are not present.

6. Kegan, R. (1994). *In over our heads: The mental demands of modern life*. Cambridge, MA: Harvard University Press.

7. Glickman, C. (1985). *Supervision of instruction: A developmental approach*. Boston: Allyn and Bacon.

8. Goleman, D. (1997). *Emotional intelligence: Why it can matter more than I.Q.* (27). New York: Bantam Books.

9. Costa, A., and Garmston, R. (2000). Peer Assistance and Review: Potentials and Pitfalls in *The Peer Assistance and Review Reader*. In Gary Bloom and Jennifer Geldstein, Eds., Santa Cruz, CA. New Teacher Center, University of California, Santa Cruz.

10. Lipton, L., and Wellman, B. with C. Humbard. (2001). *Mentoring matters: A practical guide to learning-focused relationships*. Sherman, CT: MiraVia.

11. Glickman, C. (1985). *Supervision of instruction: A developmental approach*. Boston: Allyn and Bacon. See also Glickman, C., Gordon, S., and Ross-Gordon, J. (2000). *Supervision and instructional*

leadership: A developmental approach (5th ed.) Boston: Allyn and Bacon.

12. New Teacher Center, University of California, Santa Cruz, www.newteachercenter.org and Center for Cognitive Coaching. Highlands Ranch, CO. www.cognitivecoaching.cc.

13. Grinder, M. (2001). Personal communication. We are grateful to Michael Grinder for his many insights on how a coach can read nonverbal cues to calibrate a teacher's cognitive and affective states.

Part IV

Integrating Cognitive Coaching Throughout the System

In this section we give practical examples of how the ideals of Cognitive Coaching can be embedded into the curriculum, culture, policies, and practices of the school. We review the most recent research examining the achievement of Cognitive Coaching goals, its effects on student learning, its impact on staff, and other dimensions. We close with our vision of an educational Renaissance in schools, school systems, communities, and the world.

13

Integrating the Ideals of Cognitive Coaching[1]

The very best organizations have a fractal quality to them. An observer of such an organization can tell what the organization's values and ways of doing business are by watching anyone, whether it be a production floor employee or a senior manager. There is consistency and predictability to the quality of behavior. No matter where we look in these organizations, self-similarity is found in its people, in spite of the complex range of roles and levels.

—Margaret Wheatley

The essence and elements of Cognitive Coaching have applications well beyond a dyadic coaching relationship. Renaissance leaders remain vigilant for opportunities to institutionalize Cognitive Coaching into the curriculum, the policies, and the practices of an organization. In this chapter, we search for ways that these ideals can be integrated into the culture of the school.[1]

INTEGRATING COGNITIVE COACHING IDEALS THROUGHOUT THE SCHOOL CULTURE

There is a greater likelihood that teachers will teach and students will learn the ideals of Cognitive Coaching if those ideals are apparent in the school's curriculum and its culture. Teachers will adopt visions of self-directed learning for their own students and will value exacting standards, flexibility, cooperation, and creativity in thoughtful, interdependent environments.

We have selected four of the major components of Cognitive Coaching around which to organize this chapter. Those components are as follows:

- **Values,** such as self-directedness and holonomy (see chapters 1, 3, and 6).

- **Beliefs,** especially the idea that humans have the capacity to draw forth the five states of mind to solve problems and resolve conflicts (see chapter 6).

- **Mental maps,** which guide all Cognitive Coaching interactions (see chapters 2, 9, and 10).

- **Coaching skills,** such as using verbal and nonverbal tools (see chapters 3, 4, and 5).

Integrating Cognitive Coaching throughout the school culture and curriculum requires valuing, understanding, and making a commitment to constructivist principles of learning. As described in chapter 7, constructivism is a theory of learning that places the natural human quest for understanding at the center of the educational enterprise.[2] Constructivist theories offer a particular challenge to Cognitive Coaches in an era of testing, uniform standards, lock-step processes, and high-stakes accountability.[3]

EMBEDDING COGNITIVE COACHING IDEALS IN CURRICULUM DECISIONS

The curriculum process is composed of three basic groups of decisions:

1. Purposes: outcomes, goals, and intentions.

2. Instruction: strategies, materials, and organizational patterns to achieve those outcomes.

3. Assessment: ways to assess progress toward and achievement of those outcomes.

Cognitive Coaching can be integrated into the curriculum through this decision-making process. Figure 13-1 contains a diagram of this dynamic process, which balances so many different ingredients.[4]

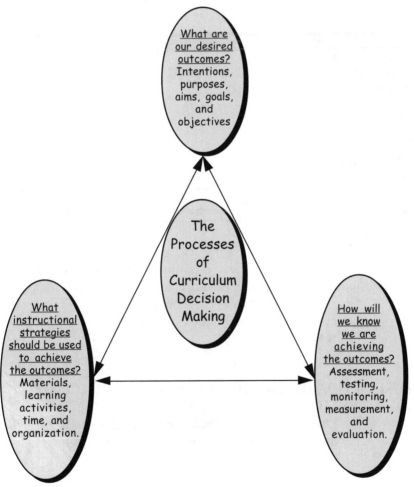

Figure 13-1.
Curriculum Decision Making Process

The matrix in Table 13-1 may serve as an organizer for this chapter. Each of the curriculum decisions (purposes, instruction, and assessment) is correlated with the four selected components of Cognitive Coaching:

TABLE 13-1.
MATRIX

Curriculum Decisions	Cognitive Coaching Ideals & Principles			
	Values	**Beliefs**	**Mental Maps**	**Coaching Skills**
	Valuing Self-Directedness and a Spirit of Community (Holomony)	Drawing on States of Mind as Resources	Applying Mental Maps	Employing Verbal and Nonverbal Tools
1. PURPOSES: Integrating into goals, outcomes, and intentions				
2. INSTRUCTION: Integrating into instruction				
3. ASSESSMENT: Integrating into assessing and reporting practices				

We provide some selected examples in each intersection of the matrix. The intent is to stimulate a staff's search for ways that Cognitive Coaching values, beliefs, maps, and skills can be integrated into the cultural values, curriculum, policies, and practices of the workplace.

INFUSING COACHING THROUGH GOALS, OUTCOMES, AND INTENTIONS

One of the sources of pride in being a human being is the ability to bear present frustrations in the interests of longer purposes.

—Helen Merrell Lynd

Because some students may come from homes or from other schools where self-directed learning was not valued, they may be dismayed by and resistant to the teacher's invitations to plan for themselves, monitor themselves, and reflect and derive meaning from their own experiences. School staffs, therefore, must clearly convey to parents and students that their goal of education is self-directed learning, including the following ideals:

- Thinking is the student's responsibility.

- Having more than one solution is desirable.

- Taking time to plan and reflect on multiple possible answers is more commendable than responding rapidly or impulsively.

- Changing an answer in the light of additional information is more desirable than holding fast to an initial answer.

Incorporating Self-Directedness and Holonomy

Children come fully equipped with an insatiable drive to explore and experiment. Unfortunately the primary institutions of our society are oriented predominantly toward controlling rather than learning, rewarding individuals for performing for others rather than cultivating their natural curiosity and impulse to learn.

—Peter Senge

Cognitive Coaching prizes self-directedness. Simultaneously, it values the reciprocal relationships between and among the individual and members of the larger community.

These values can be clearly communicated throughout the school's mission statements, standards, outcomes, reports to parents, student handbooks, orientation materials, and newsletters.

For example, Encinal High School in Alameda, California, composed and adopted the following mission statement. Although this mission statement does not use exactly the same terminology found in this book, the thoughts are clearly congruent with the ideals of Cognitive Coaching:

> Encinal High School is a home for the active mind—a cooperative community promoting knowledge, self-understanding, mutual respect, global understanding, adaptability to change, and a love for lifelong learning.

Table 13-2 contains a statement of student exit outcomes from the Tahoma School District. The ideals embodied in this statement are also highly congruent with the values of Cognitive Coaching.

TABLE 13-2.[5]

TAHOMA SCHOOL DISTRICT STUDENT OUTCOMES

The Tahoma School District in Maple Valley, Washington, has adopted the following outcomes for students. Becoming:

- Collaborative   Workers
- Complex   Thinkers
- Quality   Producers
- Effective   Communicators
- Self-directed   Learners
- Community   Contributors

Incorporating States of Mind

Instruction in various content areas and at various grade levels provides numerous opportunities to experience, reflect on, and build a disposition for the five states of mind. Students are more likely to habituate the five states of mind if they encounter them repeatedly across all content areas and all grade levels throughout the school years. Following are some examples of standards of learning[6] showing how craftsmanship may be applied throughout several grade levels and across various subjects.

In elementary grade social sciences, an outcome might be:

> Understands the historical perspective. Evaluates historical fiction according to the accuracy of its content and the author's bias and interpretation.

In middle school mathematics, an outcome might be stated like this:

> Understands and applies basic and advanced properties of the concepts of measurement. Selects and uses appropriate units and tools, depending on degree of accuracy required, to find measurements for real-world problems.

A high school language arts department might create an outcome like this:

> Uses the general skills and strategies of the writing process. Drafting and revising: Uses a variety of strategies to draft and revise written work (e.g., highlights individual voice; rethinks content, organization, and style; checks accuracy and depth of information; redrafts for readability and needs of readers; reviews writing to ensure that content and linguistic structures are consistent with purpose).

In all the transdisciplinary examples above, there is a recurring theme of craftsmanship: striving for accuracy, precision, and refinement.

Incorporating Mental Maps

Working with technology provides a powerful opportunity to practice the maps of planning, monitoring, and reflecting. Following is one example of a middle school standard of learning that supports the use of the planning map:

> Understands the nature of technological design: Implements a proposed design (e.g., organizes materials and other resources, plans one's work, makes use of group collaboration when appropriate, chooses suitable tools and techniques, works with appropriate measurement methods to ensure accuracy).

Incorporating Verbal and Nonverbal Tools

The language arts provide a natural avenue for learning and practicing verbal and nonverbal tools. Here is an example of a language arts standard for grades 3–5:

> Uses listening and speaking strategies for different purposes. Uses a variety of nonverbal communication skills (e.g., eye contact, gestures, facial expressions, posture). Uses a variety of verbal communication skills (e.g., projection, tone, volume, rate, articulation, pace, phrasing).

INTEGRATING COACHING PRINCIPLES INTO INSTRUCTION[7]

Good teachers are passionate about ideas, learning and their relationship with students. These teachers did more than teach to set standards or use approved techniques. Their classroom relationships are built on interest, enthusiasm, inquiry, excitement, discovery, risk-taking and fun. Their cognitive scaffolding of concepts and teaching strategies was held together with emotional bonds.

—P. Woods and B. Jeffrey[8]

The values, beliefs, maps, and tools of Cognitive Coaching guide teachers in making daily decisions about teaching. Teachers will want to seize opportunities to help students become aware of, practice and reflect on the elements of Cognitive Coaching.

Integrating Self-Directedness and Holonomy

Working in cooperative groups provides the context for learning about holonomy. To help students experience positive interdependence, teachers structure cooperative learning situations in which individual students not only learn the content but are also responsible for ensuring that all members of the group succeed. The learning task is structured to be cooperative and reciprocal. Each member can succeed individually only if all members succeed collectively.[9]

Purposely structuring groups heterogeneously to supply a mixture of cultures, languages, styles, modalities, points of view, and maturity levels is another way to provide rich opportunities to experience the tensions that arise through a pursuit of holonomy. Students learn to draw upon the states of mind to resolve conflicts that arise in these heterogeneous groups. Following is one example:

> In the wake of El Nino's visit to Africa in 1997, there was severe drought in the south of Tanzania. A Social Studies teacher "wanted 10th graders to develop a meaningful personal project that would bring home to them what it meant for people to live at the mercy of unpredictable weather patterns." Together with his students, he planned a pilot, small-scale permaculture farm project in a leprosy village some six hours south of Dar es Salaam. These students [from many nations] were involved at every stage of the project: in discussion with village elders, in clearing land, planning drought resistant crops and thinking of ingenious ways to defend the crops against bands of marauding wild bush pigs. This [teacher] had found a way to combine the curriculum with existing weather conditions and make the program personally meaningful to the students. He had been flexible in his thinking.[10]

Operational descriptions of effective group work may be elicited from the students before the work is begun. Then students can monitor their own and each other's contributions. After the cooperative task is completed, time should be provided to reflect on how well individuals in a group worked together. What contributed to the group's success? How did each group member contribute to and learn from the experience? Encourage students to give nonjudgmental feedback to each other about their observations.[11]

Integrating the States of Mind

Effective teachers seize every opportunity to engage, reinforce, illuminate, practice, reflect on and model the states of mind. For example, teachers can display their own flexibility in valuing student differences. Because teachers know that all students are different, they draw upon a repertoire of learning and teaching strategies to fit a wide range of student styles, preferences, and intelligences.[12] Students are rarely aware of these teaching strategies unless someone has taken the time to teach them about them.

Knowing about cultural differences, teachers help students learn to understand, accept, and value communal traits of humility, respecting and listening to others, and taking responsibility for others' welfare. At the same time they instill the intellectual standards of independence, accuracy, clarity, and rational thought.

Teachers help students to become aware of the states of mind by posing questions designed to call attention to and to use one or more of these states. For example, before a learning activity the teacher might ask the following:

- As you anticipate your projects, which states of mind might we need to use?

- In working these math problems, which of the states of mind will help us?

- As we are reading, which of the states of mind will we be using to help understand the story?

After a learning activity, ask such questions as the following:

- As you reflect on your work on this project, which of the states of mind did you find yourself using?

- As you were solving these problems, which of the states of mind did you employ?

- As you were working in groups to design your plan, what metacognitive strategies did you use to monitor your performance of the states of mind?

The teacher can also cue transference and applications of the states of mind to other settings:

- In what other classes might you use these states of mind?

- What other situations in your life would your use of these states of mind be beneficial?

- In what careers or professions would people have to draw forth these states of mind?

Pose intriguing questions like the following to stimulate discussion:

- How might an intelligent person use the states of mind to choose a doctor?

- Which states of mind were primary resources for Martin Luther King?

- Which of the states of mind would be helpful in reading a newspaper (or watching television)?

Literature is a perfect conduit to an understanding of the states of mind. In the primary grades, reading such books as *The True Story of the Three Little Pigs from the Wolf's Point of View* can foster flexibility.[13] This book causes students to assume an allocentric stance. In the middle grades, students can discover the true meaning of interdependence through books such as *My Side of the Mountain* by Jean Craighead George.[14] High school students can discover craftsmanship with such books as Robert Persig's *Zen and the Art of Motorcycle Maintenance.*[15] Many teachers report that using the states of mind as a template to understand characters and stories assists students in comprehension, analysis of metaphor, and linking literature to their own lives.

Integrating Mental Maps

The mental maps of planning and reflecting can be taught directly as students prepare for projects, field trips, and lab experiments. Upon completion, students may be invited to reflect on the experience, analyze the causes of success, construct new learnings, and make commitments to apply learnings to future tasks. For example, in San Francisco, Bill Baker and Pat Forte have been teaching fourth-grade students to use the planning and reflecting maps in their own projects and to take the lead in facilitating parent-teacher conferences during reporting periods.

Integrating Verbal and Nonverbal Tools

Practicing skills related to listening and questioning can begin in the early grades: taking turns talking, facing the speaker, questioning to gather data, and empathizing with others. Here are a few examples of how these skills can be integrated into the classroom.

Whatever the subject area, it is useful for students to pose study questions for themselves before and during their reading of textual material. Self-generating questions facilitate comprehension and create a more focused mind. Questioning while reading, for example, provides an opportunity to predict what is coming next in the story.[16]

Students also gain much by keeping their questions in a response log or a reading log. They can begin to answer the questions raised as they reflect on the reading and seek other sources. Students may compose questions that will be used in a study guide or on a test. Teachers might list and compare the questions that students compose: What makes them powerful? How are they alike and different grammatically? What kind of data do they yield? When is it appropriate to ask each type?[17]

Sometimes the most significant questions are generated through the research process. A thoughtful way to end a research paper is with a set of questions that have arisen as a result of the research. It is valuable for students to know that there is always more to know!

ASSESSING GROWTH IN COGNITIVE COACHING IDEALS

How much do students really love to learn, to persist, to passionately attack a problem or a task? . . . to watch some of their prized ideas explode and to start anew? . . . to go beyond being merely dutiful or long-winded?
Let us assess such things.

—Grant Wiggins

Assessment is the heart of any organizational improvement process. Feedback data energizes learning. The Cognitive Coach's intent is to consciously build a culture that attends to and is guided by indicators (what to look for) and feedback systems (how to describe to the persons who need to learn what the focus of learning must be).

Below are a variety of assessment tools and techniques intended to help students and staff generate data about their increased use of the principles and ideals of Cognitive Coaching.

Assessing Self-Directedness and Holonomy

When confronted with problematic situations, self-directed persons consciously and habitually draw upon the states of mind as mental disciplines to resolve personal and organizational tensions. They reflect on their own experiences and pose questions for them-

TABLE 13-3.
SELF-MEDIATION

Self-Managing To what degree do I:	Often	Sometimes	Not Yet
Draw from prior knowledge, sensory data, and intuition to guide, hone, and refine my actions?			
Display an internal locus of control?			
Thoughtfully plan and initiate my actions?			
Manage my time effectively?			
Produce new knowledge through my own research and experimentation?			
Reflect on and learn from my experiences?			
Use clear and precise language?			
Balance solitude and togetherness, action and reflection, and personal and professional growth?			
Display a sense of humor?			
Self-Monitoring **To what degree do I:**			
Seek perspectives beyond myself and others to generate adaptively resourceful responses?			
Generate new and innovative ideas and problem-solving strategies?			
Pursue ambiguities and possibilities to create new meanings?			
Subjugate my own desires in deference to group needs?			
Monitor my awareness of what is known and not known and develop metacognitive strategies to fill in the gaps?			
Self-Modifying **To what degree do I:**			
Explore choice points between asserting myself and integrating with others?			
Seek feedback from colleagues for improved performance?			
Continue to learn new skills and strategies?			

selves. Growth toward self-directedness is assessed by the degree to which they become habitually self-managing, self-monitoring, and self-modifying. Table 13-3 contains a checklist for self-evaluation of employment of the five states of mind. The rubric is intended for use by a staff, team, or group to assess itss capacity to work interdependently.

Assessing States of Mind

One way of self-assessing growth in the states of mind is to develop with students a rubric for scoring. The descriptions for each scoring category can be developed with students and staff. Each category should be sufficiently clear so that students can learn from the feedback about their behavior and how to improve. The rubrics in Tables 13-4, 13-5, and 13-6 were developed with an elementary school staff and refined by their students.[18]

Assessing Use of Mental Maps

One way to assist students in becoming aware of and employing mental maps is through the use of journals. Journals provide an opportunity to track one's progress over time and across a variety

TABLE 13-4.

SAMPLE RUBRIC FOR ASSESSING STUDENT LEVELS OF CONSCIOUSNESS

	CONSCIOUSNESS
EXPERT	• Describes in detail the steps of thinking when solving a problem or doing other kinds of mental tasks. Explains in detail how thinking about thinking helps to improve work and how it helps to be a better learner. • Describes a plan before starting to solve a problem; monitors steps in the plan or strategy; reflects on the efficiency of the problem-solving strategy.
PRACTITIONER	• Describes thinking while solving a problem or doing other kinds of mental tasks. • Explains how thinking about thinking helps learning and helps to improve work.
APPRENTICE	• Includes only sparse or incomplete information when describing thinking and solving a problem or doing other kinds of mental tasks. • Sees only small benefits gained from thinking about thinking and learning.
NOVICE	• Is confused about the relationship between thinking and problem solving. • Sees no relationship between thinking and learning. • Is unable to describe thinking when problem solving.

TABLE 13-5.

Sample Rubric for Assessing Efficacy in Self-Management

	EFFICACY
EXPERT	• Sets clear goals and describes each step to be taken to achieve goals. • Schedules each step and monitors progress.
PRACTITIONER	• Sets clear goals. • Describes some of the steps to be taken to achieve the goals and sequences some of the steps.
APPRENTICE	• Begins to work with unclear goals. • Describes only a few of the steps to be taken to achieve the goals. • Becomes distracted from the schedule.
NOVICE	• Begins to work in random fashion. • Is unclear about or unable to state goals or outcomes or steps in achieving goals.

TABLE 13-6.

Sample Rubric for Assessing Student Flexibility

	FLEXIBILITY	
	In Repertoire	**In Perspective**
EXPERT	• Uses time and resources creatively to find as many ways as possible to look at a situation. • Evaluates these many ways to see how useful they might be. • Expresses appreciation for others' points of view. • Changes mind and incorporates others' point of view in own thinking.	• Consistently explores as many alternatives as time and resources will allow and analyzes how the identified alternatives will affect outcomes. • The alternatives illustrate extremely diverse but highly useful ways of looking at situations.
PRACTITIONER	• Finds a variety of ways of looking at a situation and evaluates how useful they are. • Describes some ways others' points of view are found to be new and different from his or her own.	• Consistently generates alternative ways of approaching tasks and analyzes how the alternatives will affect those tasks. • Some alternatives show originality in the approach.
APPRENTICE	• Describes different ways of looking at a situation from own perspective.	• Sporadically generates alternative ways of approaching tasks and analyzes how the alternative will affect those tasks. • Some alternatives show originality in the approach to the tasks.
NOVICE	• Looks at a situation in only one way and that way is often his or her own. • Looks no further, even when it is clear that it would be helpful to do so.	• Rarely generates alternative ways of approaching tasks. • The few alternatives lack originality.

of classes and settings. Below is a structured invitation to students to plan for, monitor, and reflect on their approach to homework assignments. The intent is to write their responses to these sentence stems in their journal and, over time, to record their improved strategies for accomplishing homework assignments and periodically to reflect on their growth in confidence and self-discipline in managing their assignments.

When planning their homework, monitoring it at home, and reflecting on it, students respond to prompts like the following:

- So that I understand what is expected of me in my homework assignments, I . . .

- To ensure that my homework is complete and accurate, I . . .

- The time and location for best accomplishing my homework is . . .

- To stay on task and avoid distractions, I . . .

- The strategies I use to ensure that my homework is complete, on time, and accurate include . . .

- In my work I look for such success indicators as . . .

Assessing Verbal and Nonverbal Tools

Table 13-7 contains a "How Am I Doing" Checklist. This may provide an opportunity to experience using, monitoring, and self-evaluating the performance of the standard of learning described above.

EMBEDDING COGNITIVE COACHING IDEALS IN THE SCHOOL CULTURE

> *You can tell the ideals of a nation by its advertisements.*
> —Norman Douglas

As schools work to reinvent themselves, they commit human resources to modify the systems in which people work.[19] Organiza-

TABLE 13-7.

"HOW AM I DOING?" CHECKLIST

STATE OF MIND: Listens with understanding	Often	Sometimes	Not Yet
Verbal			
Restates or paraphrases a person's idea before offering personal opinion.			
Clarifies a person's ideas, concepts, or terminology.			
Expresses empathy for other's feelings and emotions.			
Poses questions intended to engage thinking and reflection.			
Expresses personal regard and interest.			
Nonverbal			
Faces the person who is speaking.			
Uses facial expressions congruent with speaker's emotional message.			
Nods head.			
Mirrors gestures.			
Mirrors posture.			

tional change is as important as the development of the individual, perhaps more important because of the incredibly powerful mediating capacity of the environment.[20] Certainly, the two interact with one another, and they mutually influence student learning.

Embedding Self-Directedness and Holonomy

In the holonomous school community, twin goals must exist: development of the organization's capacities for growth, and the development of the individual's capacities for learning.[21]

Limitations of time, isolation, and minimal peer interaction in traditional school settings often prevent teachers of different departments, grade levels, and disciplines from meeting together. Traditional content and subject matter boundaries, however, have become increasingly obscure and selectively abandoned. In their place, relevant, problem-centered, integrative themes are judiciously selected because of their contributions to the thinking, learning, and community-building processes. Thus, teachers bring their unique talents, knowledge, and expertise into an interdisciplinary transformation of lesson planning to help students find connections and relationships among diverse subject matter.

Crossing Boundaries

Boundaries are the intangible lines that separate person from person, team from team, and team from organization. People cross boundaries when they solicit help, collaborate with others to accomplish some end, or actively listen to another's opinion. Learning is shared with others, which leads to better thinking and action. People may cross boundaries for a specific purpose, or they may incidentally pick up ideas "more or less by osmosis."

When people cross the boundaries of their teams, organizational learning can take place. A high-involvement team talked about learning by going as guests to meetings in other installations and inviting others into their own meetings as guests. They considered themselves missionaries whose task was to empower the workers through workshops, consultation, and other kinds of interaction. [22]

Embedding States of Mind

The states of mind pervade the school culture in the day-to-day interactions among staff and parents, in problem solving, and in resolving conflicts. Following is one example of how one school defined flexibility in its culture:

> Interdependent learning communities are built not by obscuring diversity but by valuing the friction those differences bring and resolving those differences in an atmosphere of trust and reciprocity. Appreciation for diversity can be choreographed by deliberately bringing together people of different political and religious persuasions, cultures, gender, cognitive styles, belief systems, modality preferences, and intelligences. In an atmosphere of trust, structuring such diversity within decision-making groups not only enhances the decisions that are made but also stretches members' capacity for flexibility and empathy. Our old perceptions of uniformity need to yield in deference to valuing diversity—the true source of power in today's world. [23]

Embedding Mental Maps

Most school staffs spend a great deal of time planning: preparing grants, implementing curriculum, scheduling parent meetings, and designing lessons. Obviously, the Cognitive Coaching maps can serve groups as well. For example, if the staff is planning a retreat prior to the opening of school, the following questions might guide the staff's thinking:

- What goals do we wish to achieve?

- What strategies will we use to achieve those goals?

- What indicators should we monitor as evidence of our success?

- How shall we collect such data?

- What might we learn from this planning process?

Unfortunately, school staffs rarely spend an equivalent amount of time on reflection. It is often easier to discard what has happened and simply move on. In schools that are integrating the principles of Cognitive Coaching, however, time is regularly devoted to reflect on how intended activities compare with actual outcomes, to evaluate metacognitive strategies, to analyze and draw causal relationships, to synthesize meanings, and to apply learnings to new and novel situations.[24] For example:

- What feelings about our staff retreat did the group express?

- What contributed to those feelings?

- What were some indicators of success of the retreat?

- What evidence of goal achievement was collected?

- How might this data inform us about next steps and future plans?

- How did our planning and reflecting further contribute to our success?

- What have we learned from the planning and reflecting process that we might carry forward to future activities?

Embedding Verbal and Nonverbal Tools

Highly developed professional communities are characterized by a staff's skillfulness in reflective dialogue.[25] Reflective dialogue implies self-awareness about one's own listening skills, awareness of one's own and others' styles and preferences, and knowing when and how to advocate and inquire. It means consciously employing positive presuppositions and monitoring intentions. It requires that participants operate from data rather than speculation or hearsay; it is enhanced when participants contribute ideas and know when to relinquish these ideas in favor of others. It means the ability to clarify and paraphrase. Most important it means knowing when to silence one's mouth and brain to make room for others' thoughts to be fully entertained.[26]

A school staff that desires to infuse the tools of Cognitive Coaching throughout the culture will want to plan for, monitor, and reflect on these dialogical tools in its members' daily interactions. The staff will make a conscious effort to improve those skills and seek ways of gathering evidence of its continued growth toward mastery.

Keeping an inventory (Table 13-8) during meetings, when solving problems, and after interacting with others can help individuals and groups gather valuable data on which to self-reflect and plan for enhancing learning to collaborate even more effectively. A staff meeting might start with a facilitator drawing from the group and listing criteria or indicators of excellence in meeting management.

During a team meeting, participants monitor their own performance and are aware of each other's. Before the end of the meeting, the facilitator asks the group to reflect on the meeting and to describe how the criteria were or were not met. Feelings are explored and indicators of how the team is working together synergistically are expressed. Consider such questions as the following:

- What decisions did you make about when and how to participate?

- What metacognitive strategies did you employ to monitor your own communicative competencies?

- What were some of the effects of your decisions for you and others in your group?

TABLE 13-8.

Meeting Inventory[27]

Decide Who Decides	Low				High
We are clear about who we are in the decision-making process.	1	2	3	4	5
We are clear about what decision-making processes are being used.	1	2	3	4	5
Define the Sandbox					
We are clear about which parts of the issue(s) we are exploring live in our area of influence.	1	2	3	4	5
Develop Standards					
We adhered to one process at a time.	1	2	3	4	5
We adhered to one topic at a time.	1	2	3	4	5
We balanced participation.	1	2	3	4	5
I felt listened to.	1	2	3	4	5
I listened to others.	1	2	3	4	5
We engaged in productive cognitive conflict.	1	2	3	4	5
We were clear about meeting roles today.	1	2	3	4	5
Design the Surround					
We managed the environment to support our work.	1	2	3	4	5

Date _____ Group _____

- As you anticipate future team meetings, what commitments might you make to strengthen the group's productiveness?

- What signals in other future situations will alert you to the need for these communicative competencies?

INSTITUTIONALIZING COGNITIVE COACHING IDEALS IN POLICIES AND PRACTICES

Cognitive Coaches constantly scrutinize district goals, policies, and practices for their consistency with and contribution to these principles. For example:

Because Cognitive Coaches believe in interdependence and flexibility, they design group assignments and composition by timing and defining tasks so that stakeholders from diverse levels of maturity, beliefs, and styles must collaborate. The confluence of these multiple perspectives enriches the thinking of diverse levels of thought within the groups. Teachers from different grade levels and departments can be paired in peer coaching and other collaborative arrangements. A diffusion of knowledge and assumptions about learning occurs when teachers from different disciplines plan together, observe in each other's classroom, share responsibilities for student learnings, or are assigned the same students for multiyear periods.

Because of their belief in self-directedness, numerous school districts have encouraged flexible pathways to continued learning. They encourage teachers to choose each year how they wish to grow. Among the choices are in-house mini-sabbaticals, coaching and being coached, evaluation, staff development, course work, curriculum revision projects, collecting portfolios of student and teacher work, or keeping reflective journals. The only option teachers cannot choose is to stagnate.

Schools may be designed so as to build flexibility into the very walls and passages of the edifice, making it necessary for the staff, students, and community to function in interdependent ways. When constructing a new high school in Crystal Lake, Illinois, Superintendent Joe Saban wrote the following:

> If I had the opportunity to support the "Renaissance School" (as envisioned in your Cognitive Coaching text) with a physical structure, (a) What would it look like? (b) How would space be arranged to support my vision for schools? (c) What kind of areas would be needed to support important professional relationships? (d) How would space look if students were engaged in coaching relationships? (e) What sort of structure could support creative and meaningful thinking? (f) What would the supportive physical building manifestations be for promoting flexibility, interdependence, efficacy, consciousness, craftsmanship, or holonomy among those who enter the structure? (g) If I could break the mold of the high school of yesteryear, what would replace it? (h) How might a building promote shared vision among its constituents? How about team learning, personal mastery, promotion and support of mental models, or systems thinking?[28]

MODELING

*Don't worry that children never listen to you. Worry that they
are always watching you.*

—Robert Fulghum

Understanding that imitation and emulation are the most basic
forms of learning, teachers, parents, and administrators realize the
importance of their own display of desirable Cognitive Coaching
maps, tools, and values in the presence of learners. Following are
some examples of how Cognitive Coaching ideals may be modeled
by adults in the presence of learners.

Modeling Self-Directedness and Holonomy

Adults are sensitive to the tensions and conflicts arising from self-
directed individuals and their relationship to group pressures.
Nowhere else is this more apparent than in classrooms where individual students (particularly adolescents) strive to assert their
autonomy while having to function effectively as a member of a
group, a class, or a student body. To model holonomy, adults will
seek out and help students to understand the external conditions
in the environment or the group that produced tensions and conflicts. Rather than blaming, judging, or advising students, adults
can pace students' feelings and lead students to draw forth the
states of mind when confronted with such tensions and conflicts.

Thus, in day-to-day events and when problems arise in schools,
classrooms, and homes, students must see adults employing the
same types of behaviors that are desired in the students.

Modeling States of Mind

Adults model efficacy when they display a "can do" spirit and view
problems as learning opportunities. They model this state of mind
when they persist until a satisfactory resolution to a problem has
been reached and they manage their own impulsivity during periods of crisis.

Adults model consciousness when they share with students their own thoughts, feelings, beliefs, values, and plans. As problems are solved, they overtly describe their reasoning and mental processes: "Right now I'm feeling . . ." or "Here's what I'm planning" or "My strategy is to . . ."

Adults model craftsmanship by constantly seeking improvement and by demanding high standards of themselves and their students. "How can we do this better next time?" is a frequent question. Or, "Let's check our process again to make sure we have done it accurately."

Adults model flexibility when they attempt to see a situation from a student's or parent's point of view, when they laugh at themselves, and when they bring innovation and creativity to their lesson design and classroom practices.

Adults model interdependence when they plan and team-teach with each other, when they deliberately form learning teams of students in classrooms, and when they become learners among learners.

Modeling Mental Maps

As teachers plan lessons and projects, they can share their planning with students: their goals, their expected outcomes, their indicators of success, where this lesson fits into the overall plan, the standards toward which they are working, and what they themselves hope to learn from this unit. During the lesson, teachers help students to monitor their own progress toward desired outcomes. Upon completion of the lesson, teachers and students reflect on the lesson, analyzing what has been learned, what in the lesson assisted in the learning processes, and how these learnings may be applied to future lessons, life, and situations beyond the classroom.

Modeling Verbal and Nonverbal Tools

If we want students to learn to listen with understanding and empathy, then adults will listen to them with understanding and empathy. If we want students to pose powerful questions, then adults will deliberately construct questions intended to engage and challenge students' intellects. Day-to-day, real-life problems are the best way to practice problem solving: what to take on the field trip, how to return the playground equipment more efficiently, how to make an equitable distribution of limited classroom supplies.

CONCLUSION

The ideals of Cognitive Coaching—its values, beliefs, maps, and tools—are valued not only for staff but also for students. In this chapter we have provided numerous practical examples intended to stimulate further inquiry into ways the principles and practices of Cognitive Coaching might be infused throughout the organization. We believe that all the inhabitants of the school community can become increasingly self-directed and that they should become more resourceful, deliberate, reflective, and skillful. We believe that teachers will teach these ideals in a culture that values these ideals as well.

NOTES

1. For an elaboration of ways to integrate the ideals and practices of Cognitive Coaching in schools and classrooms, see, Ellison, J. and Hayes, C. (Eds.). (In preparation). *Applying cognitive coaching in a system.* Norwood, MA: Christopher-Gordon.

2. Brooks, J., and Brooks, M. (2001). Becoming a constructivist teacher. In A. Costa (Ed.), *Developing minds: A resource book for teaching thinking* (p. 150–157). Alexandria VA: Association for Supervision and Curriculum Development. See also Lambert, L., Walker, D., Zimmerman, D., Cooper, J., Lambert, M., Gardner, M., and Slack, P. J. (1995). *The constructivist leader.* New York: Teachers College Press.

3. Franklin, J. (May 2001). Trying too hard? How accountability and testing are affecting constructivist teaching. *Education Update 43* (3), 1–8.

4. Costa, A. (1997). Curriculum: A decision-making process. In A. Costa and R. Liebmann (Eds.), *Envisioning process as content: To-*

ward a Renaissance curriculum (pp. 41–59). Thousand Oaks, CA: Corwin Press.

5. Skerrit, N., and Hard, E. (2000). An Integrated Approach to the Habits of Mind. In Costa, A., and Kallick, B. C. (Eds.), *Activating and Engaging Habits of Mind.* Alexandria, VA. Association for Supervision and Curriculum Development.

6. The Mid-Continent Regional Educational Laboratory has synthesized standards of learning from many states as well as learned professional organizations. They have been adapted and adopted by local school districts. The standards of learning included in this chapter are congruent with the principles, maps, tools, and values of Cognitive Coaching. We express appreciation to the Mid-Continent Regional Educational Laboratory for its contribution.

7. Costa, A., and Kallick, B. (2000). *Activating and engaging habits of mind.* Alexandria, VA: Association for Supervision and Curriculum Development.

8. Woods, P., and Jeffrey, B. (1996). *Teachable moments* (p. 71). Buckingham: Open University Press.

9. Johnson, D., and Johnson, R. (2001). Cooperation, conflict, cognition, and meta-cognition. In Costa, *Developing minds,* pp. 455–458.

10. Powell, W. (2000). Recruiting educators for an inclusive school. In O. Powell and W. Powell. (Eds.), *Count me in: Developing inclusive international schools* (p. 194). Washington, DC: Overseas Advisory Council.

11. Costa, A. and Kallick, B. (Eds.) (2000). *Assessing and reporting on habits of mind* (pp. 29–53). Alexandria, VA: Association for Supervision and Curriculum Development.

12. Costa, *Developing minds,* pp. 190–245.

13. Scieszka, J. (1996). *The true story of the three little pigs from the wolf's point of view.* New York: Penguin Putnam.

14. George, J. C. (2000). *My side of the mountain.* New York: Penguin.

15. Pirsig, R. (1974). *Zen and the art of motorcycle maintenance.* New York: Bantam Books.

16. DePinto-Piercy, T. (2000). Enhancing reading comprehension instruction through habits of mind. In Costa and Kallick, *Activating and engaging,* pp. 137–142.

17. Costa and Kallick, *Activating and engaging.*

18. Adapted from Costa and Kallick, *Assessing and reporting on habits of mind.* Alexandria, VA Association for Supervision and Curriculum Development. Kallick, B. (2000) T*echpaths for math,* Guilford, CT.

19. Glickman, C. (1993). *Renewing America's schools.* San Francisco: Jossey-Bass. Frymier, J. (1987). Bureaucracy and the neutering of teachers. *Phi Delta Kappan 69* (1), 9–14.

20. Costa, A. (1999). Mediative environments: Creating environments for intellectual growth. In B. Presseissen (Ed.), *Teaching for intelligence.* Pallatine, IL: Skylights.

21. Garmston, R., and Wellman, B. (1999.) *The adaptive school: A sourcebook for developing collaborative groups.* Norwood, MA: Christopher-Gordon.

22. Watkins K. E., and Marsick, V. J. (1993). *Sculpting the learning organization* (p. 102). San Francisco: Jossey-Bass.

23. Tomlinson, CA. (1999). *The differentiated classroom: Responding to the needs of all learners.* Alexandria, VA: Association for Supervision and Curriculum Development.

24. For an extensive discussion of reflection as a schoolwide practice, see York-Barr, J., Sommers, W., Ghere, G., and Montie, J. (2001). *Reflective practice to improve schools: An action guide for educators.* Thousand Oaks, CA: Corwin Press.

25. Louis, K., Marks, H., and Kruse, S. (1996). Teachers' professional community in restructuring schools. *American Educational Research Journal 33* (4), 757–798.

26. Baker, B., Costa, A., and Shalit, S. (1997). Norms of collaboration: Attaining communicative competence. In A. Costa and R. Liebmann (Eds.), *The process-centered school: Sustaining a Renaissance community* (pp. 119–142). Thousand Oaks, CA: Corwin Press. See also Garmston, and Wellman, *The adaptive school.*

27. Garmston and Wellman, *The adaptive school,* p. 139.

28. Saban, J. (1995). Personal communication.

14

Research on Cognitive Coaching[1]

As you've read the other chapters in this book, you might have wondered, "Does Cognitive Coaching achieve its goals? What is the evidence that Cognitive Coaching is making a difference?" Numerous studies have investigated the impact of Cognitive Coaching since it was first developed in 1984. The first study examined the influence of Cognitive Coaching on teachers' thought processes; and the second study investigated its impact on first-year teachers' conceptual development and reflective thinking. Studies have also investigated the effects of Cognitive Coaching on students, on school culture, and on the personal and professional lives of teachers. Other researchers have examined the use of Cognitive Coaching in supervisory relationships, university classes, and teacher preparation programs. Many of the studies investigated a number of areas associated with Cognitive Coaching and reported multiple findings.

We are extremely grateful to Jenny Edwards for developing this chapter. In addition to her own research, Dr. Edwards has maintained a clearinghouse for studies about Cognitive Coaching and has been an important contributor to our learning.

This chapter begins by presenting findings from studies that have shown benefits in the goals of self-directed learning and the five states of mind. It continues with information about the benefits of Cognitive Coaching for students, for school staffs as teams, for individual teachers professionally, and for individual teachers personally. The chapter closes with questions and suggestions for further research.

SELF-DIRECTED LEARNING

One of the major goals of Cognitive Coaching is to create self-directed learners, and research evidence suggests that it achieves this goal. One study found that teachers who had taken Cognitive Coaching training, when compared with a control group, spent more hours in workshops, both during school time and outside school time. In addition, they had implemented more new teaching practices in the previous two years than teachers who had not taken the training. They also had more positive attitudes toward Cognitive Coaching and toward Professional Growth Planning, a method of self-evaluation that their district was using.[2]

In another study, teachers who were involved in a year-long Cognitive Coaching program took on more leadership positions during that year, such as giving presentations to the faculty, increasing their involvement in state activities, and joining the school leadership team.[3]

When principals commented on the portfolios of teachers who were using Cognitive Coaching to help them reach their goals, they emphasized their teachers' increased desire to learn and grow professionally.[4]

Cognitive Coaching has been associated with teachers expanding their repertoire of teaching strategies with their students. In one study, two middle school English teachers who received Cognitive Coaching expanded their teaching repertoires, requested greater student accountability, exhibited more power as they planned lessons, and became more conscious of their behaviors and options as they worked with students. They also began to use the coaching behaviors of paraphrasing, probing, and gathering data with their students as they internalized the coaching process.[5]

In another study, teachers expanded their teaching practices over the course of a year, adopting such practices as team teaching, use of learning logs, peer tutoring, marketing strategies, student choices, multiple forms of assessment, exhibitions, interviews, and developing lessons based on learning styles.[6]

Teachers have indicated that an advantage of being involved in Cognitive Coaching is having the opportunity to learn and grow. Teachers who have taken Cognitive Coaching training mention the following sources of satisfaction with teaching as a profession more often than those who have not taken the training: learning and growth, the ever-changing nature of the profession, the opportunity to make a difference, the opportunity to be creative, and relationships with school staff.[7]

In another study, second-, third-, and fourth-year elementary school teachers grew significantly in seven months over a matched control group in expressions of how they had developed professionally. Those who participated in Cognitive Coaching indicated that they grew in awareness of their teaching practices as a result of coaching. They indicated that they had numerous opportunities to grow and change professionally.[8]

Awakuni's research found that teachers trained in Cognitive Coaching who used it over the course of a year reported that they made changes in their teaching. Both interview data and observations confirmed that they increased the use of inquiry methods, including asking more higher-level questions, varying their explanations and feedback to students, and involving students more in discussions. They also made changes in their classroom management, using more strategies to work with misbehavior, organizing the classroom to prevent behavior problems from occurring, motivating students with grades, and rethinking how curriculum was aligned. In addition, they adopted new strategies for teaching and assessing students, such as using cooperative learning, helping students to clarify their thinking in writing projects, and attempting to accommodate different learning styles through art, video, music, projects, and demonstrations.

Poole[9] and Poole and Okeafor[10] reported that higher levels of efficacy when coupled with more frequent task-focused interactions among teachers predicted higher levels of curricular change. In a three-year project that utilized Cognitive Coaching to increase teachers' implementation of standards-based education, teachers who coached each other increased significantly in their reported levels of use of standards-based education than did teachers in a matched control group.[11]

Cognitive Coaching has also been used to increase growth in self-directed learning in university professors. Professors trained in Cognitive Coaching showed substantial improvement in using language more precisely in their teaching, as well as in expanding their teaching repertoires.[12]

Training in Cognitive Coaching has been associated with increases in the ability to solve problems. Teacher interns who received mentoring for a year by experienced teachers who had been trained in Cognitive Coaching wrote that they felt confident that they could solve problems, and they wrote evaluations of how they solved the various problems that they encountered. They were able to draw their own conclusions rather than looking outside themselves for answers.[13] Along those same lines, first-year teachers who received Cognitive Coaching grew significantly on the conceptual level question, "When I am told what to do . . ." [14] They moved from "black and white" thinking to having more "shades of gray" in their thinking and to thinking more on their own.

Administrators trained in Cognitive Coaching were asked to reflect on an event in which they used their Cognitive Coaching skills in order to obtain an outcome in their administrative positions. They made conscious choices and used paraphrasing, pacing and leading, and elements of rapport. They kept the five states of mind in their awareness, identified goals for their own growth, related their positive results to specific coaching maps and tools, and reflected on their growth in coaching. In addition, they identified the next steps for their own growth, recognized their own growth as well as the growth of the person they were coaching, reflected on the importance of coaching for their staff, and expressed appreciation for being asked to reflect in writing on the event.[15]

STATES OF MIND

Cognitive Coaching especially seeks to help teachers increase awareness of and skill with the five states of mind: efficacy, flexibility, consciousness, craftsmanship, and interdependence. A number of researchers have measured teacher growth in those areas. Ushijima[16] and Alseike[17] developed instruments to measure the five states of mind. Studies that were focused on measuring all of the five states of mind will be presented first, followed by studies on specific states of mind.

Studies on All Five States of Mind

Alseike focused specifically on measuring the five states of mind in her study, and she investigated various factors that could have been associated with teacher growth in them. She found that teachers who had received Cognitive Coaching from experienced coaches scored significantly higher than teachers who had not received Cognitive Coaching on measures of efficacy, flexibility, consciousness, interdependence, and overall holonomy. No significant differences were found between males and females who received Cognitive Coaching in their receptivity to coaching, nor in their states of mind of efficacy, flexibility, consciousness, interdependence, and overall holonomy. Males scored higher than females on craftsmanship.

No differences were found in the impact of Cognitive Coaching on the states of mind between teachers who had been coached by the principal, a building resource teacher, another teacher, or a combination of the three. In addition, no differences were reported by number of years of teaching experience for the states of mind of flexibility, craftsmanship, consciousness, and interdependence. Teachers with 16 to 20 years of teaching experience had higher overall states of mind, and teachers with 6 to 20 years of experience had higher efficacy than did teachers with under 6 years of experience or teachers with 21 years or more of experience.[18]

Liebmann[19] investigated how human resource developers from product and service organizations perceived the five states of mind. She found that they identified the states of mind of consciousness and interdependence, followed by flexibility, as critical attributes for all employees to have. They also placed a high value on holonomy for a democratic society.

Another study examined teachers who used Cognitive Coaching for a year and a half. They showed a 40 percent increase in efficacy, a 33 percent increase in flexibility, a 27 percent increase in consciousness, and a 37 percent increase in craftsmanship. Quantitative measures were supported by qualitative measures. When teachers used the coaching process at least four times, they showed gains in the states of mind.[20]

Studies on Efficacy

Perhaps the most frequently investigated area in Cognitive Coaching research has been teacher efficacy. Numerous studies have found benefits for students that were associated with higher levels of efficacy in teachers. These included student achievement in reading, language, and mathematics,[21] greater use of cooperative learning by teachers,[22] teacher use of fewer control tactics with students,[23] more time in large-group instruction,[24] more teacher enthusiasm and higher student grades at the middle school level,[25] fewer referrals of children from low socioeconomic status to special education,[26] more parental involvement and support,[27] and less anger for student misbehavior.[28]

The majority of the studies investigating teacher efficacy used the Teacher Efficacy Scale, developed by Gibson and Dembo.[29] Krpan and Smith used the Teacher Efficacy Scale developed by Guskey and Passaro,[30] while Alseike used a self-developed measure of efficacy.

The first study found that teachers who had been trained in Cognitive Coaching showed higher levels of teaching efficacy than did teachers in a matched control group.[31] In addition, teachers who frequently used Cognitive Coaching scored significantly higher in teaching efficacy than did teachers who used it less often.[32] In a follow-up study in the same school district, teachers who were trained in Cognitive Coaching had grown significantly in teaching efficacy between 1993 and 1996. Growth in teaching efficacy was correlated with length of time in the district, more positive attitudes toward Cognitive Coaching, implementation of a larger number of teaching practices in the previous two years, and more positive attitudes toward Professional Growth Planning.[33]

Teachers who participated in a three-year project utilizing Cognitive Coaching to help them implement standards-based education grew significantly more in teaching efficacy on the Gibson and Dembo Teacher Efficacy Scale than did teachers in a matched control group. Teachers with higher levels of teaching efficacy indicated that they used paraphrasing more frequently, asked questions more often, coached students and parents more, and generally used coaching skills more often than did teachers with lower levels of teaching efficacy.[34]

Second-year, third-year, and fourth-year teachers who participated in a seven-month program of Cognitive Coaching grew significantly on the Teacher Efficacy Scale developed by Guskey and Passaro, compared to a matched control group. They also grew significantly over the control group during the same period of time on written expressions of efficacy.[35] In addition to scoring higher on the measure, teachers in the seven-month study grew significantly over a matched control group in their perceptions of their abilities to bring about purposeful change.[36]

Alseike[37] investigated whether teachers who were coached by experienced Cognitive Coaches would score higher on a measure of the state of mind of efficacy that she developed for the study. She found that they did score significantly higher on efficacy than did a matched control group. She also found that teachers who had attended seven or more trainings given by experienced Cognitive Coaching trainers scored significantly higher on the measure of efficacy than did teachers who hadn't attended any trainings or who had attended one or two trainings, even though they had received coaching from experienced coaches. In addition, teachers who received Cognitive Coaching from experienced coaches yet had never coached another teacher scored significantly lower in efficacy than did teachers who had coached another teacher seven or more times.

One study examined teacher growth in empowerment as a result of Cognitive Coaching. Teachers who participated in Cognitive Coaching scored higher than a control group on all subscales of the Vincenz Empowerment Scale[38] and on total empowerment.[39] Teachers who grew more in total empowerment on the Vincenz Empowerment Scale indicated that they informally coached their colleagues more frequently, built rapport with colleagues more frequently, paraphrased colleagues more often, asked questions of their colleagues more often, and used pacing and leading more frequently. In another study, higher levels of empowerment were also associated with more frequent coaching conversations.[40]

Studies on Flexibility

Although teacher flexibility has not been a specific research agenda, some indications that Cognitive Coaching is associated with increased flexibility were evident in two studies. Garmston, Linder, and Whitaker[41] conducted a study in which Garmston used Cognitive Coaching with Linder and Whitaker, who were teaching. As a result of the process, Linder and Whitaker became more flexible in their thinking and teaching styles as they began to use the side of their brains that they formerly hadn't used as much. They became more balanced in using analytic and intuitive styles. In another study, teachers reported that they increased in creativity and flexibility as a result of being involved with Cognitive Coaching.[42] When asked about their sources of satisfaction in their teaching positions, teachers trained in Cognitive Coaching were more likely to mention autonomy and flexibility, as well as the opportunity to contribute to students.[43] Thus, they valued the flexibility that comes with teaching.

Studies on Consciousness

Teachers in several studies became more conscious of their teaching as they reflected on their practices. More training in Cognitive Coaching correlated with higher levels of consciousness in one study.[44] Teachers who participated in seven or more training sessions scored significantly higher in the state of mind of consciousness than did teachers who hadn't attended any trainings or had attended one or two trainings, even though they had received coaching from experienced coaches.

Cognitive Coaching has been associated with teacher growth in reflective thinking in numerous studies. In their comments on the portfolios of teachers who were using Cognitive Coaching to help them reach their goals, principals emphasized their teachers' growth in self-reflection.[45]

In another study of first-year teachers who received Cognitive Coaching from trained coaches, higher numbers of formal and informal interactions with coaches were correlated with increased growth on the Reflective Pedagogical Thinking Instrument (RPT),[46] a measure of reflective thinking about teaching.[47] In addition, the first-year teachers who filled out more interaction sheets, which were their reflections on their coaching conferences, grew more on the RPT than did those who filled out fewer interaction sheets.[48]

In another study of teacher reflection, Jewish day school teachers who received three cycles of Cognitive Coaching over a period of seven months were compared with a group of teachers who received traditional evaluation, which included observations by administrators and letters containing suggestions after the observations. They were also compared with a group of teachers who participated in informal discussions about their classroom instruction. Although all of the teachers grew on the RPT, teachers who received Cognitive Coaching grew significantly more than did the control groups.[49]

Schlosser[50] found that teachers who participated in Cognitive Coaching training and coached each other reported that Cognitive Coaching assisted them in thinking more precisely about their teaching. They hypothesized that they had become more reflective as a result.

Teachers who were supervising student teachers indicated that using Cognitive Coaching with their student teachers impacted their own teaching, and they found themselves using nonjudgmental feedback with their students and reflecting more on their lessons.[51]

In another study, teachers using Cognitive Coaching reflected more deeply on their practice at the end of the project than at the beginning.[52] In yet another study, second-year, third-year, and fourth-year teachers who participated in Cognitive Coaching over a seven-month period increased their ability to think reflectively on qualitative measures. They grew in awareness about their teaching practices, became more observant, and gained greater insights into their teaching. This self-reflection helped them to re-define their perceptions about their teaching roles. They also grew in their appreciation for the value of self-reflection.[53]

Teachers indicated that they had become more conscious of their teaching practices. In a study of second-, third-, and fourth-year teachers, teachers indicated that they grew in awareness of their teaching practices as a result of coaching.[54]

Graduate students in educational administration and leadership who used formative portfolio assessment, reflective practice, and Cognitive Coaching indicated that they deepened in their under-standing, had opportunities to create meaning, and were able to engage in metacognitive analysis. They also said that their ability to link theory and practice was enhanced, that they became more open to exploring complex problems because they were in a safe environment, and that they redefined and reaffirmed themselves as developing leaders.[55]

Over an eight-month period, special education interns in a mas-ters program who met monthly to learn and practice Cognitive Coaching skills grew significantly in awareness, skill development, and application of those skills. At the end, they had also grown in their ability to think reflectively, to self-analyze and self-evaluate, and to apply the coaching skills in their teaching.[56]

In a peer coaching program in which professors received 42 hours of training in Cognitive Coaching, they showed a maximum im-provement in their ability to analyze and evaluate themselves. They also grew in self-perception and the ability to autonomously perform cognitive activities.[57]

Studies on Craftsmanship

Teaching is a craft, and another goal of Cognitive Coaching is to help teachers grow in their craftsmanship. As with the other states of mind, research evidence suggests that teachers do, in fact, grow in craftsmanship as a result of Cognitive Coaching.

In chapters 2 and 7, it was suggested that teaching consists of planning, teaching, analyzing, evaluating, and applying. Foster[58] conducted a study in which she examined the impact of Cognitive Coaching on teacher perceptions of their thought processes in those areas. She found that teachers who participated in seven or more coaching conferences perceived that Cognitive Coaching had a high level of impact on their thought processes in the areas of planning, teaching, analyzing, evaluating, and applying. Teachers who participated in four to six coaching conferences reported that Cognitive Coaching had an average impact on planning, teaching, and applying, and a high impact on analyzing and evaluating. Teachers who participated in one to three coaching conferences reported that Cognitive Coaching had an average impact on their thought processes in the areas, and teachers who participated in no coaching conferences reported that Cognitive Coaching had a low impact on their thought processes in the areas. No differences were found between elementary and secondary teachers in their perceptions of the impact that Cognitive Coaching had on their thought processes. Furthermore, no differences were found in the perceptions of impact on thought processes between teachers who were coached by an administrator and teachers who were coached by another teacher.

Alseike[59] built on Foster's study and examined the impact of cognitive coaching on teacher thought processes. Teachers who participated in seven or more Cognitive Coaching training sessions scored significantly higher on teaching, applying, and overall instructional processes than those who hadn't attended any sessions or only one or two sessions. All of the teachers received Cognitive Coaching from experienced trainers.

Alseike also examined the effects of Cognitive Coaching in a variety of coaching situations and found that teachers who had been coached by experienced coaches scored significantly higher on measures of planning, teaching, analyzing, and applying than did teachers who had not received Cognitive Coaching. No differences were found according to years of experience in how teachers reported that Cognitive Coaching impacted their instructional processes in the areas of planning, teaching, analyzing, applying, or overall instructional process. Furthermore, teachers who received Cognitive Coaching from experienced coaches yet had never coached another teacher scored significantly lower in teaching and applying than did teachers who had coached another teacher seven or more times.

Whether teachers were coached formally—including planning conversations, classroom observations, and reflecting conversations—or informally, they identified Cognitive Coaching as having a positive impact on their teaching. No significant differences were found between males and females who received Cognitive Coaching on their report of its impact on their planning, analyzing, and applying. Females scored higher than males on teaching. No differences were found in the impact of Cognitive Coaching on the instructional processes of planning, teaching, analyzing, and applying between teachers who had been coached by the principal, a building resource teacher, another teacher, or a combination of the three.

As a result of being coached for a year, senior high teachers reported that the coaching facilitated the achievement of their goals because they changed the strategies they used in teaching their students.[60] In other words, they grew in craftsmanship. Teachers who used Cognitive Coaching more frequently obtained significantly higher scores on the Self-Reflection Survey: Cognitive Coaching Rating Scale[61] than did those who used it less. Subscales included planning, teaching, analyzing and evaluating, and applying.[62] Edwards and Green[63] found that practice in using Cognitive Coaching skills is essential in order to bring about the growth that is possible through Cognitive Coaching.

Studies on Interdependence

Cognitive Coaching has also been found to affect interdependence. Principals identified collaboration with supervisors on work goals, frequent interaction with and observation by supervisors, responsive practices, and trusting relationships as contributing to their growth.[64]

In the study by Alseike,[65] teachers who were coached formally—including the planning conversation, observation, and reflecting conversation—scored significantly higher on a measure of interdependence. She also found that teachers who were coached by experienced Cognitive Coaches scored significantly higher on interdependence than did a matched control group of teachers who had never experienced Cognitive Coaching. In another study, teachers involved in a year-long Cognitive Coaching program indicated that they were satisfied with their positions because of the support that they gave to one another.[66]

In yet another study, Cognitive Coaching impacted the amount of time that teachers talked with one another. As a result of being coached for a year, senior high teachers talked more with their colleagues about their teaching and ceased being concerned about the extra time involved in coaching.[67]

Teachers who participated in Cognitive Coaching scored significantly higher than a control group on the relatedness subscale equivalent to the state of mind of interdependence of the Vincenz Empowerment Scale.[68]

THE IMPACT OF COGNITIVE COACHING ON STUDENTS

The goal of every school initiative is to benefit students, and research evidence exists to suggest that Cognitive Coaching achieves this goal as well. In a three-year project utilizing Cognitive Coaching, monthly dialogue groups, and nonverbal classroom management to assist teachers in implementing standards-based education, differences in changes for the treatment and control schools were found on the Iowa Test of Basic Skills (ITBS) for the Total ITBS Score and the Integrated Writing Total Score between year 1 and year 3, for Math Advanced Skills and Integrated Writing Advanced Skills between years 1 and 2 and between years 1 and 3, and for the Math Total Score between years 1 and 2. No marked differences were found for Reading Advanced Skills or for the Reading Total Score. Although the scores for control schools improved over time, the improvements found for treatment schools exceeded the changes for control schools.[69]

In that same study, teachers who used Cognitive Coaching decreased significantly in referring students to special education, compared with teachers in a matched control group. This finding was substantiated in the focus groups when teachers said, "In the past when I had a student who was having difficulty, I would have referred him or her to special education right away. Now I ask a colleague to come in and coach me on how to make him success-ful. As a result, we are able to make him successful in the regular classroom."

The use of Cognitive Coaching was associated with teacher use of more higher-order thinking skills in other studies. In one study, teachers trained in Cognitive Coaching grew significantly on the Encouragement of Higher Order Thinking Skills subscale of the Teacher Survey[70] over a matched control group.[71]

In another study, as a result of being coached for a year, senior high teachers taught more thinking skills to their students and modeled the skills of coaching.[72] In their comments on the portfo-lios of teachers who were using Cognitive Coaching to help them reach their goals, principals emphasized their teachers' increased used of higher-level questions with students and their growth in communicating with and working with students.[73]

In a study by McLymont and da Costa,[74] teachers trained in Cog-nitive Coaching found themselves consciously creating an atmo-sphere of trust and nonjudgmentalness in their classrooms, seeking to help their students arrive at decisions on their own.

Students of teachers who were trained in Cognitive Coaching were assessed in their question asking skills for quantity and quality. In one semester, 78 percent of the students increased the quantity of questions asked, 74 percent of the students improved the quality of the questions they asked, and 65 percent of the students reduced the number of irrelevant responses they gave. In one year, 85 per-cent of the students increased the quantity of questions asked, 91 percent of the students improved the quality of the questions they asked, and 46 percent of the students reduced the number of irrel-evant responses they gave. Students of teachers who participated in more coaching cycles gained more than did students of teachers who participated in fewer coaching cycles.[75]

In that same study, students of teachers who were trained in Cog-nitive Coaching were also assessed in their math problem-solving skills. In one year, 86 percent of the students showed gains in their math problem-solving skills. Students of teachers who participated in more coaching gained more than did students of teachers who participated in less coaching.

In yet another study, high school sophomores viewed 10- to 15-minute videotapes of their teacher being cognitively coached twice a week for six weeks, and the control group of students viewed videotapes of the teacher reporting the results of the coaching conversation for the same period of time. Those who viewed the tapes of the Cognitive Coaching conversations increased in the use of verification behaviors in problem solving. The differences approached significance.[76]

THE IMPACT OF COGNITIVE COACHING ON INDIVIDUAL TEACHERS PROFESSIONALLY

Studies have shown that Cognitive Coaching affects individual teachers professionally. Teachers grew significantly on Saphier's teacher professionalism and goal-setting subscale of the School Culture Survey over a matched control group.[77] Teachers who had higher scores on teacher professionalism and goal setting built rapport with others more frequently and participated in more coaching cycles. Supervising teachers indicated that by supervising student teachers using Cognitive Coaching, they increased in their sense of professionalism.[78] Teachers who had been trained in Cognitive Coaching said that some of the reasons they liked Cognitive Coaching were that it was respectful of teachers, it was nonjudgmental, and it made sense.[79]

Teachers who participated in a three-year project utilizing Cognitive Coaching increased in satisfaction with their positions, and with their choice of teaching as a profession, compared to teachers in a matched control group.[80] In other studies, teachers who engaged in Cognitive Coaching were significantly more satisfied with teaching as a profession than were teachers in a matched control group who had not taken Cognitive Coaching training.[81]

In a peer coaching program for professors in which they received 42 hours of training in Cognitive Coaching, the professors showed a maximum improvement in their ability to analyze and evaluate themselves. They also grew in self-perception and the ability to autonomously perform cognitive activities. In addition, they developed increased confidence in themselves and greater enthusiasm for teaching.[82] In another study, second-year, third-year, and fourth-year teachers grew significantly in seven months over a matched control group in expressions of how they had grown professionally. They indicated that they had numerous opportunities to grow and change professionally.[83]

COGNITIVE COACHING AND SUPERVISORY RELATIONSHIPS

The use of Cognitive Coaching in supervisory relationships has also been explored. Mackie[84] compared teachers who used the Cognitive Coaching format with teachers who received traditional supervision. Those who used Cognitive Coaching rated the overall quality of the observation process significantly higher. They also indicated that the collegial coaching process had more impact on their teaching practices as well as on their attitudes toward teaching.

In another study, first-year teachers who received Cognitive Coaching from trained coaches expressed more satisfaction with the supervision they received than did first-year teachers who received traditional supervision.[85]

THE IMPACT OF COGNITIVE COACHING ON STAFF AS A TEAM

According to several studies, as Cognitive Coaching was practiced and used, teamwork of the staff was enhanced and school cultures became more collaborative. In one study, teachers reported that, as a result of Cognitive Coaching training and implementation, they noticed more of a sense of community in the school, they talked more with each other about teaching, and the atmosphere in the school was more positive. Teachers also indicated that they had more rapport with each other, they seemed more open to growth and new ideas, and they tended to evaluate themselves more frequently.[86] In a study by McLymont and da Costa,[87] teachers using Cognitive Coaching to improve their teaching of mathematics developed a collaborative coaching community as they worked together to discover new insights about their teaching.

The School Culture Survey[88] was used in a three-year study.[89] In this study, teachers trained in Cognitive Coaching grew significantly on the Administrator Professional Treatment of Teachers subscale over a matched control group. Teachers who felt that their administrators treated them more professionally also participated in more coaching cycles. In addition, teachers grew significantly on Saphier's collaboration subscale of the School Culture Survey over a matched control group. Teachers who had higher scores in collaboration built rapport more frequently, participated in more coaching cycles, and believed that they had changed more as a result of their use of Cognitive Coaching.

A year-long study of teachers using Cognitive Coaching found that team teaching improved, teachers had more of a sense of community, they trusted each other more, they had greater resiliency, they shared ideas more, they felt more comfortable with taking risks, they solved problems together, they were more accepting of differences because of mutual respect, they communicated more across grade levels, and they gave and received more support and feedback in their work with children.[90]

Teachers who supervised student teachers using Cognitive Coaching indicated that they benefited because they were able to network with other educators.[91] Teachers reported that positive influences on their attitudes toward Cognitive Coaching included the fact that it positively influenced their school's culture and that they were able to work together in coaching triads to support each other.[92]

Teachers were more positive in their comments about teaching and expressed more positive feelings about all aspects of their experiences as teachers than did teachers who did not take Cognitive Coaching training. Those trained in Cognitive Coaching listed 16 sources of dissatisfaction with their positions, and those who hadn't taken the training listed 57 sources of dissatisfaction.[93]

COGNITIVE COACHING IN MENTORING AND TEACHER PREPARATION PROGRAMS

Cognitive Coaching has been examined in mentoring and teacher preparation programs. In one study, teachers in a graduate program of educational administration and leadership focusing on collaboration were coached each semester on their formative portfolios. In addition, they wrote reflectively on each document or artifact. They reported that Cognitive Coaching was one of the most powerful aspects of the program. In addition, they said that later in their careers, when they were in difficult situations, they found themselves thinking about their coaching experiences and realizing that they had the resources they needed within themselves to be successful.[94]

Beginning teachers in the Student-Teacher Expanded Program (STEP), an alternative teacher training program, participated in one-year internships and received mentoring from teachers who had been trained in Cognitive Coaching. They were compared with teachers in a traditional 12-week student teaching program. Those who participated in the STEP program increased significantly over the control group on ratings by self, supervising teacher, and university supervisor on all subscales of the Proficiencies for Teachers Survey, including Learner-Centered Knowledge, Learner-Centered Instruction, Equity in Excellence, Learner-Centered Communications, and Learner-Centered Professional Development. The areas of Learner-Centered Knowledge and Equity in Excellence were the most robust.[95]

Student teachers who had received 10 hours of training along with their supervising teachers reported that Cognitive Coaching provided them with a greater understanding of why teaching occurs the way it does, facilitated trust with their cooperating teacher, caused them to think deeply as they planned lessons, provided a common language for them to share with their cooperating teachers, and helped them anticipate the lesson in the planning conversation and bring closure to the lesson in the reflecting conversation. In addition, Cognitive Coaching provided a structure that gave them time to think about their teaching, required the supervising teacher to use the recommended coaching practices of nonjudgmental responses, helped them to own the lesson and to feel a sense of power, helped them when they received support, and worked best when the supervising teacher had confidence in Cognitive Coaching.[96]

In the same study, cooperating teachers who had received 10 hours of training in Cognitive Coaching along with their student teachers reported that Cognitive Coaching helped them to become more conscious about their teaching, validated their beliefs about teaching, worked well for both progressive and traditional teachers, encouraged them to have collegial relationships with other coaches, enhanced the reflection of teachers who were already reflective, and helped them to realize the value of listening by using paraphrasing and probing. In addition, the success of the program depended on the ability of the cooperating teachers to use the Cognitive Coaching strategies effectively.

A study in which supervising teacher mentors used Cognitive Coaching with student teachers found that the training was an excellent way to prepare mentor teachers. These authors concluded that Cognitive Coaching impacted mentors in all areas, including their work with student teachers, their own students, and other teachers. In the same study, supervising teachers indicated that by supervising student teachers using Cognitive Coaching, they increased their sense of professionalism and were able to network with other educators.[97]

THE IMPACT OF COGNITIVE COACHING ON TEACHERS' PERSONAL LIVES

Teachers reported that Cognitive Coaching not only impacted them professionally, it impacted them personally. In an early study, they listed usability of skills in all areas of their lives as the number one source of satisfaction with Cognitive Coaching. They listed self-growth as the second source of satisfaction.[98]

In another study, teachers indicated that they first used Cognitive Coaching in their personal lives before using it in their professional lives because trust had already been established in those relationships.[99]

In a study by Awakuni[100] in which teachers participated in Cognitive Coaching for a year, teachers reported having increased confidence in themselves and a greater sense of self.

QUESTIONS FOR ADDITIONAL RESEARCH

Many areas have been investigated so far in Cognitive Coaching research, and many areas remain to be investigated. The following sections include ideas for additional studies to investigate its impacts on students, school teams, and teachers, both professionally and personally.

Questions About the Impact on Students

So far, researchers have studied the outcomes of teachers coaching each other, or the outcomes of teachers being coached by administrators, university professors, or full-time coaches. A major area for future research involves studying what might happen when teachers coach students. What might be some of the outcomes if teachers taught coaching skills to students so that they could coach each other? In what ways might that impact student growth and thinking? How might student learning be accelerated through the process?

Some possible areas to explore could be student time on task, self-directedness of students, students' views of themselves as self-directed learners, student identity, student interactions with one another in general, student interactions in terms of problem solving when conflicts arise, frequency of students asking questions, number of discipline referrals, student grades, student development of higher-order thinking skills, and student growth in the five states of mind. Other possible areas to explore might be how student relationships with each other would change, how student relationships with the teacher could change, how student relationships with their parents might change, and how students resolved difficulties. What might happen at the different grade levels? Would similar outcomes occur at all grade levels, or would students in some grade levels change more quickly?

Questions About the Impact on School Staff

More research could be done to investigate the effects of Cognitive Coaching on entire schools. Some investigations might examine principal-teacher interactions in the school. For example, what changes might occur in the ways that the principal interacts with individual staff members? What changes could occur in the ways that the principal interacts with the staff as a group? What might be some changes in the ways that the staff members interact with the principal? What could be some changes in the ways that staff members interact with each other? What changes might occur in weekly staff meetings?

Other possibilities might be to investigate how personal relationships between teachers in the school could change. What changes might occur in how teams of teachers interacted with other teams? What could be some of the changes in how teams interacted within their teams? What changes might teachers notice in their friendships with other teachers in the school? Would fewer arguments and disagreements occur?

Further possibilities could include investigations of the impact on schoolwide problems. When problems occur, what are some of the strategies that teachers and administrators use to resolve them? Would fewer difficulties and issues arise as a result of all staff using Cognitive Coaching? Fewer major problems and conflicts should occur, because Cognitive Coaching training and use could provide teachers with the skills to be able to work together and coach each other in an atmosphere of trust and rapport in order to solve problems while they were still small.

Still other investigations might examine how Cognitive Coaching might contribute to schools becoming Learning Organizations.[101] What might happen to teachers' desire to learn? How could that desire be passed on to students?

Questions About the Impact on Teachers' Professional Lives

In what other ways does Cognitive Coaching impact teacher professionalism? What might be some contributing factors giving teachers more enjoyment of teaching as a profession? In what ways would teacher-parent conferences be different in schools in which teachers used Cognitive Coaching on a regular basis? How might Cognitive Coaching impact the number of conflicts that teachers had with parents or that teachers had with children? What changes could occur in the ways that teachers viewed themselves professionally? In what ways might Cognitive Coaching impact teachers' desire to learn and try new skills, to get higher degrees, and to take more classes? How might Cognitive Coaching impact teachers' emphasis with students on the five states of mind? How might teachers grow in the five states of mind? What impact would Cognitive Coaching have on teachers' sense of being isolated?

Still other studies could investigate the progression that teachers make as they learn to coach and as they implement and internalize Cognitive Coaching values, beliefs, maps, and skills.

Questions About the Impact on Teachers' Personal Lives

Studies could also address the impact of Cognitive Coaching on teachers' personal lives. How might relationships with spouses or significant others change? In what ways could their relationships with their children change? Might relationships change in different ways depending on the ages of the teachers' children? What could be some trends in how teachers' friendships outside school might change?

Other investigations might examine the teacher as a person. What impact could Cognitive Coaching have on teacher emotions, such as happiness, sadness, enthusiasm, or anger? How might Cognitive Coaching impact teacher curiosity and creativity? What might be some changes in teacher self-concept? What changes could occur in teacher identity and how teachers see themselves? What might be some possible changes in teachers' abilities, desires, and inclinations to be self-directed learners?

Questions About Cognitive Coaching and the Larger Community

An even larger systemic inquiry might involve examining the impact of a school's use of Cognitive Coaching on the surrounding community. How might schools change in their interactions and relationships with the local community? What changes might begin to occur in families as a result of students experiencing coaching at school?

Other studies might investigate what happens in other schools in a school district in which one school begins using Cognitive Coaching. What impact might one school's use of Cognitive Coaching have on teachers in other schools? When teachers at a school that uses Cognitive Coaching interact with teachers in other schools at district-wide inservices and at other meetings, what might be some of the effects?

Possible Avenues for Collecting Data

A range of possibilities exists for collecting data on the above-mentioned research questions. Possible avenues for collecting data might be in-depth interviews with teachers, students, parents, and members of the community, videos or audiotapes of coaching conversations, teacher journals, teacher testimony, lesson plans, teacher language, teacher questions, commercially prepared instruments, and instruments in educational journals or papers. Other possibilities include measuring levels of use and stages of concern from the Concerns-Based Adoption Model (CBAM),[102] and observing interactions in schools and classrooms.

CONCLUSION

Much research has been done to investigate the impacts of Cognitive Coaching, and much remains to be done. As school districts involve teachers in investigating the outcomes of Cognitive Coaching training and use on students, teachers, the school, and the community, the field will advance even further. More research is needed in order to learn more about why Cognitive Coaching is producing the kinds of results reported here.

NOTES

1. Dr. Edwards can be reached at jedwards@fielding.edu or jedwards23@yahoo.com.

2. Edwards, J. L., and Green, K. (1997). *The effects of Cognitive Coaching on teacher efficacy and empowerment* (Research Rep. No. 1997-1). Evergreen, CO: Authors.

3. Awakuni, G. (1995). *The impact of Cognitive Coaching as perceived by the Kalani high school core team.* Doctoral dissertation, The Union Institute. Dissertation Abstracts International, 9613169.

4. Edwards, J. L., and Newton, R. R. (October 1994). *Qualitative assessment of the effects of Cognitive Coaching training as evidenced through teacher portfolios and journals.* (Research Rep. No. 1994-3). Evergreen, CO: Authors.

✕ 5. Garmston, R., Linder, C., and Whitaker, J. (October, 1993). Reflections on Cognitive Coaching. *Educational Leadership, 51* (2), 57–61.

6. Awakuni, G. *The impact of Cognitive Coaching.*

✠ 7. Edwards, J. L., and Newton, R. R. (February, 1994). *The effects of Cognitive Coaching on teacher efficacy and empowerment.* (Research Rep. No. 1994–1). Evergreen, CO: Authors.

8. Krpan, M. M. (1997). *Cognitive Coaching and efficacy, growth, and change for second-, third-, and fourth-year elementary school educators.* Master's thesis, California State University at Fullerton. Masters Abstracts International, 35/04, AAD13-84152.

9. Poole, M. G. (1987). *Implementing change: The effects of teacher efficacy and interactions among educators.* Doctoral dissertation, University of New Orleans. Dissertation Abstracts International, 52/03-A, AAD91-21469.

✕ 10. Poole, M. G., and Okeafor, K. R. (Winter, 1989). The effects of teacher efficacy and interactions among educators on curriculum implementation. *Journal of Curriculum and Supervision 4* (2), 146–161.

11. Hull, J., Edwards, J. L., Rogers, M. S., and Swords, M. E. (1998). *The Pleasant View experience.* Golden, CO: Jefferson County Schools.

12. Garmston, R., and Hyerle, D. (August, 1988). *Professors' peer coaching program: Report on a 1987-88 pilot project to develop and test a staff development model for improving instruction at California State University.* Sacramento: Authors.

13. Burk, J., Ford, M. B., Guffy, T., and Mann, G. (February, 1996). *Reconceptualizing student teaching: A STEP forward.* Paper presented at the annual meeting of the American Association of Colleges for Teacher Education, Chicago.

14. Edwards, J. L. (1993). *The effect of Cognitive Coaching on the conceptual development and reflective thinking of first year teachers.* Doctoral dissertation, The Fielding Institute. Dissertation Abstracts International, 54/03-A, AAD93-20751.

15. Lipton, L. (1993). *Transforming information into knowledge: Structured reflection in administrative practice.* Paper presented at the annual meeting of the American Educational Research Association, New Orleans.

16. Ushijima, T. M. (1996). *Five states of mind scale for Cognitive Coaching: A measurement study.* Doctoral dissertation, University of Southern California. Dissertation Abstracts International, AAT9720306.

17. Alseike, B. U. (1997). *Cognitive Coaching: Its influences on teachers.* Doctoral dissertation, University of Denver. Dissertation Abstracts International, 9804083.

18. Ibid.

19. Liebmann, R. M. (1993). *Perceptions of human resource developers as to the initial and desired states of holonomy of managerial and manual employees.* Doctoral dissertation, Seton Hall University. Dissertation Abstracts International, 54/05-A, AAD93-27374.

20. Ushijima, T. (Spring, 1996). *The impact of Cognitive Coaching as a staff development process on student question asking and math problem solving skills.* (Research Rep. No. 1996-1). Honolulu: Author.

21. Tracz, S. M., and Gibson, S. (November, 1986). *Effects of efficacy on academic achievement.* Paper presented at the annual meeting of the California Educational Research Association, Marina del Rey.

22. Dutton, M. M. (1990). *Learning and teacher job satisfaction.* Portland State University. Dissertation Abstracts International, 51/05-A, AAD90-26940.

23. Ashton, P., Webb, R., and Doda, C. (1983). *A study of teachers' sense of efficacy.* Gainesville: University of Florida.

24. Gibson, S., and Dembo, M. H. (1984). Teacher efficacy: A construct validation. *Journal of Educational Psychology 36* (4), 569–582.

25. Newman, E. J. (1993). The effect of teacher efficacy, locus-of-control, and teacher enthusiasm on student on-task behavior and achievement. Doctoral dissertation, Florida State University. Dissertation Abstracts International, 54/07A, AAD93-34264.

26. Podell, D. M., and Soodak, L. C. (March/April, 1993). Teacher efficacy and bias in special education referrals. *Journal of Educational Research, 86* (4), 247–253.

27. Hoover-Dempsey, K. V., Bassler, O. C., and Brissie, J. S. (Fall, 1987). Parent involvement: Contributions of teacher efficacy, school socioeconomic status, and other school characteristics. *American Educational Research Journal 24* (3), 417–435.

28. Glenn, R. A. (1993). Teacher attribution: Affect linkages as a function of student academic and behavior failure and teacher efficacy (academic failure). Doctoral dissertation, Memphis State University. Dissertation Abstracts International, 54/12-A, AAD94014958.

29. Gibson and Dembo, Teacher efficacy: A construct validation.

30. Guskey, T. R., and Passaro, P. (1993). *Teacher efficacy: A study of construct dimensions.* Lexington, KY: University of Kentucky.

31. Edwards, J. L., and Newton, R. R. (1995). *The effects of Cognitive Coaching on teacher efficacy and empowerment.* Paper presented at the annual meeting of the American Educational Research Association, San Francisco.

32. Edwards, J. L., and Newton, R. R. (July, 1994). *The effects of Cognitive Coaching on teacher efficacy and thinking about teaching.* (Research Rep. No. 1994-2). Evergreen, CO: Authors.

33. Edwards and Green, K. (1997). *The effects of Cognitive Coaching.*

34. Edwards, J. L., Green, K., Lyons, C. A., Rogers, M. S., and Swords, M. (1998). *The effects of Cognitive Coaching and nonverbal classroom management on teacher efficacy and perceptions of school culture.* Paper presented at the annual meeting of the American Educational Research Association, San Diego.

35. Krpan, *Cognitive Coaching.*

36. Smith, M. C. (1997). *Self-reflection as a means of increasing teacher efficacy through Cognitive Coaching.* Master's thesis, California

State University at Fullerton. Masters Abstracts International, 1384304.

37. Alseike, *Cognitive Coaching.*

38. Vincenz, L. (1990). *Development of the Vincenz empowerment scale.* Doctoral Dissertation, Dissertation Abstracts International, 9031010 University of Marland, College Park, MY.

39. Edwards and Green (1997), *The effects of Cognitive Coaching.*

40. Edwards and Newton (1995), *The effects of Cognitive Coaching.*

41. Garmston, et al. Reflections on Cognitive Coaching.

42. McLymont, E. F., and da Costa, J. L. (1998). *Cognitive Coaching: The vehicle for professional development and teacher collaboration.* Paper presented at the annual meeting of the American Educational Research Association, San Diego.

43. Edwards and Newton, *Qualitative assessment.*

44. Alseike, *Cognitive Coaching.*

45. Edwards and Newton, *Qualitative assessment.*

46. Simmons, J. M., Sparks, G. M., Starko, A., Pasch, M., and Colton, A. (1989). *Pedagogical language acquisition and conceptual development taxonomy of teacher reflective thought: Interview and questions format.*

47. Edwards, *The effect of Cognitive Coaching.*

48. Ibid.

49. Moche, R. (1999). *Cognitive Coaching and reflective thinking of Jewish day school teachers.* Doctoral dissertation, Yeshiva University. Dissertation Abstracts International, 9919383.

50. Schlosser, J. L. (1998). *The impact of Cognitive Coaching on the thinking processes of elementary school teachers.* Doctoral dissertation, Brigham Young University. Dissertation Abstracts International, 9821080.

51. Clinard, L. M, Mirón, L., Ariav, T., Botzer, I., Conroy, J., Laycock, K., and Yule, K. (March, 1997). *A cross-cultural perspective of teachers' perceptions: What contributions are exchanged between cooperating teachers and student teachers?* Paper presented at the annual

meeting of the American Educational Research Association, Chicago.

52. McLymont and da Costa, *Cognitive Coaching.*

53. Smith, *Self-reflection.*

54. Krpan, *Cognitive Coaching.*

55. Geltner, B. B. (1994). *The power of structural and symbolic redesign: Creating a collaborative learning community in higher education* (Descriptive Report #141). Rochester, MI. Oakland University.

56. McMahon, P. J. (1997). *Cognitive Coaching and special education advanced practicum interns: A study in peer coaching.* Master's thesis, University of Hawaii. Masters Abstracts International, 1385959.

57. Garmston and Hyerle, *Professors' peer coaching program.*

58. Foster, N. J. (1989). *The impact of Cognitive Coaching on teachers' thought processes as perceived by cognitively coached teachers in the Plymouth-Canton Community School District.* Doctoral dissertation, Michigan State University. Dissertation Abstracts International, 27, 54381.

59. Alseike, *Cognitive Coaching.*

60. Sommers, W., and Costa, A. (1993). Bo Peep was wrong. *NASSP Bulletin. 77* (557), 110–113.

61. Schuman, S. (1991). *Self-reflection survey: Cognitive Coaching rating scale.* Federal Way, WA: Federal Way Public Schools.

62. Edwards and Newton, *The effects of Cognitive Coaching on teacher efficacy and thinking about teaching.*

63. Edwards, J. L., and Green, K. (1999). *Persisters versus nonpersisters: Characteristics of teachers who stay in a professional development program.* Paper presented at the annual meeting of the American Educational Research Association, Montreal.

64. McDonough, S. (1991). *The supervision of principals: A comparison of existing and desired supervisory practices as perceived by principals trained in Cognitive Coaching and those without Cognitive Coaching training.* Unpublished master's thesis, California State University, Sacramento.

65. Alseike, *Cognitive Coaching.*

66. Awakuni, *The impact of Cognitive Coaching.*

67. Sommers and Costa, Bo Peep.

68. Edwards and Green (1997), *The effects of Cognitive Coaching.*

69. Hull et al., *The Pleasant View Experience.* See also Grinder, M. (1996). *ENVoY: A personal guide to classroom management* (3rd ed.). Battle Ground, WA: Michael Grinder and Associates for information about nonverbal classroom management.

70. McCombs, B. (1995). *Teacher survey.* Aurora, CO: Mid-Continent Regional Educational Laboratory.

71. Hull, et al., *The Pleasant View Experience.*

72. Sommers and Costa, Bo Peep.

73. Edwards and Newton, *Qualitative assessment.*

74. McLymont and da Costa, Cognitive Coaching.

75. Ushijima, *The impact of Cognitive Coaching.*

76. Muchlinski, T. E. (1995). *Using Cognitive Coaching to model metacognition during instruction.* Doctoral Dissertation, University of North Carolina at Chapel Hill. Dissertation Abstracts International, 56/07-A, AADAA-19538459.

77. Edwards et al., *The effects of Cognitive Coaching and nonverbal classroom management.* See also Saphier, J. (1989). *The school culture survey.* Acton, MA: Research for Better Teaching.

78. Clinard et al., *A cross-cultural perspective.*

79. Edwards and Newton, (February, 1994), *The effects of Cognitive Coaching.*

80. Edwards et al. *The effects of Cognitive Coaching and nonverbal classroom management.*

81. Edwards and Newton (February, 1994), *The effects of Cognitive Coaching*; Edwards and Newton (July, 1994), *The effects of Cognitive Coaching*; Edwards and Newton, *Qualitative assessment*; Edwards and Newton (1995), *The effects of Cognitive Coaching.*

82. Garmston and Hyerle, *Professors' peer coaching program.*

83. Krpan, *Cognitive Coaching.*

84. Mackie, D. J. (1998). *Collegial observation: An alternative teacher evaluation strategy using Cognitive Coaching to promote professional growth and development.* Doctoral dissertation, Wilmington College. Dissertation Abstracts International, 9826689.

85. Edwards, *The effect of Cognitive Coaching.*

86. Edwards and Newton (July, 1994), *The effects of Cognitive Coaching.*

87. McLymont and da Costa, *Cognitive Coaching.*

88. Saphier, *The School Culture Survey.* Acton, MA: Research for Better Teaching.

89. Edwards et al., *The effects of Cognitive Coaching and nonverbal classroom management.*

90. Ushijima, *The impact of Cognitive Coaching.*

91. Clinard et al., *A cross-cultural perspective.*

92. Edwards and Newton (February, 1994), *The effects of Cognitive Coaching.*

93. Edwards and Newton (1995), *The effects of Cognitive Coaching.*

94. Geltner, *The power of structural and symbolic redesign.*

95. Burk, J., Ford M.B., Guffy, T., and Mann, G. (February, 1996). *Reconceptualizing student teaching; A STEP forward.* Paper presented at the annual meeting of the American Association of Colleges for Teacher Education, Chicago.

96. Townsend, S. (1995). *Understanding the effects of Cognitive Coaching on student teachers and cooperating teachers.* Doctoral dissertation, University of Denver. Dissertation Abstracts International, 9544000.

97. Clinard, et al., *A cross-cultural perspective.*

98. Edwards, and Newton (February, 1994), *The effects of Cognitive Coaching.*

99. Schlosser, *The impact of Cognitive Coaching.*

100. Awakuni, *The impact of Cognitive Coaching.*

101. Senge, P., Cambron-McCabe, N., Lucas, T., Smith, B., Dutton, J., and Kleiner, A. (2000). *Schools that learn: A fifth discipline fieldbook for educators, parents, and everyone who cares about education.* New York: Doubleday.

102. Hall, G. E., and Hord, S. M. (2001). *Implementing change: Patterns, principles, and potholes.* Boston: Allyn and Bacon.

15

Toward an Educational Renaissance

How wonderful it is that nobody need wait a single moment to improve the world.

—Anne Frank

What do we mean when we speak of an "educational Renaissance" and "Renaissance schools"? Let us first begin with the idea that the word *renaissance* means a rebirth or revival. The term is most often associated with the great European revival of art, literature, science, and learning from the 14th to the 17th centuries. These years saw a return to classical Greek and Roman values: the laws of Plato, the logic of Aristotle, and the inquiry of Socrates. The Renaissance was the age of European voyages of exploration; Gutenberg's gift of mass literacy; Leonardo da Vinci's inventiveness; Martin Luther's challenging perspectives; and Michelangelo's profound artistic innovations.

The Renaissance was especially a time for new perspectives, as embodied in Galileo's bold theories about the earth, the planets, motion, and space. In architecture, the prevailing Gothic flatness, austerity, and severity gave way to soaring, innovative lines and shapes. New forms of artistic expression also flowered. Experimental science began to challenge existing fatalistic beliefs in the occult, magic, and astrology.

Humanism became the major intellectual movement of the period (and achieved a permanence that flourishes today). Humanism emphasizes a flexible approach to society's problems and an active life in service to one's fellow human beings. Humanism also emphasizes human consciousness and emotion along with the idea that we all are a part of a larger system and have control over the environment and ourselves.

Perhaps the best and most widely known example of Renaissance art is Michelangelo's statue of David. This 18-foot titan not only portrays the triumph of divine victory over evil but also a new era and a new outlook. The figure of David comes from the Bible story of the Israelites surrounded by barbarian hordes. The brutish giant Goliath challenges the Israelites to send someone to fight him. A young shepherd boy, David, volunteers, armed with a simple sling in one hand and some stones in the other.

Michelangelo's David captures the essence of Renaissance optimism: he is a civilized, thoughtful, confident individual who can grapple with and overcome obstacles, yet he is also vulnerable. David's gaze is shaded by thoughtful contemplation. He is gathering data and sizing up his adversary. He has no armor to protect him, only his internal resources. His strength is in his body and his intellect, and his simple weapons are of minor importance. (The stones held in his left hand are barely visible, and the sling is draped out of sight over his shoulder.)

Poised, unabashed, and vulnerable, Michelangelo's David goes forth to protect his community. David truly represents the values of the Renaissance: a sense of autonomy and self-assurance, with a commitment to the larger group. David is thoughtful, courageous, unfettered, and resourceful.

The spirit of holonomy is revealed in David's inner strength and dedication to community. We can find the five states of mind in the Renaissance attributes he portrays: efficacy, consciousness, craftsmanship, flexibility, and interdependence.

Some of the adjectives that describe historical Renaissance values also describe the renaissance we see in today's schools:

diverse	flexible	conscious
experimental	contemplative	civilized
thoughtful	bold	courageous
confident	committed	vulnerable
resourceful	interdependent	open
logical	autonomous	inventive
principled	inquiring	adventuresome

Renaissance schools are neither places to be visited nor specific locations to be described. Renaissance schools flourish in many different educational settings and programs throughout North America and beyond. Renaissance elements go by many different names: constructivist curriculum, character education, habits of mind,[1] professional communities, and standards of excellence. Renaissance schools are learning organizations engaged in a journey, moving toward fresher, clearer visions of educational settings as places of rebirth. They are communities collaborating for the best interests of students, in which all inhabitants are respected as learners.

Renaissance thought and achievement did not emerge overnight. Neither did current developments in Renaissance schools, although change is happening at a rate far faster than before. Physicists have adopted the word *jerk* to describe this rate of change. Velocity measures speed; acceleration measures the rate of increase in speed. Jerk measures the rate of increased acceleration. Futurist Joseph Pelton[2] describes humanity's current situation as "cyberjerk." *Cyberjerk* means that current changes are 10 times faster, deeper, and more profound than any revolution in human history. Today, as in the classical Renaissance period, we have a merging of many evolving economic, political, technical, artistic, and religious elements.

THE RENAISSANCE SPIRIT TODAY

Renaissance schools are works in progress. In the same way that the Renaissance spanned several centuries, the work of creating Renaissance schools will continue for many years as long as "medieval" practices abound. In too many schools, children's and teachers' spirits are compromised, creativity is stifled, inquiry is quashed, conformity is coerced, and freedom is jeopardized.[3] Still, we hear valiant stories of the Renaissance spirit as educators talk about their work, even though they often struggle under repressive systems governed by the most current fad in school reform.

For example, some educators face accountability practices based on narrow sets of numerical indicators that drive curriculum and instructional decisions. In some places, merit pay is tied to students' test scores. Other teachers struggle with instructional materials that have little value beyond practicing for the tests and curricula that stifle the learning goals and aspirations of teachers and students alike. Sometimes educators simply battle to overcome historical limits on practice: the idea that "we have always done it this way" or that "schools in our grandparents' day were basic and it was good enough."

Even amid these conditions, Renaissance energies flourish in a number of settings. Such efforts go by many names; some don't have special names heralding their efforts. The Coalition for Essential Schools, The League of Professional Schools, Adaptive Schools, Harvard's Project Zero, the School as a Home for the Mind,[4] and Multiple Intelligences Schools are examples of programs in which educators and communities coalesce around courageous visions of learning. These schools are not driven by state-mandated accountability measures. They emphasize accountability based on the belief that all human beings can continue to learn throughout their lifetime and that the responsibility of educational leaders is to see that it happens.

Renaissance schools like these embrace a vision about human potential, set exacting standards, gather data about results, and refine their practices. They are constructively dissatisfied with current performance, and they consistently seek improvement. They value thoughtful collaboration and reflective dialogue. They engage parents as partners. They view and converse about one another's work. They adopt and construct learning practices founded in current knowledge about learning, instruction, and curriculum. They dare to dream, and they dare to try to make those dreams reality.

COMMON RENAISSANCE AIMS

Love is a potent instrument for social and collective transformation.

—Martin Luther King, Jr.

Forms of renewal differ from program to program, but we have found many similarities among the models. One common aim is to develop and sustain professional communities in which collective responsibility drives school renewal and student achievement. Each program is open to the community as part of the conversation shaping students' lives in school. (However, some programs emphasize this more than others do.)

Each renewal model reflecting Renaissance energies is data-driven. Non-Renaissance models are often data-driven, too, but with a difference. In Renaissance schools, the norms, values, and procedures for using data come from within the school. In non-Renaissance settings, the reporting and analysis of data usually occurs as a function of compliance rather than a craftsmanlike quest for improvement.[5]

In non-Renaissance schools, teachers typically act in isolation. Where Renaissance energies thrive, collective teacher work is the norm. If you are reading efficacy, consciousness, flexibility, craftsmanship, and interdependence into this description, you are discerning. They are the energy sources for all right-minded renewal.

If only two things could be said to characterize schools in which Renaissance energies are at work, we would cite cultures of inquiry and communities of collaboration. Gone are the days of teacher isolation, in which instructional programs were carried out in systems like egg cartons, side by side but without communication or mutual influence. Michael Fullan observes that the good work many schools are doing is merely tinkering unless educators come to see themselves as inquirers and collaborators.[6] Education is just too complex for linear responses to tenacious problems in which cause and effect are not closely related in time, and too fluid for only centralized leadership.

PRINCIPLES THAT GUIDE RENAISSANCE WORK

The three questions asked most frequently in Renaissance schools are: Who are we? Why are we doing this? Why are we doing it this way? These questions are asked within the context of clear norms and values, reflective dialogue about practice, five states of mind as nurtured energy sources, professional collaboration, and shared responsibility for student learning. In such schools, there are no longer "your" students and "my" students. Colleagues speak only of "our" students. As much as is possible in large organizational settings, there is also a spirit of *gemeinschaft*, the term Thomas Sergiovanni used to mark the difference between a community of beings in which norms were voluntary and an organization in which policies and laws were required to frame human behavior.[7]

The adaptive schools model[8] is one renewal approach that draws specifically from Cognitive Coaching values, principles, and tools. Certain tenets guide the work of adaptive schools, and we offer them here as an example of principles that can inform all Renaissance work.

Schools are dynamical systems. Dynamic systems can be complex yet linear. Dynamical systems are nonlinear and operate in much the same way as weather patterns or national economies. They are complex, interacting arrangements in which cause-and-effect are difficult to ascertain. Small events cause major disturbances, and both things and energy matter. Because of this, both nonlinear logic and the linear logic of traditional Western reasoning is required for renewal to be successful.

Consistent energy is given to twin goals. These goals are (1) developing the production capacity of individuals, and (2) developing the capacity of the organization to be holonomously self-renewing. Ongoing, varied professional development activities are considered a normal, essential part of program refinements. School teams inquire about how they might work more efficiently. They let go of historical practices that have no current value and adopt those with greater relevance. For example, one way they emphasize production is by placing student learning at the center of the school's mission. To back this up, teacher teams share many conversations in which they intensively examine student work.

Leadership is distributed. All players are leaders. Colleagues are strong role models for one another. They are informed and skillful members of dialogue groups (talking to inquire and understand) and discussion events (decision making). They take turns as facilitators of meetings. They have skill in presenting concepts to each other. They coach one another, and they consult one another.

Frequent, rigorous, collective self-examination occurs. Reflection on data supports self-directed learning for individuals and teams. Coaching skills are so embedded in the culture that people often "self-coach," an ultimate goal of Cognitive Coaching. Modifications in practices and programs evolve from these practices, increasing individual and collective efficacy and craftsmanship as time goes on.

Learning is for everyone, adults *and* students. School teams construct new knowledge. They plan action research and how to share it. Graduate study is encouraged for all staff members, and the school finds creative ways to foster community learning.

Collaborative skills are practiced, refined, and taught to students. Collaboration can be defined as people with different resources (cognitive style, role, culture, gender, age) valuing and drawing upon each other's uniqueness and working together as equals to produce extraordinary results. Collaboration requires certain skills, and faculty members working at the edges of their own learning invest in building the capacity for skillful collaboration.

Some of the collaborative skills acquired in Renaissance schools are as follows:

1. Communicative competencies, drawn from Cognitive Coaching, which become normal behavior within the organization (pausing, paraphrasing, probing, paying attention to self and others, presuming positive intentions, and providing nonjudgmental feedback).[9]

2. Facility in two ways of talking: dialogue for collective inquiry and discussion for decision making. The metacognitive skills of being an effective group member are especially important: knowing one's intentions and choosing congruent behaviors, knowing when to self-assert and when to integrate, setting aside unproductive patterns of listening or responding, and being flexible in communication styles.

3. Distinguishing between "tame" problems, which can be resolved with linear logic, and "wicked" problems, in which new sciences of understanding and seeking solutions are required.[10]

4. Understanding and working to manifest the ideals of holonomy: individual autonomy and a simultaneous sense of community.

THE IMPORTANCE OF PRAGMATIC IDEALISM

Schools cannot achieve the above without certain resources. Leaders are right to work on the human energy, to "reculture" before they restructure schools for improvement. Yet leaders at the political, organizational, and community levels must ensure that practical resources are available to improve schooling. One study of reform and innovation found three major, necessary resources: human, social, and fiscal-capital.[11] The districts in that study represented a range of size, urban and rural locations, social and ethnic composition, and reputations for reform and innovation. The authors drew the following conclusions:

- Districts that made the greatest strides were those with a strong sense of trust among educators.

- Learning substantive ideas was at the heart of a new initiative, and helping teachers and others learn and build on these ideas was a primary capacity.

- Funding, staffing, time, and materials were necessary to support the reforms. However, without district leaders with the right commitments, connections to sources of knowledge, and trustworthiness, no amount of money, staff, time, and materials will help.

Although the soul and fire of Renaissance work lies within the hearts and minds of the participants in an educational unit, time and fiscal resources to support that work must be present. Without such resources, schools cannot undertake meaningful, lasting change.

RENAISSANCE LEADERSHIP DEFINED

Some people think you are strong when you hold on. Others think it is when you let go.

—Sylvia Robinson

Educational renaissance is a reorientation that requires courage, service, sacrifice, and intellectual vigor. A Renaissance demands that we reexamine our beliefs, values, sense of purpose, and impact. We must let go of what is safe and comfortable and proceed into the unknown with trust in our ability to learn and adapt. Uncertainty is a constant companion as we find our way into the light of our vast potential. Slowly, we learn to live anew according to Renaissance values and new inner maps of reality.

Enlightened educators in Renaissance schools believe in altruism, idealism, and activism. They are perceptually flexible, simultaneously focusing on minute details and elements of the larger system. They reject "either-or" solutions and seek to optimize systems through creative, "both-and" thinking. They integrate intuition with rationality. They understand that life itself is a work in progress, constantly transformed by new information, new connections, and new relationships.

Many of us were neither born to these ideals nor have we developed the skills to embrace them. We must find the courage to face the external critics and doubters and our own disbelief. Renaissance leaders stay the course and strive to live by Renaissance ideals:

- They know they can control only their own choices, decisions, and mental maps.

- They transcend their own existence by believing in, revering, and communing with something greater than themselves.

- They are honest with themselves and about themselves, and they strive to live by their deepest authenticity.

- They choose an active life of service to the community and seek to learn with and from others.

- They search for and reflect on their impact on others and the environment, thus continually modifying their own actions.

Renaissance leaders do not rely on mindless, mechanical formulas for change. Instead, they draw on their wisdom, maturity, and judgment to do the right thing, in the right way, at the right time. They are servants who set a direction, live their values, and mediate others to create meaning and change. Most of the time, the only reward for this hard work is the refreshing enlightenment that accompanies an internal shift of thinking, perception, and disposition. However, lack of external rewards matters little to the Renaissance leader, who is focused on a broader goal.

Whereas less committed leaders falter under the pressure of constant change, Renaissance leaders unite to use their power to liberate life-sustaining change under a shared vision: to encourage schools and the people who inhabit them to become continuously learning, generative individuals dedicated to creating a more compassionate community for future generations. This journey begins with a highly personal intellectual, psychological, and spiritual shift of consciousness that each of us must make if we want to lead Renaissance schools toward a Renaissance world.[12]

A NEW AND LARGER VISION

In essentials unity; in nonessentials freedom; in all things charity.

—St. Augustine

The work of Cognitive Coaching is dedicated to a vision of self-directed learning, not only for individuals but also for families, organizations, and cultures. We dream of classrooms, schools, and communities (and, indeed, a world) that represent a more thoughtful place in which humans reflect, learn from experience, and modify practice. As Cognitive Coaches, we feel a larger, more spiritual calling: to build the future world as an interdependent learning community in which all people are continually seeking ways to trust, solve problems, and learn together.

We envision a time in which individuals become increasingly adept at effective holonomous living, achieving personal potential while working for the betterment of the larger society. We imagine the states of mind of efficacy, flexibility, craftsmanship, consciousness, and interdependence as mutually valued and supported. We see a world in which many have coaching skills and in which coaches strive toward personal states of holonomy and help others to grow toward holonomous expressions of living together.

This is a challenge of major proportions. There are more human beings to be educated and fed on planet earth in the next 35 years than there have been up to this point in history. For this current population of six billion souls, the global economy works for only one billion of them. Over the next 30 years, the majority of people joining the planet will be born in poorer places. We dream of educators who constantly create conditions to produce ever more effective economic, social, and political systems and the conditions to produce ever more holonomous organizations and community. We envision a more actualized, holonomous world community. We envision a world in which various communities (and the world community collectively) value and work toward the goals described below.

Worldwide efficacy in continually generating more effective approaches to solving world problems in peaceful ways rather than resorting to violence and terrorism to resolve differences. There are no immutable reasons why lessons learned in the Indian province of Uttar Pradesh cannot be applied throughout the developing world to help eradicate the crises of hunger, health, and shelter. Applications of space geomatics have transformed this area from a semiarid desert to a green and agriculturally productive area. In humanity's five-million-year history, 95 percent of human knowledge has been developed during the last half-century. Surely we can turn our emerging knowledge to support a world culture of efficacy.

Worldwide flexibility in understanding and valuing the diversity of other cultures, races, religions, language systems, time perspectives, and political and economic views in an effort to develop a more stable world community. Scientists speculate that the future of Homo sapiens may be charted by the same life-force formula that moved us from single-celled organisms to multiple-cell organisms and so on. This chain of life, according to theorists at the Santa Fe Institute, consistently follows nonlinear formulas in which one stage, after certain conditions are met, builds upon previous stages. One conclusion being considered is that humanity must overcome illogical thinking and cultural intolerance to evolve to the next stage of human development. Education remains a major resource for achieving this goal.[13]

Worldwide consciousness of our human effects on each other and on the earth's limited resources in an effort to live more respectfully, graciously, and harmoniously in our delicate environment. "There is no hiding place for bad corporate behavior in world of globally connected activism," says Glenn Prickett, vice-president for corporate partnerships at Conservation International.[14] Capacities exist now, and will increase, to reduce air pollution, preserve diverse species, recycle arable land, reverse desertification, conserve wetlands, and create new, "clean" jobs in industry and services. At this writing, some scientists have predicted that the snows on Mount Kilimanjaro, the majestic mountain on the African continent, will be gone in 15 years as a result of global warming. Biologically, humans are wired to respond to immediate, present threats. Enhanced consciousness is required to overcome this neurological given, and efficacy is needed to approach major problems and make a difference.

Worldwide craftsmanship in our communication with other peoples, regardless of what language they speak. We must dream dreams together, understand complex issues together, and use dialogue instead of weapons to resolve misunderstandings. The world's rate of person-to-person communication is shrinking in relative volume, whereas person-to-machine communication is on the rise. The majority of international communication is in English, but perhaps not for long. Joseph Pelton predicts that in 20 years, the top tier of national economies will shift, and Asia will become the top economic region. Precision in language and thought are even more demanding goals in a world of electronic communications. Language precision as a focus of craftsmanship will become increasingly essential.

Worldwide interdependence by sharing the riches and resources in one part of the globe to help the less fortunate achieve their fullest potential. By 2035, the earth will house 8.5 billion souls, an increase of 2.5 billion in less than 30 years. Interdependence will bring us meaningful survival; wars will bring more and more destruction. Renaissance work is about building the human capacity for caring for and learning from others. The communication technology is already in place. In India, Indonesia, and China, literally millions of students are linked via satellite to tele-education systems that stretch to the most remote villages. Information flows to us and from us via cell phones, fiber-optic cables, high-performance and personal computers, satellites, and the Internet.

As Alan Kay states: "The best way to predict the future is to invent it."[15] If we want a future that is much more thoughtful, vastly more cooperative, greatly more compassionate, and a lot more loving, then we have to invent it. The future is in our schools and classrooms today. We must consciously seek, nurture, and celebrate that future until all children, students, families, and citizens around the world share in the Renaissance we seek.

NOTES

1. Costa, A., and Kallick, B. (200) *Habits of mind: A developmental series.* Alexandria, VA: Association for Supervision and Curriculum Development.

2. Pelton, J. (2000). *e-Sphere: The rise of the worldwide mind.* Westport, CT: Quorum Books.

3. Franklin, J. (May, 2001). Trying too hard? How accountability and testing are affecting constructivist teaching. *Education Update 43* (3), 1–8.

4. Costa, A. (1991). *The school as a home for the mind.* Pallatine, IL: Skylights.

5. Fuhrman, S. (1999). *The new accountability* (pp. 1–11). Philadelphia: University of Pennsylvania Consortium for Policy Research in Education.

6. Fullan, M. (1993). *Change forces: Probing the depths of educational reform.* New York: Falmer Press.

7. Sergiovanni, T. (1996). *Leadership for the schoolhouse.* San Francisco: Jossey-Bass.

8. Garmston, R., and Wellman, B. (1999). *The adaptive school: A sourcebook for developing collaborative groups.* Norwood, MA: Christopher-Gordon.

9. Ibid. See also Baker, W., Costa, A., and Shalit, S. (1997). The norms of collaboration: Attaining communicative competence. In A. Costa and R. Liebmann, (Eds.), *The process-centered school* (pp. 119–142). Thousand Oaks CA: Corwin Press.

10. Garmston, and Wellman, *The adaptive school,* pp. 219–242.

11. Spillane, J., and Thompson, C. (1997). *Reconsidering conceptions of local capacity: The local agency's capacity for ambitious instructional reform.* Philadelphia, PA: Educational Evaluation and Analysis.

12. Ray, P., and Anderson, S. (2000). *The cultural creatives: How 50 million people are changing the world.* New York: Crown.

13. Pelton, *e-Sphere,* p. 142.

14. Freidman, T. (2000). The *lexus and the olive tree: understanding globalization* (p. 288.) New York: Anchor Books.

15. Kay, A. (1990). The best way to predict the future is to invent it. Keynote presentation at the Annual Conference of the Association for Supervision and Curriculum Development, San Francisco.

Appendix A

Transcript of a Coaching Cycle

Teacher's Comments	Coach's Comments	Language Skills Used	Areas of the Planning Map	Additional Comments
Hi, Pete. Thanks for agreeing to come into my class today. I appreciate the time together.				The teacher has invited the coach in to observe— a strong indicator of a high level of trust.
	I'm looking forward to it. Tell me, Trish, what's your lesson going to be about?	The coach begins with an open-ended question to evoke the teacher's intentions.	Clarify goals and outcomes.	
Today I'm going to try a concept attainment lesson. I hadn't tried one before I attended the worksop that the District Thinking Skills (cont'd)				Another indicator of trust. The teacher is risking a new lesson format with the coach.

continued on next page

THE PLANNING CONFERENCE

Teacher's Comments	Coach's Comments	Language Skills Used	Areas of the Planning Map	Additional Comments
Committee presented, and I thought it would be great fun. I've tried it once with this class but they didn't respond too well and I think I need some help.				
	So you're experimenting with some new techniques. Tell me what you hope to accomplish.	The coach paraphrases by labeling the teacher's behaviors and intentions, then probes for outcomes.		Draws forth craftsmanship. This paraphrase both acknowledges and clarifies and lifts logical levels by offering conceptual language to match teacher statements.
Well, I want the kids to verbalize their metacognition—to talk about their thinking. We've never really done that before, and I don't know if they will be able to talk about their thinking.				
	So you're interested in metacognition—having them talk about what's going on inside their heads when they are thinking?	Paraphrasing/ labeling intentions.	Clarify goals.	Matches verbal modality in language.
Exactly. But I don't know if they can do that at this age.				
	You're uncertain as to whether students this young are capable *(cont'd)*	Paraphrases and probes for specific student behaviors.	Determine success indicators.	Draws forth the state of mind of craftsmanship Causes *(cont'd)*

THE PLANNING CONFERENCE

Teacher's Comments	Coach's Comments	Language Skills Used	Areas of the Planning Map	Additional Comments
	of talking about their thinking. What would you hear students saying if they were able to verbalize their inner thought processes?			images of the event.
Well, if they reported that they were "observing" or "hypothesizing" or "changing their mind with more information." Something like that.				
	So you're going to be alert for students describing in words what they're doing cognitively; you're listening for their use of cognitive terminology.	Paraphrases to acknowledge and gain clarity. Probes for greater precision regarding teacher's criteria for success. Employs positive presuppositions.	Determine success indicators.	Exacts success criteria. Draws forth craftsmanship.
I want everyone to use at least two cognitive terms. For half the class I would expect to hear four or five.	So your goal of this lesson is kids verbalizing their metacognition. You're listening for a couple of comments from everyone and for half the class to make four or five.	Paraphrases to summarize and organize.		The coach mediates by helping the teacher set up a monitoring system. She will be alert to and conscious of certain student behaviors as indicators of metacognitive capabilities.
Exactly!				
	What will you do to make that happen?	Questions to elicit intended teacher behaviors.	Anticipate approaches, strategies, and decisions.	Invites teacher to draw upon her own efficacy.
Well, I'll ask them to talk about *(cont'd)*				

continued on next page

THE PLANNING CONFERENCE

Teacher's Comments	Coach's Comments	Language Skills Used	Areas of the Planning Map	Additional Comments
what they're doing inside their head— their confusion, their strategies, their reasoning.				
	In other words, you'll invite them to talk out loud about their thought processes.	Paraphrases.	Anticipate approaches, strategies, and decisions.	
Yes.				
	And you have a concern that they will not be able to do that?	Empathizes with the teacher's concern.		
Yes. It's a new way of thinking for them—and for me. I've not asked them before. Or, if I have asked them to share their planning or their strategies, they just say, "I , don't know I just did it."				
	As you've thought about the challenges in this lesson, how are you thinking about structuring your plan?	The coach clarifies the teacher's strategies. Uses positive presupposition. She has considered the challenges and has a plan.	Anticipate approaches, strategies, and decisions.	
I'll start by reviewing our past concept attainment lesson. I'll tell them we're going to add to it. I'll explain the word *metacognition* (they love those *(cont'd)*				

THE PLANNING CONFERENCE

Teacher's Comments	Coach's Comments	Language Skills Used	Areas of the Planning Map	Additional Comments
big words at this age). And I'll model it for them and ask them to explain to me what they are thinking as they are solving a sample problem that I'll give them. Next I'll introduce another concept attainment lesson I've planned. I'll remind them of the rules about the two columns—the examples and non-examples—and how they must not give the concept but rather another example as a test. I'm going to stop along the way and ask them to share their thinking and to describe why they are keeping or changing their hypotheses.				
	How will you know when to listen for their metacognition?	Probes for criteria and specific time to make teaching decision.	Anticipate approaches, strategies, decisions, and how to monitor them.	Facilitates teacher becoming specific as to when to look for behaviors: craftsmanship.
After I have presented them with the two columns of the "examples" and "not examples," I'll have them work in small groups. I hope to make them curious so they have to gather data more to support their conclusions.				

continued on next page

THE PLANNING CONFERENCE

Teacher's Comments	Coach's Comments	Language Skills Used	Areas of the Planning Map	Additional Comments
	What would you like me to pay attention to while I'm in your classroom?	Establishes his role as observer.	Anticipate approaches, strategies, decisions, and how to monitor them.	The teacher is in charge of setting the parameters and focus for data gathering.
I want you to listen to the students and collect evidence of their metacognitive vocabulary. Are they expressing what they're thinking using cognitive terminology?				
	So you want me to observe them. How should I collect the data in a way that would be most useful to you?	Paraphrases; then probes for specific format of data collection.	Anticipate approaches, strategies, decisions, and how to monitor them.	
I'll give you a seating chart, and I'd like you to record all the cognitive words you hear each student expressing.				
	Okay. By each student's name on the seating chart, I'll record the cognitive terminology the student uses. Is there anything else?	Paraphrases the role of the coach. Asks an open-ended question.		Had the teacher not identified a personal learning focus, then the coach probably would have asked for one.
Yes. I'd also like to have you record my use of cognitive terminology. I want to know if I am modeling in my own language *(cont'd)*			Identify personal learning focus and processes for self-assessment.	The teacher has identified an area for personal learning and stated why it is important to her.

THE PLANNING CONFERENCE

Teacher's Comments	Coach's Comments	Language Skills Used	Areas of the Planning Map	Additional Comments
and labeling their cognitive language.				
	So you are going to be aware of your own use of cognitive language. How should I record that information for you?	Uses positive presupposition. Clarifies the task of the coach.	Identify personal learning focus and process for self-assessment.	Draws on consciousness.
Well, I'd like you to record my use of thinking terms when I am modeling at the beginning. Then, during the discussion, do I label their cognitive processes? For example, if a kid says, "Well before I thought . . . but now I'm thinking . . . ", I'd say, "Okay, you're demonstrating flexibility; you've changed your mind with the addition of more information."				
	So my job will be to keep track of when you place a label on student's behaviors. If I discover I'm having trouble recording both student language and your language, and cannot do both, which is more important to you?	Shares personal information and seeks role clarification.		Taps relative values; keeps teacher in charge of data-gathering process.
Oh, the students' labeling their own thinking process is most important to me.				

continued on next page

THE REFLECTING CONFERENCE

Teacher's Comments	Coach's Comments	Language Skills Used	Areas of the Planning Map	Additional Comments
	Well, Trish, as you reflect on your lesson, how do you think it went?	Asks an open-ended question. Employs positive presupposition.	Summarize impressions.	Poses an open-ended question that allows the teacher to take the lead in interpreting the lesson from any approach. This open question also provides the teacher an opportunity to talk about her emotional reactions, always a component in assessment, analysis, and decision making. Positive presupposition invites reflection.
I think it went pretty well, actually. I was impressed by how well these students could explain and describe their thought processes.				
	What were you aware of in your students' descriptions that make you think they succeeded?	Probes for recall of specific student behaviors to support interpretation.	Recall supporting information.	Positive presupposition draws upon the teacher's consciousness.
I heard a lot of students saying things like "theory," "I'm changing my mind," "attribute" —words like that.				
	So you heard your students using metacognitive terminology. From what you *(cont'd)*	Paraphrases. Invites the cognitive process of inferring from the data.	Compare, analyze, infer.	

THE REFLECTING CONFERENCE

Teacher's Comments	Coach's Comments	Language Skills Used	Areas of the Planning Map	Additional Comments
	heard, what inferences would you make about your students' capacity to verbalize their internal thought processes?			
They really are aware of their internal thought processes. I wasn't sure they could put them into words, but I now think they can. This opens up all kinds of possibilities for our discussion.				
	Would you be interested in seeing which students used which words?	Invites the teacher to consider the data that was requested.		Does not dump the data; rather, the coach asks permission to share it if the teacher so desires.
Yes, I would.				
	You asked me to keep a seating chart and to record which students used which words. Here's what I recorded.	Provides nonjudgmental data that was collected.		Hands the record of observations to the teacher.
Hmm. I didn't realize so many students used so many thinking words. Especially Roberto. And here, Mingwa and Mark, too.				The teacher observes and analyzes the recorded data for herself.
	So, you are finding that many of the students did respond *(cont'd)*	Paraphrases the teacher's interpretations. Poses a question *(cont'd)*	Determine cause-and-effect relationships.	Such a question stimulates growth toward even greater *(cont'd)*

continued on next page

THE REFLECTING CONFERENCE

Teacher's Comments	Coach's Comments	Language Skills Used	Areas of the Planning Map	Additional Comments
	and did use thinking vocabulary. What did you do to make that happen?	intended to have the teacher state a causal relationship between the teacher's behavior and the student's performance.		consciousness, efficacy, and an internal locus of control.
Well, I did try to model it, and, uh, I guess in this lesson I stated it as a goal at the beginning. I told students that that's what I wanted them to do. Then when I modeled it, I think they caught on. It freed them up to talk about what they were thinking because I modeled what I was thinking.				
	Why do you think that's so?	Questions to cause the teacher to infer a causal relationship.	Invite analysis.	
Well, I guess making your objectives explicit and modeling the desired behaviors encourages them to do it themselves.				The teacher infers a relationship for herself.
	You were also interested in your own use of cognitive terminology and whether you labeled student's thinking. How do you feel you did?	Recalls the teacher's concern about her own behavior from the planning conference.	Invite comparison of intended with actual behaviors.	Does not yet volunteer the data; rather, invites the teacher to first share her own recollections.
Well, as a result of talking with you in the planning *(cont'd)*				The teacher talks about her own metacognition and

THE REFLECTING CONFERENCE

Teacher's Comments	Coach's Comments	Language Skills Used	Areas of the Planning Map	Additional Comments
conference, I found I was more aware of my own labeling. I was more alert to the students' cognitive per-formances and could identify which behaviors the stud-ents were using while I was teaching				thinks about her own thinking.
	As you reflect on the lesson, what were some examples of your labeling of stu-dents' thought processes?	Positive presup-position ("You are reflective") and questions to cause the teacher to provide data.	Recall supporting information.	To recall accurately what occurred in a lesson is a cog-nitive skill. It is developed by practice. It is essential to reflection and self-directed learning.
Hmmm. Well, one time was when Elena said, "I think the concept is 'ani-mals with wings,'" and I said, "So you have a theory. How could you test it?" Then she said some-thing like, "I could test it by adding another winged animal to the exam-ples list, and if it stays there, then I will think my theory is a good one."				
	You're feeling good about their per-formance. Would you be interested in knowing how many times you labeled students' cognition?	Paraphrases. Offers data to the teacher.	Provide nonjudgmental data for comparison and analysis.	

continued on next page

THE REFLECTING CONFERENCE

Teacher's Comments	Coach's Comments	Language Skills Used	Areas of the Planning Map	Additional Comments
Yes, I would.				
	I counted 11 times that you labeled students' thought processes.	Provides the data.	Provide nonjudgmental data for comparison and analysis.	
I did that 11 times? Wow! Hmm. Maybe as students hear those words repeated and attach the names to their behaviors, they get used to hearing them and start using them.				The teacher forms her own inference about the effects of her behavior on the student's performance.
	Given this experience, what next steps are you considering for these students in learning about thinking?	Questions to cause application and prediction toward the future.	Construct new learning and applications.	Uses positive presuppositions of envisioning and planning.
Well, I've been thinking that it's not enough to just use the terminology. I want them also to apply these thinking processes to other situations in life.				
	So, you want them to use these words elsewhere?	Probe for clarity of purpose.		
No, not just the words. I want them to talk about when they would use the processes of theorizing, experimenting, and changing their mind with additional data. That's the real purpose for these types of thinking skills lessons.				The teacher clarifies the coach's misinterpretation.

THE REFLECTING CONFERENCE

Teacher's Comments	Coach's Comments	Language Skills Used	Areas of the Planning Map	Additional Comments
	So, you want them to not only improve in their thinking but be in charge of their own thinking processes. As you are planning those lessons, I'd be interested in having you share your thoughts about how you'll do that.	Paraphrases to a higher logical level. Leaves door open for future inter-actions.	Construct new learning and applications.	Positive presup-position about carrying forth the learnings from this analysis to planning future lessons. If time permitted, this might be an opportunity to initiate a planning conference.
Yes. I'd enjoy that.				
	Tell me, Trish, as you reflect on our coaching today, what did this process do for you?	Invites the teacher to evaluate use-fulness of the coaching process.	Reflect on the coaching process and explore refinements.	
It really helped. Our planning conference made me more aware of the behav-iors I wanted from the students. I also found that when I made them clear to you, I made them clear to me. You know, we've done this coaching four times now, and I'm beginning to see that when I think through the lesson objectives as I plan, the clearer I become about what I'm try-ing to accomplish, and the greater the likelihood is that I'll accomplish them.				
	So becoming precise in your planning is helpful to you.	Paraphrases the teacher's conclusion.		Draws forth state of mind of crafts-manship.

continued on next page

THE REFLECTING CONFERENCE

Teacher's Comments	Coach's Comments	Language Skills Used	Areas of the Planning Map	Additional Comments
Yes. In some ways, I need you more to think through the plan with me; then I can analyze whether I've achieved my purposes for myself.				
	Thank you, Trish. I'd be happy to think through more lessons with you.			

Appendix B

What Teachers Want Observed

Teachers generally request that coaches observe two rather distinct categories of behaviors: their own and their students'. The following is a list of verbal and nonverbal behaviors, with examples of factors teachers most often want coaches to observe in the classroom.

NONVERBAL FEEDBACK ABOUT TEACHERS

1. Mannerisms
   - Pencil tapping
   - Hair twisting
   - Handling coins in pocket

2. Use of Time
   - Interruptions
   - Transitions from one activity to another
   - Time spent with each group
   - Time spent getting class started (e.g., dealing with routines such as attendance)
   - Punctuality of starting and ending times

3. Movement Throughout the Classroom
   - Favoring one side of the room over another
   - Monitoring student progress and seat work

4. Modality Preference
   - Using balanced visual, kinesthetic, and auditory modes of instruction

5. Use of Handouts
   - Clarity, meaningfulness, adequacy, or complexity

6. Use of Audiovisual Equipment
   - Placement, appropriateness, operation

7. Pacing
   - Too fast, too slow, "beating a dead horse" (tempo, rhythm)
   - Coverage of desired material in time allotted (synchronicity)
   - Time spent in each section of lesson sequence (duration)

8. Meeting Diverse Student Needs
   - Making allowances for gifted, slow, cognitive styles
   - Considering emotional needs, modality strengths, languages, and cultures

9. Nonverbal Feedback
   - Body language, gestures, proximity
   - Moving toward or leaning into students when addressing them
   - Eye contact

10. Classroom Arrangements
    - Furniture placement
    - Bulletin board space
    - Environment for learning
    - Provision for multiple uses of space

VERBAL FEEDBACK ABOUT TEACHERS

1. Mannerisms
   - Saying "okay" or "ya know"
   - Nodding the head excessively while speaking

2. Sarcasm During Negative Feedback
   - Gender references
   - Criticism
   - Put-downs
   - Critical intonation of voice

3. Other Positive and Negative Feedback
   - Use of praise and criticism
   - Ignoring distracting student responses

4. Response Behaviors
   - Silence
   - Accepting, paraphrasing, clarifying, empathizing
   - Responding to students who give "wrong" answers

5. Questioning Strategies
   - Posing questions at appropriate taxonomy level
   - Asking questions in sequence

6. Clarity of Presentation
   - Giving clear directions
   - Clarifying assignments
   - Checking for understanding
   - Modeling

7. Interactive Patterns
   - Teacher to Student to Teacher to Student
   - Teacher to Student to Student to Student

8. Equitable Distribution of Responses
   - Favoring gender
   - Favoring language proficiency, race, perception of abilities, placement in room

9. Specific Activities, Teaching Strategies
   - Lectures, group activities, lab exercises, discussion
   - Movies, slide shows

NONVERBAL FEEDBACK ABOUT STUDENTS

1. Attentiveness
   - On task, off task
   - Note taking
   - Volunteering for tasks

2. Preparedness
   - Participation
   - Sharing
   - Homework
   - Materials
   - Volunteering knowledge

3. Movement
   - Negative: getting out of seat, squirming, fidgeting, causing discomfort, interfering with others
   - Positive: following directions, transitioning, following self-direction, taking initiative, consulting reference books

4. Managing Materials
   - Audiovisual equipment, textbooks, art supplies, musical instruments, lab equipment
   - Care of library books
   - Returning supplies

VERBAL FEEDBACK ABOUT STUDENTS

1. Positive Participation
   - Volunteering responses
   - Speaking out while on task
   - On-task student-to-student interaction
   - Requesting assistance

2. Negative Participation
   - Speaking out while off task
   - Off-task student-to-student interaction

3. Positive Social Interaction
   - Taking turns
   - Listening and allowing for differences
   - Sharing and establishing ground rules
   - Assuming and carrying out roles
   - Following rules of games, interactions

4. Negative Social Interaction
   - Interrupting, interfering, hitting
   - Name-calling, put-downs, racial slurs, foul language
   - Hoarding, stealing

5. Performing Lesson Objectives
   - Using correct terminology
   - Applying knowledge learned before or elsewhere
   - Performing task correctly
   - Conducting experiments
   - Applying rules, algorithms, procedures, formulas
   - Recalling information
   - Supplying supportive details, rationale, elaborations

6. Language Patterns
   - Using correct syntax
   - Using correct grammar, spelling, and punctuation
   - Using correct numbers and mathematical terms
   - Supplying examples

7. Insights Into Student Behaviors and Difficulties
   - Learning styles: verbal, auditory, kinesthetic
   - Cognitive styles: field-dependent, field-independent
   - Friendships, animosities
   - Tolerance for ambiguity and chaos
   - Distractibility

Appendix C

Why Cognitive Coaches Do What They Do: Applying Principles of Constructivism

Meaning-making is not a spectator sport. Knowledge is a constructive process. The activity of constructing content is what gets stored in memory. Humans don't *get* ideas; they *make* ideas.

Constructivism is a theory of learning based on a belief that human beings have an innate quest to make meaning from their experiences. When humans are perplexed with anomalies, discrepancies, or new information, they have a natural inclination to make sense of it. This process of making sense is enhanced in environments when certain coaching behaviors are practiced, such as seeking and valuing others' points of view, challenging others' suppositions, focusing on "big" ideas and long-range outcomes, creating conditions for self-assessment, and providing opportunities for reflection on experience.

The following 12 principles of constructivism guide Cognitive Coaches. The development of these descriptors has been informed by the work of several researchers and theoreticians, including Irving Sigel, Thomas Kuhn, John Dewey, and Jacqueline Brooks and Martin Brooks.

1. Constructivist environments encourage self-directedness. Autonomy empowers the pursuit of making connections among ideas and concepts. When participants raise issues and frame questions, then analyze and answer those issues and questions themselves, they take responsibility for their own learning, becoming problem solvers and problem finders. In the pursuit of new understandings, they are led by their own ideas and informed by the ideas of others.

As such, constructivist environments must be safe as they provide freedom to experiment with ideas, explore issues, and encounter new information. When learners anticipate that their thoughts will be judged, their thinking mode shifts from open to closed. Nonjudgmental feedback encourages others to pursue their ideas more deeply and less defensively. Nonjudgmental feedback also helps others to develop the capacity for evaluating the worth of their own and others' ideas. Listening to, paraphrasing, and clarifying ideas indicates that the other person's brain has the power to produce meaning.

2. Coaches view themselves as mediators of others' meaning-making. Because learning is viewed as a continual process of engaging the mind that transforms the mind, constructivist coaches cast others in the role of producers of knowledge rather than consumers of knowledge. They see themselves as facilitators of meaning-making, interposing themselves between the learner and the learning so as to cause others to approach activities in a strategic way, to help them monitor their own progress in the learning, to construct meaning from the learning and from the process of learning, and then to apply the learnings to other contexts and settings.

Coaches' mediational questioning and problem posing stimulate the brain to engage in higher-order and creative cognitive functions. Coaches help others to raise and illuminate perplexing situations, problems, discrepancies, and intriguing phenomena—the answers to which are not readily apparent. Day-to-day, real-life problems are the best way to practice problem solving.

Constructivist coaches seek elaboration of initial responses. Initial responses are just that—*initial*. People's first thoughts about issues are not necessarily their final thoughts or their best thoughts. Inviting elaboration causes others to reconceptualize and assess their own language, concepts, and strategies.

In dialogue, constructivist coaches use cognitive terminology. The words we hear and use in dialogue affect our way of thinking and ultimately our actions. Cognitive Coaches deliberately choose words intended to activate and engage mental processes. Finding relationships, predicting outcomes, analyzing, and synthesizing are mental processes that require others to draw forth their knowledge, make connections, and create new understandings.

3. Constructivist approaches begin with raw data and direct experiences from which abstractions can be made. Concepts, theorems, laws, criteria, and guidelines are abstractions that the human mind generates through interaction with previous information, new ideas, experiences, and data. The constructivist approach draws on primary sources, information from memory and past experiences, manipulatives, and real-life situations. Then, the constructivist approach helps learners generate abstractions from all of these data sources. Learners gather data from a variety of sources and are than asked to compare, analyze, synthesize, and evaluate. Learning becomes the result of research related to real problems.

Providing information is also valid for coaches. Providing information is appropriate when the information is linked (scaffolded) to previous learnings. Providing information is also appropriate when the learners express a need for the information and the data are then delivered in a manner that matches the learner's learning style. Data also should be relevant to the learner's developmental levels and drawn from multiple sources: visual, auditory, kinesthetic, tactile. With a coach's guidance, this data can then be acted upon and processed as the colleague makes inferences, forms concepts, synthesizes theorems, induces algorithms, generates laws, and creates guidelines so that learning is applied in and beyond the context in which it was learned.

4. Constructivism suggests a sequence of learning. Constructivists such as Hilda Taba, Jerome Bruner, and Jean Piaget believe that there is a sequence to concept formation in which learning begins with gathering sensory data, then making sense of the data by finding patterns and relationships, and then applying those concepts to new problems.

The first stage is the input, or "discovery," stage in which data is taken in through the senses and drawn from memory. This is an open-ended opportunity to experiment and become familiar with materials and to generate questions and hypotheses.

Next is the processing stage in which patterns are found, meaningful relationships are drawn, and concepts are constructed from those data. New labels for concepts are formed, hypotheses are drawn, and inferences are made.

The third step is the output, or "concept application." Further iterations of the discovery are made, then generalizations and principles are formed and used as models to explain problems and predict consequences in settings beyond the one in which learning it was formed.

5. **Constructivist coaches challenge others' mental models.** Humans often develop and refine ideas about phenomena and then tenaciously hold on to these ideas as eternal truths. Much of what we think happens simply by virtue of our agreement that it should, not because of our close examination of our bounded assumptions, limited history, and existing mental models. Constructivist coaches realize that cognitive growth occurs when individuals revisit and reformulate a current perspective. Therefore, coaches provide data, present realities, and pose questions for the purpose of engendering contradictions to others' initial hypotheses, challenging present conceptions, illuminating another perspective, and breaching crystallized thinking. Coaches must listen to and understand the other person's present conceptions or points of view to help him understand which notions might be accepted or rejected as contradictory.

6. **Constructivist coaches support on-demand learning.** In the meaning-making process, humans direct the need for information in the moment. Because they feel a need for information or skills to fulfill the gaps and inadequacies in their process of meaning-

making, there is a greater openness to learning. (Computers assist in this process, as they allow the pursuit of interests through browsing, tapping varied data bases in a random and nonlinear way. Coaches, therefore, allow others' responses to drive the interaction, shift the focus, and alter the content.)

Being alert to such verbal and nonverbal signals as eye movements; facial expressions; postural shifts; gestures; breathing rates; and changes in pitch, speed, volume of speech, and overt expressions of interest and enthusiasm, the coach may shift the topic or approach. (We all know of a "teachable moment," when our planned lesson was derailed by an event of greater interest.) Learners' in-the-moment insights, experiences, motivations, and interests may intersect around an urgent theme. When magnetic events exert an irresistible pull on a learner's mind, the coach may hold his or her planned strategy in abeyance and "go with the flow."

7. Constructivism involves communities of learners. Constructivist learning is a reciprocal process of the individual's influence on the group and the group's influence on the individual. Meaning making is not only an individual operation. The individual also constructs meaning interactively with others to construct shared knowledge. Meaning-making may be an individual experience, one's unique way of constructing knowledge. Meaning-making also is a sociocultural phenomenon. Social processes of interaction and participation enhance, refine, and amplify meanings. An empowering way to change conceptions is to present one's own ideas to others as well as to hear and reflect on the ideas of others. Discourse with others, particularly with peers, activates the meaning-making process. The constructivist environment encourages questioning of each other and rich dialogue within and among groups and teams of learners as they resolve differences in perceptions and styles and synthesize alternative viewpoints.

8. Process *is* the content with constructivism. A constructivist curriculum challenges the basic educational views of "knowledge" and "learning" with which most schools are comfortable. It causes us to expand our focus from educational outcomes, which are primarily collections of subskills. A constructivist curriculum embraces successful processes of participation in socially organized activities and the development of students' identities as conscious, flexible, efficacious, interdependent, and continual learners.

A constructivist curriculum lets go of having learners acquire predetermined meaning and has faith in the processes of individuals' construction of shared meanings through social interaction. Constructivist coaches, therefore, inquire about their colleagues' understandings of concepts before sharing their own understandings of those concepts. When coaches share their ideas and theories before others have an opportunity to develop their own, questioning of theories is essentially eliminated. People being coached assume that the coach knows more than they do. Consequently, most often they stop thinking about a concept or theory once they hear "the correct answer."

9. Constructing meaning takes time. As such, constructivist coaches invite colleagues to construct relationships and create metaphors. When sufficient time is given to activities, learners go beyond initial relationships to create novel relationships, find patterns, and generate theories for themselves. This also means that coaches allow wait time after posing questions.

With constructivism, failures are never dismissed as mistakes. Rather, time is taken to reflect on their learning, to compare intended with actual outcomes, to analyze and draw causal relationships, to synthesize meanings, and to apply their learnings to novel situations.

Unlike many other quick-fix educational innovations and experiments, constructivism remains focused on the longer view. Constructivist educators realize that assisting others to habituate self-directed learning takes years of coaching, well-defined instruction with qualified teachers, and carefully constructed curriculum before a significant and enduring change is observed.

We know that the amount of time on task affects learning. As self-directed learning becomes a goal of education, we must place greater value is placed on allocating time for learning activities intended to stimulate, to practice the construction, or for personal meaning.

10. Constructivist coaches invite metacognition. They invite colleagues to think about their thinking. Time is taken to monitor and discuss thinking skills and problem-solving processes. They invite colleagues to share their metacognition—to reveal their intentions, strategies, and plans for solving a problem; to describe their mental maps for monitoring their strategy during the problem solving; and to reflect on the strategy to determine its adequacy.

11. Assessment is viewed as another opportunity to accelerate self-directed learning. In the constructivist environment, what matters most is whether the inhabitants are learning to become increasingly more self-managing, self-monitoring, and self-modifying. Coaches help others design diverse ways of gathering, organizing, and reporting evidence of continual learning and meaning making.

In the current politics of education, the key to school success is higher test scores. Most states in the United States have developed standards for learning. Many have implemented new assessments tied to these standards or linked high school graduation to passing these new assessments. Others are beginning to link teacher evaluation and even merit pay to increases in test scores. These educational practices shift the focus toward the transmission of test-related information and to judging teachers on how well their students score. In such a climate, it is difficult to embrace and sustain constructive practices designed for individual meaning-making.

The intent of constructivist assessment is to support others in becoming self-managing, self-monitoring, and self-modifying. Self-knowledge is the first step in self-assessment. Much of the work of self-evaluation is developed through the metacognitive process of reflection. This process of self-assessment provides internal and external data that promotes one's own learning and growth.

12. Modeling (through imitation and emulation) is the most basic form of constructivist learning. Teachers, coaches, parents, and administrators realize the importance of their own display of desirable learning behaviors in the presence of others with whom they work. If coaches want their colleagues to value inquiry, then they must also value it. If coaches pose questions with the orientation that there is only one correct response, then how can others be expected to develop either the interest in or the analytic skills necessary for more diverse modes of inquiry?

In day-to-day events, and when problems arise in schools, classrooms, and homes, the same types of constructivist learning listed above can be used. Without this consistency, there is likely to be a credibility gap. As Mahatma Ghandi said, "You must be the change you wish to see in the world."

These principles of constructivism may serve as a basis for understanding why Cognitive Coaches do what they do. They provide the theoretical underpinnings of the model of Cognitive Coaching. These principles also can be used as a template to determine the degree to which schools embrace a constructivist philosophy and as a vision that Renaissance schools might strive to achieve.

Appendix D

Mediative Questioning

Effective Cognitive Coaches are aware of the direct correlation between the structure of their questions and the production of thought processes. As such, they deliberately use language and syntax to construct questions in ways that mediate desired mental processes in the other person's mind.

The following sample questions come from planning and reflective conversations. The questions are designed to mediate specific mental processes. These questions are only examples, however, and they are not meant to be prescriptive.

The coach's intent with these questions is to engage, mediate, and thereby enhance another's cognitive functions. The questions are adroitly designed and posed to deliberately engage the intellectual functions of teaching. The long-range intent, of course, is self-coaching: to help the other person reach a point where he or she habitually and autonomously initiates such questions without the coach's intervention.

The left-hand column in each chart contains desired cognitive thoughts and processes. The right-hand column contains sample questions. Specific syntax cues in the questions are in boldface type. As you analyze these examples, you may wish to refer to chapter 4 to review the criteria for constructing powerful, mediative questions.

PLANNING CONVERSATION

If the desired cognitive thought or process is to:	Then the coach might ask:
Describe (State the purpose of the lesson.)	What outcomes do you have in mind for your lesson today?
Envision (Translate the lesson purposes into descriptions of desirable, observable student behaviors.)	As you see this lesson unfolding, what will students be doing?
Predict (Envision teaching strategies and behaviors to facilitate students' performance of desired behaviors.)	As you envision this lesson, what do you see yourself doing to produce those student outcomes?
Sequence (Describe the sequence in which the lesson will occur.)	What will you be doing first? Next? Last? How will you close the lesson?
Estimate (Anticipate the duration of activities.)	As you consider the opening of the lesson, how long do you anticipate that will take?
Define (Formulate procedures for assessing outcomes by envisioning, defining, and setting success indicators.)	What will you see students doing or hear them saying that will indicate to you that your lesson is successful?
Metacogitate (Monitor his or her own behavior during the lesson.)	What will you be aware of in students' reaction to know if your directions are understood?
Self-Assess (Identify a process for personal learning.)	As a professional, what are you hoping to learn about your own practices as a result of this lesson?
Describe (Depict the data-collecting role of the observer.)	What will you want me to look for and give you feedback about while I am in your classroom?

REFLECTING CONVERSATION

If the desired cognitive process is to:	Then the coach might ask:
Assess (Express feelings about the lesson.)	As you reflect on your lesson, how do you feel it went?
Recall and Relate (Recollect student behaviors observed during the lesson to support those feelings.)	What did you see students doing (or hear them saying) that made you feel that way?
Recall (Recollect their own behavior during the lesson.)	What do you recall about your own behavior during the lesson?
Compare (Draw a comparison between student behavior performed with student behavior desired.)	How did what you observe compare with what you planned?
Infer (Abstract meaning from data.)	Given this information, what do you make of it?
Draw Conclusions (Assess the achievement of the lesson purposes.)	As you reflect on the goals for this lesson, what can you say about your students' achievement of them?
Metacogitate (Become aware of and monitor their own thinking during the lesson.)	What were you thinking when you decided to change the design of the lesson? OR What were you aware of that students were doing that signaled you to change the format of the lesson?
Infer from Data (Draw hypotheses and explanations from the data provided.)	What inferences might you draw from these data?
Analyze (Examine why the student behaviors were or were not achieved.)	What hunches do you have to explain why some students performed as you had hoped while others did not?
Describe Cause and Effect (Draw causal relationships.)	What did you do (or not do) to produce the results you obtained?
Synthesize (Make meaning from analysis of the lesson.)	As you reflect on this discussion, what big ideas or insights are you discovering?
Self-Assess (Construct personal learnings.)	What did you gain personal learnings from this experience?
Apply (Prescribe alternative teaching strategies, behaviors, or conditions.)	As you plan future lessons, what insights have you developed that might be carried forth to the next lesson or other lessons?
Evaluate (Give feedback about the effects of this coaching session and the coach's conferencing skills.)	As you think back over our conversation, what has this coaching session done for you? What is it that I did (or didn't) do that was of benefit to you? What assisted you? What could I do different in future coaching sessions?

Glossary

Autobiographical Listening: Occurs when the listener associates a colleague's story with his or her own experiences. This kind of listening includes making judgments and comparisons. (See also Set Asides.)

Capabilities: How one uses knowledge and skill. For the coach, these metacognitive functions include knowing one's intentions and choosing congruent behaviors, setting aside unproductive patterns of listening and responding, adjusting personal style preferences, and navigating within and among various coaching maps and support functions.

Coaching Cycle: Describes how a coach uses both the planning and reflective maps before and after an event in which the coach will be present as observer and data collector.

Cognitive Coaching: A nonjudgmental, interactive strategy focused on developing and utilizing cognitive processes, liberating internal resources, and accessing the five states of mind as a means of more effectively achieving goals while enhancing self-directed learning.

Collaborating: Providing support in a mentoring or collegial relationship in which coach and colleague share and test ideas, determine focus for inquiry, and gather and interpret data to inform collaborative practice.

Consulting: A support service in which the colleague develops teaching effectiveness by drawing on the more extensive experience of the consulting educator.

Consciousness: The human capacity to represent information about what is happening outside and inside the body in such a way that it can be evaluated and acted upon by the body. To be conscious is to be aware of one's thoughts, feelings, points of view, and behaviors and the effect they have on the self and others. (See also *States of Mind.*)

Constructivism: A theory of learning based on a belief that human beings have an innate quest to make meaning from their experiences. When humans are perplexed by anomalies, discrepancies, or new information, they have a natural inclination to make sense of it. This theory is used to guide pedagogy, curriculum, and assessment of learning.

Craftsmanship: The human drive to hone, refine, and constantly work for improvement. Includes striving for precision, elegance, refinement, and fidelity. (See also *States of Mind.*)

Efficacy: Engaging in cause and effect thinking, spending energy on tasks, setting challenging goals, persevering in the face of barriers and occasional failure, and forecasting future performances accurately. Efficacy is linked to a belief that one's work will make a difference and is related to being optimistic, confident, and knowledgeable. Efficacy is also linked to having an internal locus of control. (See also *States of Mind.*)

Evaluation: Measurement of and judgment about performance based on external criteria or standards.

Flexibility: The human capacity to perceive from multiple perspectives and to endeavor to change, adapt, and expand the repertoire of response patterns. Involves humor, creativity, risk-taking, and adaptability. (See also *States of Mind.*)

Holonomy: An individual's cognitive capacity to be autonomous and interdependent at the same time. The ability to function as a member of the whole while still maintaining separateness. A person's cognitive capacity to accept the concept that he or she is whole in terms of self and yet subordinate to a higher system. The idea of holonomy is based on Arthur Koestler's work.

Identity: An autobiographical sense of self in this time and space constructed from the meanings we make of our interactions with others and how we perceive that others see us.

Interdependence: The human need for reciprocity, belonging, and connectedness. The inclination to become one with the larger system and community. (See also *States of Mind.*)

Inquisitive Listening: Occurs when the listener becomes curious about portions of a colleague's story that are not relevant to the problem at hand. Inquisitive listening sometimes involves mind reading and scrutinizing. (See also *Set Asides.*)

Mediate: To be the medium of bringing about a result. Literally it means "middle."

Mediator: One who interposes himself or herself in the middle between a person and some event, problem, conflict, or other perplexing situation and intervenes in such a way as to enhance meaning and self-directed learning. Based on Feuerstein's "Mediated Learning Experience."

Mental Map: A pathway held in the mind and used by a coach as a guide to interaction; a scaffold for a conversation. For example, Bloom's taxonomy is a mental map guiding a sequence of cognitive tasks.

Pace and Lead: A coaching map used to restore a colleague's resourcefulness. Pacing and leading validates perceptions of a problematic state and helps the person envision a desired state. (See also *Problem Resolving Conversation.*)

Paralanguage: Describes what is communicated and understood by the qualities of voice, body, gestures, and other nonverbal behaviors that exist alongside the words we speak. (The prefix para means "alongside.")

Planning Conversation: A structured interaction conducted before participating in an event, resolving a challenge, or attempting some task. The intent is to mediate the cognitive processes of planning. The coach may or may not be present during the event or available for a follow-up conversation. (See also *Coaching Cycle.*)

Problem Resolving Conversation: A conversation conducted when a colleague feels stuck, helpless, unclear, or lacking in resourcefulness; experiences a crisis; or requests assistance. The coach's aim is to have the colleague access the necessary internal resources. (See also *Pace and Lead.*)

Reflecting Conversation: A structured interaction conducted after participating in an event or completing a task, the intent of which is to mediate the cognitive processes of reflection. The coach may or may not have participated or witnessed. (See also *Coaching Cycle.*)

Renaissance: In the context of this book, refers to the current revolution of relationships and the intellect, placing a premium on our greatest resource: human minds in relationship with one another.

Resources: Internal elements used for decision making, problem solving, and effective action. Resources include electrochemical energy released by neurotransmitters and peptides related to accessing states of efficacy, flexibility, craftsmanship, consciousness, and interdependence. (See also *Problem Solving Conversation* and *Pace and Lead.*)

Self-Directed Learning: The capacity for self-managing, self-monitoring, and self-modifying.

Set Asides: Noticing and freeing oneself from several normal ways of listening and responding in order to be more effective as a Cognitive Coach. Three set asides are described in this glossary: autobiographical listening, inquisitive listening, and solution listening. Three special set asides are used during pacing and leading. They are:

- **Closure** is setting aside the need to understand the end of the story and instead looking for nonverbal cues indicating that a colleague has achieved the necessary internal resources.

- **Comfort** is setting aside the need for feeling at ease in pacing-and-leading conversations and being willing to embrace ambiguity as a resource for both parties.

- **Comprehension** is setting aside a coach's need to know the history, background, and context of a problem. Seeking this information is useful when consulting, but it may be counterproductive when pacing and leading.

Solution Listening: Occurs when a listener tries to solve a problem for another. It may involve interpretation and rehearsing. (See also *Set Asides.*)

States of Mind: Basic human forces that drive, influence, motivate, and inspire our intellectual capacities, emotional responsiveness, high performance, and productive human action. Specifically, this book describes five states of mind: efficacy, flexibility, craftsmanship, consciousness, and interdependence. (See also the separate entry for each in this glossary.) States of mind are transitory depending on a variety of personal and situational factors, but they can be mediated by helping a colleague become conscious of them and accessing them. They can also be strengthened and made more accessible to self-coaching over time.

Support Functions: Three services coaches may select from to further the aim of self-directed learning: Cognitive Coaching, collaborating, or consulting. (See definitions in this glossary.)

Arthur L. Costa

Arthur L. Costa is an Emeritus Professor of Educational Administration at California State University, Sacramento, and Co-Founder of the Institute for Intelligent Behavior. He has served as a classroom teacher, a curriculum consultant, and an assistant superintendent for instruction and as the Director of Educational Programs for the National Aeronautics and Space Administration. He has made presentations and conducted workshops in all 50 states as well as Mexico, Central and South America, Canada, Australia, New Zealand, Africa, Europe, Asia and the Islands of the South Pacific.

He earned his Bachelor's and Master's of Science in Education Degrees from the University of Southern California and his Doctorate in Education from the University of California at Berkeley.

Art has written and edited numerous articles and books, including *Techniques for Teaching Thinking,* and *The School as a Home for the Mind.* He is editor of *Developing Minds: A Resource Book for Teaching Thinking* and co-editor of the *Process as Content Trilogy* and the four book series, *Habits of Mind.*

Active in many professional organizations, Art served as president of the California Association for Supervision and Curriculum Development and was the National President of Association for Supervision and Curriculum Development, 1988 to 1989.

Photo by Bruce M. Wellman

Robert J. Garmston

Robert J. Garmston is an Emeritus Professor of Educational Administration at California State University, Sacramento and Co-Founder of the Institute for Intelligent Behavior in California. Formerly a classroom teacher, principal, director of instruction and superintendent, he works as an educational consultant and is director of Facilitation Associates, a consulting firm specializing in leadership, learning, personal and organizational development. He has made presentations and conducted workshops for teachers, administrators and staff developers throughout the United States as well as in Canada, Africa, Asia, and the Middle East.

He earned a Bachelor's and Master's of Art in Education Degrees from California State University, San Francisco and an Ed.D. from the University of Southern California.

Bob has written and co-authored a number of books including *How to Make Presentations That Teach and Transform,* and *A Presenter's Fieldbook: A Practical Guide.* In 1999, the National Staff Development Council (NSDC) selected *The Adaptive School: A Sourcebook for Developing Collaborative Groups,* coauthored with Bruce Wellman, as book of the year.

Active in many professional organizations, Bob was president of the California Associationf or Supervision and Curriculum Development from 1989–1991 and served as a member of the Executive Council for the Association for Supervision and Curriculum Development (ASCD) at the international level from 1991–1994.

Index